THE ORGAN WORKS OF BACH

A CONTRIBUTION TO THEIR HISTORY, FORM, INTERPRETATION AND PERFORMANCE

by

HERMANN KELLER

Translated from the German

by

Helen Hewitt

C. F. PETERS CORPORATION

NEW YORK - LONDON - FRANKFURT

HERMANN KELLER

THE ORGAN WORKS OF BACH

Translated from the German by Helen Hewitt

Library of Congress Catalog Card No. 67-28433

Printed in the United States of America

Translator's Preface

Hermann Keller's book *Die Orgelwerke Bachs* has remained virtually unknown to the average undergraduate organ student in America because of the latter's unfamiliarity with the German language. From 1956 to 1960, the organ students of North Texas State University presented a series of recitals tracing the history of organ music, the second year's seven recitals being devoted exclusively to Bach's organ works. During that year, in particular, Dr. Keller's book proved indispensable. It seemed imperative to provide an English translation of this book which should be in the library of every serious student of the organ.

Owing to the unusual difficulties surrounding publication of the original German book, errors crept in unavoidably. The firm of C. F. Peters Corporation has been most cooperative about the correction of musical examples when necessary, and Dr. Keller has been very helpful concerning any mistakes in the text. He has rewritten some passages and has brought the bibliography up to date. The present book is, then, a revised edition as well as a translation of the original.

The translator wishes to acknowledge her indebtedness to two colleagues at North Texas State University: Professor Jacob Hieble of the German Department read the first draft of the translation, and Professor Oma Stanley read that as well as later ones, contributing greatly to the form of the present version.

Helen Hewitt

TABLE OF CONTENTS

TABLE OF CONTENTS

B. Arrangements of Chorales

TABLE OF CONTENTS

APPENDIX

INTRODUCTION

THE TASK

This book has been written by a musician and for musicians. It is the result of an earnest effort to understand Bach's organ works: their inner logic, their form, their interpretation, and their performance. Its hope is to be of service to all those who attach importance to the same matters; its aim is to be a counselor and guide to "beginning organists"[1] as well as to "those already proficient in this field."[2]

Up to now, anyone who endeavored, on his own initiative, to search for the spiritual bond that unites all these works and that assigns to Bach's entire creative work for the organ a position in a broader context, was obliged to collect his materials for this purpose from abroad, for there still exists no monograph on Bach's organ works even halfway satisfactory in the German language, although there are some in French and in English.

This situation is disgraceful enough in itself, but is all the more so since no other department of Bach's entire production seems to lend itself so admirably to a study of this kind. It is implicit in the exceptional position that the organ holds, as a means of producing tone and as an instrument for the church service, that Bach's organ works constitute a province with fixed boundaries on all sides, except that border communication on the side of the stringed keyboard instruments remains open. In their range of forms, as well as in their capacity for expression, they are a law unto themselves.

In addition there is their unique greatness, a quality recognized from the start: if the organ comes into fullest flower during the Baroque, Bach's works, within the organ music of the Baroque, represent a culmination never reached before or since. The general effect of his choral works, sacred as well as secular, is severely impaired partly by their time-bound texts. Moreover, Bach was obliged to share with Scarlatti and Couperin the distinction of being the greatest harpsichord composer of his time, the former surpassing him in splendor and fire, the latter in elegance and grace, although both failed to equal him in depth. As a composer for the organ, however, as his contemporaries were aware, Bach had no equal.

1. See the title-page of the *Little Organ Book (Orgelbüchlein)*.
2. See the title-page of the *Well-Tempered Clavier*.

The beautiful pleases "without concepts,"[3] but no one who studies old music (and Bach's, of course, belongs in this category) can do without scholarship and its concepts.

Therefore I have tried first to sketch the culture of the Baroque and baroque organ music in concise summaries; afterwards, to present a survey of the organ works of Bach in a chronological order based on the inner development they reveal; and then to state a few fundamental principles relating to their performance. Following this, the general part of the book, will come in the second part the discussion of the individual works. These fall into two groups: free compositions and those based on a *cantus firmus*. They are dealt with chronologically within each group.

Each individual composition will be treated here as something unique, not as something referrable to the collective work of the composer. Here I felt obliged to make judgments of value, however conditional; the scholar may let them alone but to the performer they are indispensable. One kind of evaluation, of course, is expressed by the amount of space allotted to a piece. In this respect, also, this book is somewhat at variance with previous research in which a number of youthfully-immature and weaker works have been discussed in detail, while some of the last preludes and fugues—works with which the performer will never be finished in his entire life—have been given only a summary treatment. But precisely here the difficulty of my task was most evident to me: it is by no means easier to write about a work one has known by heart for years or decades than about another to which one feels inwardly less attracted.

Because of restrictions imposed, I had to forego breadth of presentation and be as concise as possible. I venture to hope, however, that this book, even in this form, may afford friendly counsel to many an organist; and I should like to thank the publisher who is making possible its publication now in spite of all difficulties.[4] For what better could we do in the tense and restricted conditions of the times than to admire again and again the timeless greatness of Johann Sebastian Bach?

SOURCES

In order to understand correctly the way in which Bach's organ works have been handed down to us, we must first remember that most of the organ music of the baroque era remained unprinted. After

3. See Immanuel Kant, *Critique of Judgment*, translated by J. H. Bernard (New York: Hafner Publishing Co., 1951), p. 54, "The *beautiful* is that which pleases universally without [requiring] a concept."

4. The work was completed in 1941, but the first printing was destroyed in 1943—an effect of the war.

the *Tabulatura Nova* of Scheidt (1624)[5]—comprising nearly 800 pages—virtually no organ works appeared in print for the next hundred years. The reason for this lacuna is to be sought not only in the impoverishment brought on by the Thirty Years' War but also in the custom of the time, of writing down music primarily for one's own use (or that of a sovereign) or, possibly, also of lending to pupils or friends for copying.

Buxtehude's organ works, for example, have been handed down to us solely in copies of this kind, as have also the majority of Bach's. Of a smaller number of Bach's works the autograph has been preserved (see p. 31). Only three collections of chorale preludes appeared in print during Bach's lifetime; these he edited himself: in 1739 the *Third Part of the Clavierübung* and, in 1746, the *Six Chorales* (the so-called "Schübler") and the *Canonic Variations on "Vom Himmel hoch, da komm ich her."*

When Bach's lifework seemed to have gone into eclipse after his death, a small number of pupils, friends, and "connoisseurs of work of this kind"[6] preserved the compositions that were in manuscript until the revival of Bach's music at the beginning of the nineteenth century. As one of the first, Haslinger in Vienna published six of Bach's preludes and fugues for organ, the so-called "Great" (Peters edition, Vol. II, Nos. 8, 10, 1, 6, 7, and 9). However, he supplied them with marks for *crescendo* and *diminuendo* in the style of Czerny; for example, he had the C Major Fugue (II, 7) close with a *diminuendo* from *ff* to *pp*. Shortly thereafter he announced a complete edition of Bach's organ works of which, however, only two installments appeared: the C Minor Fugue on a Theme of Legrenzi (IV, 6) and the Canonic Variations.

A little later (1844) Friedrich Conrad Griepenkerl and Ferdinand August Roitzsch began their critical edition of the collected works for the firm of C. F. Peters, an achievement of truly historical importance. Its authority remains unshaken even today. Moreover, it is by far the most widely used edition; therefore citations will be made from it.[7] The editors had estimated the edition at seven volumes: Vol. I contained the works which they assumed were intended for the pedal-harpsichord; Vols. II-IV, preludes, fugues, and toccatas; Vols. V-VII, the arrangements of chorales; but as early as 1852 an eighth volume appeared, and in 1881 a ninth, edited by Roitzsch. This last volume was re-edited by Max Seiffert in 1904 and reorganized by me once again in 1940; citations from Vol. IX will follow this last edition only.

---

5. Three vols.; mod. ed. pub. in 1892 as Vol. I of *Denkmäler deutscher Tonkunst.*
6. See the title-page of the *Third Part of the Clavierübung.*
7. See the List of Abbreviations, p. 312.

Griepenkerl and Roitzsch had separated Bach's arrangements of chorales into "large" and "small," though not with complete success; they had also arranged them in alphabetical order and thus destroyed the original, intended order in the collections which Bach had himself assembled. The Peters firm restored this order by publishing the *Little Organ Book*, the *Third Part of the Clavierübung*, and the *Six Chorales* together with the *Eighteen Chorales*, in three volumes in the order of the autograph.

The second great critical edition of the collected organ works is that contained in the complete edition of Bach's works by the *Bach Gesellschaft* (BG). Volume III contains the *Third Part of the Clavierübung* (ed., C. F. Becker), Vols. XV (Wilhelm Rust) and XXXVIII (Karl Ernst Naumann) the free works, and Vols. XXV (Rust) and XL (Naumann) the arrangements of chorales. It is true that additional manuscripts were available to the Bach Gesellschaft, but many of these were of lesser worth, while various important manuscripts that Griepenkerl had still been able to use had later disappeared. Nevertheless, this edition forms an important supplement to the Peters edition.

In 1950, the anniversary year of Bach's death, a hundred years after the beginning of the old edition of Bach, the corner stone was laid for a new edition of Bach's works, the *Neue Bach-Ausgabe* (NBA). Today the philological apparatus has become so voluminous that it can no longer be accommodated in a preface or appendix but requires its own supplements.

In connection with the NBA a standard work should be mentioned: the "thematic-systematic index of the works of Bach," the *Bach-Werke-Verzeichnis* (BWV) which Wolfgang Schmieder published through the firm of Breitkopf & Härtel in 1950; a 2nd, revised edition is expected shortly.[8] The BWV has the same importance for Bach as the Köchel Verzeichnis has for Mozart. In the present book, therefore, each work will be identified, along with its title, not only by its location in one of the nine volumes of the Peters edition but also by its number in the BWV.

All editions without their own textual criticism which have appeared since the Peters edition and the Bach Gesellschaft go back to these two editions. Most of the practical editions prior to the reform "Organ Movement" must be viewed today as antiquated; for example, the edition of Karl Ernst Naumann published by Breitkopf & Härtel in nine volumes (the order not agreeing with that in the Peters edition, however), the four-volume selection of Paul Homeyer (Steingräber), and others. Only the interpretive edition of the second Peters volume,

8. Another useful index is that prepared by May deForest McAll, a *Melodic Index to the Works of J. S. Bach: New Complete Tabulation of the Themes, with a Cross Reference to the Schmieder Index* (Peters No. 6300).

published in 1913 by Karl Straube, still deserves to be used today—or at least to be consulted—in spite of the radical change in style that has taken place meanwhile. This edition has the same value as have the editions of Beethoven's last piano sonatas by Hans von Bülow and the edition of Bach's clavier works by Busoni.

Besides the Peters edition and the Bach Gesellschaft or NBA, of which the former serves chiefly a practical purpose, the latter a scholarly one, we should like to mention certain editions prepared outside Germany. The Novello edition (London) in 15 volumes,[9] is not only an excellent example of the printer's art, but also includes the words of the chorales and simple four-part settings of the chorale melodies. The edition by Marcel Dupré (Paris) has a pedagogical aim and gives the student the most careful fingering and pedalling as well as directions for registration and changes of manual. Valuable as the fingering and pedalling are, the suggestions for registration reflect the state of the French art of playing the organ around the turn of the century. The change in Bach's musical picture is also disturbing. Dupré shortens to half-value notes of equal length which need to be detached—something like this: instead of ♩ ♩ ♩ ♩ he writes ♪𝄾 ♪𝄾 ♪𝄾 ♪𝄾. Before the First World War, Charles-Marie Widor and Albert Schweitzer began publishing organ works of Bach after the text of the BG, without markings, but with instructions for performance in a preface; up to 1914 four volumes had appeared (the free organ works). Recently, from Lambarene, in Africa, Albert Schweitzer alone followed these volumes with arrangements of chorales. His suggestions for performance are based on the principles of the Alsatian-French organ reform, which Schweitzer himself had initiated.

Of the more recent German editions I should like to mention my edition of the chorale preludes with texts, chorale harmonizations, and comments on origin and performance (Kassel: Bärenreiter-Verlag), of which two volumes appeared up to 1940: the *Orgelbüchlein* and the *Orgelchoräle Manualiter*.

Although marked editions may be instructive and interesting (or even convenient), I am of the same opinion as Schweitzer, that "a true organist does not submit to the instruction of a practical edition, but keeps for himself some first edition in which he enters his own observations and experiments."[10] Since entries of this kind spoil the neat appearance of a volume, it is my advice never to write registrations in the volume of music but in a separate notebook. The organ-

9. A revised edition is now in progress under the general editorship of Walter Emery. Emery also issues *Notes on Bach's Organ Works* in the form of separate pamphlets, each "A Companion to the Revised Novello Edition."

10. Cf. the Widor-Schweitzer edition of Bach's *Organ Works*, I, iii.

ist who concertizes should always have two notebooks: one for use at his own organ, the other for use on tour.

LITERATURE

Since the literature on Bach has become virtually limitless, it is impossible to give an even approximately complete bibliography relating to the organ works. In any event, however, this would be futile, for, among all the comprehensive works dealing with Bach, only three contain material that is indispensable to the organist: the great biography by Philipp Spitta,[11] still standard even today, the valuable book on Bach by Albert Schweitzer,[12] and the book by Rudolf Steglich.[13] Spitta's opinions, though colored by romanticism and classicism, still deserve to be read over and over again. Since all organists do not possess the large biography of Spitta, I have quoted it word for word in a number of places. (The so-called *Volks-Spitta* is comparatively worthless, for it lacks precisely the material that is most important, namely, the aesthetic appraisals of the works.) Of the older literature, the biography of Johann Nicolaus Forkel (1802; modern edition, Bärenreiter-Verlag, 1925)[14] contains the most valuable summary of what Friedemann and Philipp Emanuel have handed down to us concerning their father's organ music.

The following monographs dealing with Bach's organ works may be mentioned. P. Jsidor Mayrhofer's *Bachstudien* (Leipzig: Breitkopf & Härtel, 1901) and Jodokus Kehrer's *Bach und der katholische Organist* (Regensburg: Pustet) are now out of print. In German: the dissertation of H. E. Huggler, *J. S. Bachs Orgelbüchlein* (Bern, 1935). In English: *The Organ Works of Bach* (London: Novello & Co., 1922) by Harvey Grace, written in a warm and stimulating style; *Bach's Organ Works* (London, 1929) by A. Eaglefield Hull, written with a lexicographer's conciseness; and Stainton de B. Taylor's handbook, *The Chorale Preludes of J. S. Bach* (London: Oxford University Press, 1942). More recently in England: *School of Bach-Playing for the Organist,* with Gordon Phillips as general editor. Of this series

---

11. *Johann Sebastian Bach: His Work and Influence on the Music of Germany, 1685-1750.* Translated from the German by Clara Bell and J. A. Fuller-Maitland. (3 vols. in 2; London: Novello & Co., Ltd., and New York: Dover Publications, Inc., 1951)
12. *J. S. Bach.* Translated by Ernest Newman; Preface by C.-M. Widor. (2 vols.; New York: The Macmillan Co., 1911, with many reprintings in later years.)
13. *Johann Sebastian Bach* (Potsdam: Athenaion, 1935).
14. An English translation may be seen in *The Bach Reader,* edited by Hans T. David and Arthur Mendel (New York: W. W. Norton & Co., 1945), Section Six, pp. 293-356.

we may mention: *Bach's Organ-Registration* by William L. Sumner, and *Tempo and Rhythm in Bach's Organ Music* by Robert Donington (Hinrichsen edition, Nos. 1002 and 1003). In the United States: *The Style of J. S. Bach's Chorale Preludes* by Robert L. Tusler (Berkeley and Los Angeles: The University of California Press, 1956). Hinrichsen's *Eighth Music Book* (London & New York: Hinrichsen Edition, 1956) is also of great value, since it is devoted exclusively to matters pertaining to the organ. It contains, among other items, *The Organ of Bach* (pp. 14-135) by William L. Sumner and *Silbermann and His Work* (pp. 217-243) also by Sumner.

In French: André Pirro, *L'Orgue de J.-S. Bach* (written 1894; published 1897; an Eng. tr. by Wallace Goodrich, New York, G. Schirmer, 1902, entitled *Johann Sebastian Bach: The Organist and His Works for the Organ*); François Florand, *J. S. Bach: L'Oeuvre d'orgue* (Paris, Éditions du Cerf, 1946; Ger. tr., Lindau, 1949); and N. Dufourcq, *J. S. Bach, le maître de l'orgue* (Paris, 1948).

We should like to mention the following articles which have appeared in periodicals and year books. In the *Bach-Jahrbücher*: 1918, Hans Luedtke's article on the chorale preludes; 1925 and 1928, Arnold Schering's contributions concerning "Bach und das Symbol"; 1929 and 1931, the two valuable articles by Fritz Dietrich on "Bachs Orgelchoral und seine geschichtlichen Wurzeln" and "Analogieformen in Bachs Toccaten und Praeludien für die Orgel"; in 1933, Friedrich Smend on the "Canonic Variations"; in 1937, Hermann Keller on "Unechte Orgelwerke Bachs"; in 1954, W. Schrammek on the Organ Sonatas. In *Musik und Kirche*, among other studies, Wilhelm Ehmann on the Third Part of the *Clavierübung* (1933); in *Musikforschung*, Hans Klotz's article "Über Bachs Orgeln und seine Orgelmusik," 1950. In the *Organ Institute Quarterly* Arthur Howes wrote on the "Schübler Chorale Preludes" (Vol. V, Nos. 1 and 2; Vol. 6, No. 4).

Most of the older periodical articles on Bach's organ works and their performance, those of Heinrich Reimann, for example, are now out of date. On the other hand, the Bach player may obtain for himself a wealth of information from the literature that the Organ Movement has produced; from many articles in *Musik und Kirche* in Germany and *The Organ Institute Quarterly* in the United States, and above all from these three works: Hans Klotz, *Über die Orgelkunst der Gotik, der Renaissance und des Barock* (Kassel: Bärenreiter-Verlag, 1934), the first thorough presentation of the old principles of specification and the registrations resulting from them; Karl Matthäi, *Vom Orgelspiel* (Leipzig: Breitkopf & Härtel, 1936), a practical book on the aesthetics of organ-playing (rhythm, phrasing, articulation, registration, ornamentation, etc.); and finally, the great handbook of Gotthold Frotscher, *Geschichte des Orgelspiels und der Orgelkomposition* (Berlin: Max Hesse's Verlag, 1935), two volumes of 1262 pages,[15] an imposing witness to the industry of German scholarship, in which once again the organ works (their formal aspect in particular) are subjected to a penetrating evaluation.

15. A third volume is in progress (1962). A second printing of the first two volumes was made in 1959 (Berlin: Merseburger).

PART I

THE WORLD OF THE ORGAN IN THE BAROQUE ERA

CHAPTER 1

THE CULTURE OF THE BAROQUE

The art of Bach reflected in his organ music is born of the culture of the Baroque, as is the whole art of his time, and a comprehension of it must start with this premise. To be sure, it draws its nourishment from still deeper sources—particularly in the arrangements of chorales—but in its perceptible form it is baroque. We must therefore reject the designation of Bach as a "Gothic" composer. This term, frequently employed, came into existence in the nineteenth century, a time which possessed no satisfactory knowledge of the real music of the Gothic era such as the Early Gothic *organa* of the Parisian school, the motets of the High Gothic, or the masses and settings of songs of the Late Gothic.

Although no culture ever asserted itself in a more absolute or dictatorial manner than did the Baroque, no one has yet succeeded in defining its character concisely and appropriately. It is more than "the art of the Counter Reformation," for the various forms it assumed linked all the European nations together in an impressive union irrespective of creed, including rich as well as poor, conqueror and conquered, and all social classes—except the peasantry, which had been condemned to impotency for centuries. Also in Germany the Baroque cast the glamour of a uniform and externally brilliant culture over the jealously guarded seclusion of its many small territories and over the high walls behind which classes and creeds entrenched themselves. Without this glamour life would often have been almost intolerable during the years of misery which followed the Thirty Years' War.

But all this still gives no conception of the real essence of the Baroque. As the immediate continuation of the High Renaissance in Italy, the Baroque continued all the great and the new produced by the preceding century but gave it a completely different and characteristic form. This may be shown by an example. One of the most valuable achievements of the Renaissance in the field of music was the revival of the classical drama accompanied by music, the birth of the opera. The forms in which this idea was realized, however, were from the very beginning baroque.

For Germany, the adoption of all these new alien art-forms meant a not inconsiderable foreign infiltration, particularly disastrous since Germany was too greatly weakened politically to be able to compete with something of its own. We notice this most keenly before Bach's time in the art that must be rooted most deeply in the common people—in poetry. On the other hand, Germany's involvement in the general European culture saved the German spiritual life from a decline which otherwise would have been unavoidable considering the moral degeneration—of the upper classes in particular—which was becoming prevalent as an aftermath of the war. At its core, however, the moral fibre of the common people, though greatly weakened, was still not completely destroyed, and it began gradually to strengthen after the war. Bach's ancestry offers an especially fine example of this slow but unswerving ascent.[16] Thus, the recovery of Germany after 1648 and a phenomenon such as Johann Sebastian Bach may be explained only by the interaction of these two factors: the uniformity existing throughout Europe in the general intellectual and moral state of culture and the slow recovery of Germany from within.

This culture revealed itself most clearly in the many royal establishments of the time. Even the most absolute prince was in reality merely a servant of this *Zeitgeist*—the cultural trend of the period. The household of the prince formed "a pyramid with the prince as its peak." In these courts life in all its splendor and drama must have seemed like one long festival.

The political philosophy of the age (the "reason of state") was baroque. The forms of social courtesy (from which the *Sie* and *Ihnen* have been maintained down to our own time) and the high-flown formulas used to express deference (notice Bach's dedications—of the Brandenburg Concertos, for example) were also baroque. Baroque was the philosophy for which Leibniz in his theory of monads erected a well-organized mansion. Baroque, also, was the predilection for mathematics, which ranked as the highest of the sciences. The arts, of course, showed more clearly than all else the mark of the era; they became, as Burckhardt observes, "subservient and monumental"—a judgment too depreciative, perhaps. This culture was indeed not only monumental but also contemplative in the metaphysical

16. See Karl Geiringer (in collaboration with Irene Geiringer), *The Bach Family: Seven Generations of Creative Genius*. (New York: Oxford University Press, 1954.)

sense, and the baroque arts gave expression to both these qualities: the compulsion toward outward display and the propensity for contemplation. Accordingly, it is no wonder that those two arts that appeal most strongly to the senses, architecture and music, came into full flower in the baroque era—ahead of the other arts.

The architecture of the Baroque was no longer dominated by cathedral and castle, as in the Middle Ages, or by the patrician dwelling, as in the German Renaissance, but rather by the palace in its setting of formal gardens. Even the churches of this period impress us as being ecclesiastical palaces, and when the history of music calls this the era of "concerted music," it is merely conveying the same meaning in the language of the musician.

The parts played by the North and the South were different, both in their cultivation of these two arts and in the preference they accorded outward pomp and inward reflection. The warmer, more sensual Catholic South achieved immortality in architecture through its palaces, with their sculpture and gardens, as well as through its cloisters; in the field of music the South cultivated primarily the most grandiose form, the opera. In contrast, the Protestant North, with its more abstract spirituality, sought a way out of the narrowness of the spatial world into the realm of contemplation, and created immortal works in the fields of absolute and of church music in particular. But the North and the South continually penetrated each other. On the boundary between the two, "when the fullness of the time was come," was born Johann Sebastian Bach.

When we examine the history of music, we find that in it, too, the Baroque is more homogeneous and self-contained than any other musical period. The "thorough-bass period" coincides amazingly with the limits of the Baroque. Accordingly, this period partly created and partly brought to full flower a great wealth of its own forms. In vocal music there were the ingenious new creations: the opera, the oratorio, the solo cantata, the church cantata, the aria, and the recitative. In instrumental music, the realm of "absolute" music was not really established until after 1600. Yet even here a wealth of forms appeared almost immediately: the trio sonata, the five-part orchestral sonata, the concerto grosso, the solo concerto, the solo sonata with thorough-bass, and the suite using all possible combinations of instruments. Along with the chamber music flourished music for keyboard instruments: the toccata, the ricercar, the fantasy, the prelude, the fugue, the passacaglia and chaconne, the song variation, and the chorale prelude in all styles.

Even in the area of instrumental music the North and the South went their own ways. Italy developed chamber music to a high point; in the North, on the other hand, there was *one* instrument, but it combined in itself all other musical instruments. From the time of Praetorius it was the *organ,* with the solemnity of its principals, the majestic brilliance of its mixtures, the burring, penetrating sound of its reeds, and the terracing of its manuals, that was meant when the Baroque said simply "the instrument." Thus, the golden age of the organ also coincided of necessity with the Baroque, not only because the organ was superior to all other instruments, even to the baroque orchestra, in magnificence and splendor, but also because its sound directs our thoughts to something more sublime. The lineage of German organ music, then, and with it the course of organ music in general, runs from Frescobaldi and Scheidt to Bach. It is only natural that the organ had to retire from the stage of music history when music descended from heaven to men and spoke warmly and intimately with them—in short, when music ceased to be contemplative and representative in the baroque sense.

CHAPTER 2

THE ORGANS OF THE BAROQUE

Soul and body form an inseparable union; and the soul as leader can communicate its thoughts only through the medium of the body. Similarly, the soul of music, which is handed down to us in musical symbols, has need of its body, the instrument belonging to it. To the organ music of the Baroque belong the organs of the Baroque.

Only the reform movements of recent decades have taught us to perceive again this simple truth, which we had heedlessly ignored for more than a hundred years. Today a whole series of excellent studies dealing specifically with the construction of baroque organs is available to the organist; yet all knowledge of specifications, old scales, and the like, remains merely book learning if the performer himself has never played on one or another of the old instruments still kept in repair. The finest names of stops listed in reform specifications must not deceive us on the point that the old stops sound quite different from the present ones with the same names.

For the sake of simplicity we shall call the three principal types of baroque organ-construction by the names "Praetorius organ" for the early-baroque type, "Schnitger organ" for the high-baroque, and "Silbermann organ" for the late-baroque type.

The first of these need not come under consideration here; these instruments are suitable for the music of Scheidt, but are of little use for Buxtehude, and of no use at all for Bach. They have a clear, hard, straight tone in which the individuality of the stop is stronger than its readiness to blend. It was this characteristic which gave rise to the rule against drawing "two equal voices"—i.e., two stops of the same pitch—simultaneously.

The large instruments in North Germany, built (or rebuilt) by Arp Schnitger, realized most magnificently the high-baroque ideal of organ-building. The number of manuals was increased to four; tonal resources were augmented; mutations and reeds became more numerous; the *Plenum* of the individual divisions of the organ became fuller and more flexible; and the rule forbidding the drawing of two equal voices at the same time was abandoned, or at least relaxed. These instruments, indeed, signify not only the crowning achievement of the Baroque, but of organ-building in general. They are the "tonal body" for the great works of the North Germans, especially for Buxtehude, and equally for the early works of Bach.

The transition to the Late Baroque, which began shortly after 1700, signified a decline; the mutations were limited, the number of reeds lessened, the *Rückpositiv* was omitted, and the foundation-stops were augmented—by string stops particularly. However, just as Bach opposed his colossal ability to the decline in organ composition in the first half of the eighteenth century, the decline in organ-building was arrested by the brothers Silbermann: Andreas, the elder, active in Alsace, and the younger Gottfried, who built a large number of instruments in Saxony and thereby became especially important for Bach. The tone of the Saxon Silbermann-organs may be considered standard for the Leipzig works of Bach.

Even if we are acquainted with the instruments of that time and have the sound of their stops in our ears, the most important question still remains open. Which stops were used together; how were pieces registered with them? Here we must first establish the curious fact that stop combinations have come down to us from the French, but hardly any at all from Germans. Dom Bedos specifies no less than 26 different combinations of stops for every possible situation in his *L'Art du facteur d'orgues* (1766):[17] for the "slow fugue," for the "fugue played in a lively manner," for reed solos, for duos, trios, etc. We do find something similar in the writings of Karl Riepp, the builder of the two organs in Ottobeuren.

In Germany, on the other hand, after Scheidt's well-known instructions at the end of the *Tabulatura Nova,* there exist only a few instances of reasonably precise directions. Perhaps the rules (and most certainly rules were known to the Baroque) were passed on from teacher to pupil through private instruction. Or was it that composers

---

17. Cited in Émile Rupp, *Entwicklungsgeschichte der Orgelbaukunst* (Einsiedeln: Benziger & Co., 1929), pp. 199ff. See also "Dom Bedos de Celles, 'L'Art du facteur d'orgues'," translation of certain passages with notes by W. L. Sumner, *Organ Institute Quarterly,* VII (1957)-VIII (1958), especially vol. VIII, No. 2, pp. 11-14.

and theorists did not wish to encroach upon the rights of the "distinguished and learned organist"? In any event, the instructions that have been preserved give us few clues.

The most important and most controversial concept relating to the old organ music is the direction *Pro Organo Pleno* (or *In Organo Pleno*, or even—with the ablative absolute—simply *Organo Pleno*). That "Full Organ" at that time did not mean all the stops of the organ, the modern *tutti*, is, I daresay, universally well-known today; on the contrary, the term meant that sound of mixtures peculiar to the organ among all instruments of sound, which arises when mutations and mixtures are combined with foundation stops of 8', 4', 2', and, occasionally, 16'.

The concept of the *Plenum* was changing constantly during the Baroque. The *Plenum* of Praetorius had fewer stops than did that of Schnitger. That of Silbermann had more foundation stops than did that of Schnitger. The *Plenum* of the *Hauptwerk* or of the *Pedal* was frequently based on 16' or 32' as fundamental, and had principals for foundation tone, while the *Plenum* of the *Rückpositiv* or of the *Brustwerk* was erected on 8' tone, as a rule, and often had only a single stop of wide scale (perhaps an 8' Gedackt) as base.

The generous provision of reeds during the Baroque, especially in the *Hauptwerk* and *Pedal*, makes it obvious that these also contributed to the *Plenum*. Usually the *Plenum* of the *Rückpositiv* was kept more brilliant, that of the *Brustwerk* milder, but so many possibilities for variety existed that no strict rules can be formulated. According to Mattheson, in *Der vollkommene Capellmeister*,[18] the following stops "belong to the full organ:[19] the principals, the sorduns, the salicionals or salicets (willow pipes), the Rausch-Pfeifen, the octaves, the quints, mixtures, scharfs (little mixtures of three pipes),[20] the quintatens *(Quintadeen)*, cymbels, Nasat, the terz *(Terzien)*, sesquialteras, superoctaves, posaunes in the Pedal, not in the manual: for the Posaunes are a reed-work, which is excluded from the manual in full organ *(bey voller Orgel)*." Matthäi[21] wishes to have drawn for the *Plenum* "the complete pyramid of principals (8', 4', 2', 1', 2 2/3', and the mixture) in addition to the open flutes, both narrow and wide, the Hohlflöte 8', the Spitzflöte 4', and the Waldflöte 2', as well as the stopped and half-stopped voices."

Through a fortunate circumstance important directions for registration by Gottfried Silbermann have been preserved.[22] The "full

---

18. Hamburg, 1739 (facs. ed., Kassel and Basel, Bärenreiter-Verlag, 1954), p. 467, par. 76.
19. Ger.: *"zum vollen Werck."*
20. This probably means three pipes to each key, i.e., three ranks.
21. Matthäi, *Vom Orgelspiel*, pp. 104f.
22. Ernst Flade, *Der Orgelbauer G. Silbermann*, pp. 94ff.; Frotscher, *op. cit.*, pp. 1023ff.

combination,"[23] the "pure, full play,"[24] consisted of the following stops: in the *Hauptwerk*, Principal 8', Octave 4', Rohrflöte 8', Quint 2 2/3', Superoctave 2', and Mixture IV rks.; in the *Oberwerk*, Gedackt 8', Rohrflöte 4', Principal 2', Quint 1 1/3', Sifflöte 1', and Cymbel II rks.; in the *Pedal*, Sub-Bass 16', Posaune 16', and Octave 8'. These were all the stops in the organ except, in the *Hauptwerk*, the Quintadena 8', Cornet III rks. (which were kept in reserve for solo effects), and the Spitzflöte 4'; in the *Oberwerk* are lacking the Nasat 2 2/3', Gemshorn 2' (since the Principal 2' is already present), and the Terz 1 3/5'; in the *Pedal* everything has been drawn, and the keyboards are assumed to be coupled. In this small organ of 21 stops, then, 15 constituted the *Plenum;* from this small registration conclusions may easily be drawn concerning larger instruments.

Along with the *Plenum*, quite a number of combinations for bringing a c.f. into prominence were known to the Baroque. Klotz[25] cites a great many combinations, some of which are astonishing. Gottfried Silbermann also divulges a few for us: e.g., the "Cornet-combination": Principal 8', Rohrflöte 8', Octave 4', and Cornet III rks.; or, Cornet as solo, accompanied by Gedackt 8' and Rohrflöte 4' or Gemshorn 2' in the *Oberwerk*. The "Cornet-combination" in the *Oberwerk* contained: Gedackt 8', Nasat 2 2/3', and Terz 1 3/5'; the "Nasat-combination" in the *Oberwerk:* Gedackt 8', Rohrflöte 4', and Nasat 2 2/3', accompanied by the Rohrflöte 8' and Spitzflöte 4' of the *Hauptwerk*. The "Terz-combination" on the *Oberwerk* contained Gedackt 8', Rohrflöte 4', Nasat 2 2/3', Principal 2', and Terz 1 3/5'—one can see how cautiously Silbermann was already "covering" the Terz. "Stahlspiel" (i.e., "Glockenspiel") he calls the following combination: Gedackt 8', Nasat 2 2/3', Terz 1 3/5', Quint 1 1/3', and Sifflöte 1', accompanied by the Rohrflöte 8' and Spitzflöte 4'. These instructions already show a very great difference from the c.f.-combinations of the outgoing seventeenth century, which occasionally leap an interval of over two octaves between the fundamental and the overtones; for example, in coupling Principal and Cymbel.

The third manner of registering possible in principle, that with foundation-stops only, gives occasion for few remarks except that, even after 1700, several 8'-voices were seldom drawn simultaneously (which was a matter of course for the organist of the nineteenth century), but that a 4' or 2' or both had to be added to a fairly weak 8'.

---

23. The German is: "der völlige Zug." In this context "Zug" refers to the "drawing" of stops; therefore here, and in the next paragraph, the more modern term "combination" is used. (*Tr.*)

24. Ger.: "das reine volle Spiel."

25. *Op. cit.*, pp. 207ff.

In performing baroque organ music the player will have to decide for himself on one of these three possibilities in each situation: *Organum Plenum,* c.f.-combinations, or foundation stops. This does not mean any limitation of the possibilities for tone color, however; within each group there are as many colors as the player may need, if he will only seek and find them. Basically, all the large free pieces—preludes, toccatas, and fugues—should be played with a *Plenum.* This, however, may be brilliant or mild, full or thin, with or without gaps in the overtone structure, etc., corresponding to the character of the piece. For bringing out a c.f., reeds may be used as solo stops, also—if they are good ones—besides the combinations cited above. Foundation stops will be used for the accompaniment of a c.f. and for small pieces, especially those without pedals; for example, movements of chorale partitas, etc.

CHAPTER 3

BACH'S ORGANS AND ORGAN-PLAYING

Not all the organs Bach played during his life were "Bach organs."[26] The Obituary[27] indeed states that "He never succeeded, as he used to lament, in having a really large and really fine organ for his regular use. This fact has deprived us of many fine ideas never heard in organ playing which he would otherwise have set down on paper and displayed just as he had them in his head." It is true that the organs he had to play on as organist were, for the most part, mediocre instruments. But if, in his youth, an instrument rich in stops and powerful in tone perhaps had inspired him to still more daring productions, the art of the mature Bach would have become

---

26. See Hans Löffler, "J. S. Bach und die Orgeln seiner Zeit," in *Bericht über die dritte Tagung für deutsche Orgelkunst in Freiberg,* 1927, p. 122; G. Frotscher, "Zur Problematik der Bach-Orgel," *Bach-Jahrbuch,* 1935. The following studies published since the present book was written have brought out new information and should be consulted: Hans Klotz, "Bachs Orgeln und seine Orgelmusik," *Musikforschung,* III (1950), 189ff.; Werner David, *Johann Sebastian Bachs Orgeln* (Berlin, 1951), written for the reopening of the Berlin collection of musical instruments; William L. Sumner, "The Organs Played by Bach," *Eighth Music Book,* pp. 71-116.

27. See *The Bach Reader,* Section Four, pp. 213-224, for an English translation of the "Obituary, of Bach," which was originally written by C.P.E. Bach and J. F. Agricola (a pupil of Bach) and published in Mizler's *Musikalische Bibliothek* in 1754. Since this obituary is short, no references to specific page numbers will be given for brief quotations made in the following pages.

continually more independent of the instrument, more abstract, and more profound. "Do you suppose that I am thinking of your wretched violin when the spirit comes over me?" exclaimed Beethoven to Schuppanzigh.

The large 4-manual organ of St. George's Church in Eisenach was to be rebuilt by G. C. Stertzing according to designs and specifications of Johann Christoph. When Johann Sebastian left his parents' home to go to Ohrdruf, however, the rebuilding had not yet started. Hans Löffler has pointed out that Bach's design for the organ in Mühlhausen was strongly influenced by that of his uncle. In Ohrdruf, also, the large organ was in bad condition; Bach practiced, indeed, on a small instrument (4 manual stops and a Sub-Bass).[28]

The organ in St. John's Church in Lüneburg, where Böhm was organist from 1698 to 1733, had been built in 1550; Praetorius describes it in his *Organographia.*[29] It was rebuilt in 1712-1715. Little is known about the organ in St. Michael's, which was rebuilt 1705-1708.[30] The obituary notice tells us that Bach "sometimes went from Lüneburg to Hamburg to hear the distinguished organist of St. Catherine's Church, Johann Adam Reinken." The famous instrument, renovated in 1670 by Johann Friedrich Besser, was a 4-manual organ of 58 stops; it had 11 in the *Hauptwerk,* 13 in the *Rückpositiv,* 10 in the *Oberwerk,* 7 in the *Brustwerk,* and 17 (among them 7 reeds) in the *Pedal.*[31] Bach admired it, as we are informed by his pupil Johann Friedrich Agricola,[32] especially the Contra-Posaune 32' and the precise speech of the Principal-Bass 32' down to C. Of the whole instrument he mentioned with highest praise the wealth of reed stops, of which the organ had 16 in all, as well as the beauty and variety of their tone.

Bach tested and approved the new organ in St. Boniface' Church in Arnstadt on July 3, 1703;[33] this instrument had been erected by Johann Friedrich Wender of Mühlhausen. Bach's certificate of appointment was dated August 9, 1703, and he was formally inducted on August 14, 1703,[34] with the relatively high salary of 84 gulden a

28. Löffler, p. 123, David, p. 79, and Sumner, p. 73, all give the list of stops on this small instrument.

29. Michael Praetorius, *De Organographia* (Vol. II of the *Syntagma Musicum,* Wolfenbüttel, 1619; facs. ed., Kassel, Bärenreiter, 1929), p. 170. Sumner, pp. 75f., gives its specifications.

30. David, p. 80, and Sumner, p. 74, give stops before this rebuilding.

31. David, p. 82, and Sumner, pp. 76f., give list of stops.

32. See Jacob Adlung, *Musica Mechanica Organoedi* (Berlin, 1768; facs. ed., Kassel, Bärenreiter, 1931), Vol. I, pp. 66, 187, and 288, for footnotes by Agricola, who made certain additions to the MS of Adlung at the request of the publisher. Adlung had died in 1762 before his work could be published.

33. See also *The Bach Reader,* p. 49.

34. These dates are after Charles Sanford Terry, *Bach: A Biography,* 2nd and rev. ed., London, Oxford University Press, 1933, pp. 62-63.

year.[35] The list of stops on this organ, for which so many of Bach's early works were written, should interest us especially. It reads:[36]

Oberwerk		*Brustwerk*		*Pedal*	
Quintaton	8' *	Gedackt	8' *	Sub-Bass	16'
Principal	8'	Principal	4'	Violon-Bass	16'
Gemshorn	8' *	Nachthorn	4' *	Principal-Bass	8'
Gedackt	8' *	Quint (2 2/3')	3'	Hohlflöte (g-d')	8'
Viola da Gamba	8' *	Spitzflöte	2'	Posaunen-Bass	16'
Octave	4'	Octave	2'		
Quint (5 1/3')	6'	Sesquialtera			
Mixture	IV rks.	Mixture	IV rks.		
Cymbel	III rks.				
Trumpet	8'				
Glocken-Accord (Cymbelstern)					

OW to Ped. and OW to BW couplers; Tremulant in the OW.

Another organ of about the same size, a 2-manual of 22 stops, stood in the Upper Church;[37] I cannot suppose, however, that either of these organs would have stimulated Bach's musical imagination. Moreover, one receives the impression that the many new constructions and reconstructions that we encounter between 1700 and 1710 not only should be attributed to external urgency (need for repair of instruments that had become defective, etc.) but arose from a change in taste. Hence, it was perhaps the reputation of the two old organs in St. Mary's Church in Lübeck quite as much as the fame of the celebrated master, Buxtehude, which attracted the young organist when he undertook his journey to Lübeck. The large organ there was a 3-manual of 54 stops (13 in the *Oberwerk*, 12 in the *Brustwerk*, 14 in the *Rückpositiv*, and 15 in the *Pedal*) and was unusually well supplied at all pitches not only in the manuals but also in the pedal. It had been built in 1516-1518 by Barthold Hering, but had been in bad condition for a long time.[38] The small organ in the Chapel of the

---

35. To obtain the money value in marks today (1940) this figure should be multiplied by perhaps anywhere from 15 to 18.
36. Six of these stops (marked with an asterisk) are included in the present instrument. The old console exists today, but names on the stop knobs have become virtually illegible. (Ill. No. 28 in Terry, *op. cit.*) Spitta, Terry, *et al.*, differ in listing the stops. David, *op. cit.*, p. 83, gives a summary of these differences. The stop list above follows David, as being a close approximation of what Bach's organ contained.
37. Adlung, I, 197ff., gives the stop list of this organ.
38. Wilhelm Stahl, *Dietrich Buxtehude* (Kassel and Basel: Bärenreiter-Verlag, 1937), p. 23. See David, *op. cit.*, pp. 85f., or Sumner, *op. cit.*, pp. 81ff., etc., for list of stops.

Dance of Death *(Totentanz)* was a 3-manual instrument of 37 stops.[39] Unfortunately, we know nothing whatsoever about the impression these famous organs made on Bach.

When Bach exchanged his position at Arnstadt for the one at Mühlhausen, he found there a 2-manual organ with the following specifications:

Hauptwerk		*Rückpositiv*		*Pedal*	
Quintadena	16'	Quintadena	8'	Principal	16'
Principal	8'	Gedackt	8'	Sub-Bass	16'
Gemshorn	8'	Principal	4'	Octave-Bass	8'
Octave	4'	Salicional	4'	Octave-Bass	4'
Gedackt	4'	Octave	2'	Cornet	2'
Quint	2 2/3'	Spitzflote	2'	Rohrflöte	1'
Octave	2'	Quint	1 1/3'	Mixture	IV rks.
Sesquialtera	II rks.	Sesquialtera	II rks.	Posaune	16'
Mixture	IV rks.	Mixture	III rks.	Trumpet	8'
Cymbel	II rks.				
Trumpet	8'				

Since this organ also was considered to be in need of renovation, Bach had here the first and only opportunity of his life to make plans himself for the reconstruction of an organ. For this reason his memorandum is of special interest to us: he proposed a Sub-Bass 32' for the pedal and a Glockenspiel of 4' pitch (which was never built); the Posaunen-Bass should produce a much more solid tone; in the *Hauptwerk,* in place of the Trumpet 8', should be installed a Fagotto 16' "which is useful for all kinds of new ideas *(inventiones)* and sounds very fine in concerted music *(in der Music)*"; in place of the Gemshorn Bach wanted a Viola da Gamba, "which will blend admirably with the Salicional 4' already present in the *Rückpositiv*"; instead of the Quint 2 2/3', a Nasat. In addition, he wanted a complete new *Brustwerk* of 7 stops: Schalmei 8', Quint 2 2/3', Octave 2' (these three "in the face," i.e., in the organ screen), a Mixture III rks., a Terz 1 3/5', "with which, by using a few other stops, one can produce a perfectly beautiful Sesquialtera," a Flauto dolce 4', and a Stillgedackt 8', "as may go well with concerted music and, made of good wood, should sound much better than a metal Gedackt"; in addition, a coupler from the *Brustwerk* to the *Hauptwerk* and, finally, "the Tremulant must be regulated to be in the correct scale for waving [the tone]."

---

39. Klotz, *Über die Orgelkunst*, p. 414, gives the list of the stops on this organ in Bach's day.

Hence the organ had the following specifications after being rebuilt:[40]

Hauptwerk (middle manual)		*Rückpositiv*	
Quintadena	16'	Quintadena	8'
Principal	8'	Gedackt	8'
Viola da Gamba	8'	Principal	4'
Octave	4'	Salicional	4'
Gedackt	4'	Octave	2'
Nasat	2 2/3'	Spitzflöte	2'
Octave	2'	Quint	1 1/3'
Sesquialtera	II rks.	Sesquialtera	II rks.
Mixture	IV rks.	Mixture	III rks.
Cymbel	II rks.		
Fagotto	16'		

Brustwerk (top manual)		*Pedal*	
Still-Gedackt	8'	Sub-Bass	32'
Flauto dolce	4'	Principal-Bass	16'
Quint	2 2/3'	Sub-Bass	16'
Octave	2'	Octave	8'
Terz	1 3/5'	Octave	4'
Mixture	III rks.	Cornet	2'
Schalmei	8'	Rohrflöte	1'
		Mixture	IV rks.
		Posaune	16'
		Trumpet	8'

Coupler from *Brustwerk* to *Hauptwerk*. Tremulant.

Noteworthy is Bach's preference for the Sesquialtera, which was now represented on each of the three manuals. But what were the "new *inventiones*" for the sake of which Bach had the Trumpet replaced by a Fagotto 16'? Is this passage perhaps related to Bach's concern for the "*Music*," i.e., for the suitability of the organ for accompanying cantatas? In these the Fagotto could be used successfully for bringing out *continuo*-basses more strongly, and the Gedackt with the Flauto dolce for delicate accompaniments.

As a solo instrument the organ now met the requirements of the organ music of the High Baroque. Spitta demonstrated cleverly the way in which Bach used the new stops.[41] He associated a memorandum on Walther's copy of the chorale-fantasy "Ein feste Burg" (VI, 22) with the reconstructed organ in Mühlhausen.[42] On this copy one

40. David, *op. cit.*, pp. 86-87, gives the specifications of this organ after Adlung, I, pp. 260-261, where the names of the stops are slightly different
41. Spitta, *op. cit.*, I, 394ff.
42. See p. 237.

reads *"a 3 Clav."*; above the beginning of the left-hand part, "Fagotto"; and above that of the right hand, "Sesquialtera." Bach was already in Weimar when the rebuilding was completed (1709) but surely had returned to approve the organ and on that occasion played this powerful-sounding fantasy. Spitta conjectured further than the first entry of the pedals in eighths would display the precise and light speech of the new 32', just as the c.f. in the pedal, four measures later, would show off the improved Posaunen-Bass. Consequently, we have here not merely the only draft of a specification from Bach's hand, but also the only extant example of his unusual and bold registrations.

In June, 1708, Bach had accepted a position at the ducal court in Weimar as chamber musician and organist of the castle church. The tiny capital was to be his home for nearly ten years. The church was very high and narrow, and the organ was installed in a "balustraded gallery in the roof."[43] The chapel had come to be known as "der Weg zur Himmelsburg," or merely "Himmelsburg" ("The Way to the City of Heaven"). The organ had the following specifications after having been rebuilt:[44]

Oberwerk		*Brustwerk*		*Pedal*	
Quintaton	16'	Principal	8'	Gross-Untersatz	32'
Principal	8'	Viola da Gamba	8'	Sub-Bass	16'
Gemshorn	8'	Gedackt	8'	Violon-Bass	16'
Gedackt	8'	Kleingedackt	4'	Principal	8'
Quintaton	4'	Octave	4'	Cornet-Bass	4'
Octave	4'	Waldflöte	2'	Posaune	16'
Mixture VI rks.		Sesquialtera IV rks.		Trumpet	8'
Cymbel III rks.		Trumpet	8'		

Tremulants, Cymbelstern, Glockenspiel (installed in 1715)

The only account of this organ that we have is found in *Historische Nachrichten von der berühmten Residenz-Stadt Weimar* by Gottfried Albin Wette.[45] The specifications given above are those known to Wette in 1737. The organ was rebuilt in 1714 and again in 1729; the specifications given here probably correspond only in part to the state of the organ during Bach's period in Weimar.[46] In Wette's book

43. Terry, *op. cit.*, p. 97. See also illustration No. 46.
44. See David, *op. cit.*, pp. 29-33 and (for the stop list) p. 88. David lists the Sesquialtera (on the *Brustwerk*) but adds, "in the octave, from 3-foot and 2-foot." See also Sumner, *op. cit.*, pp. 85-87; Sumner lists the Sesquialtera as "II rks."
45. 2 Vols., Weimar, 1737-1739. See Vol. I, p. 174.
46. See Hans Klotz, "Bachs Orgeln," pp. 189ff.

Bach's name is not mentioned at all. The organ is described there as "incomparable," but that it could have satisfied Bach with its specifications, which were as clumsy as they were poor, cannot be imagined.

Possibly the stops given for the opening of the D Minor Concerto after Vivaldi referred to this organ. On both the *Oberwerk* and *Brustwerk* an Octave 4' was to be drawn; in the *Pedal*, a Principal 8'; in m. 21, a Principal 8' was to be added on the *Oberwerk* and a Sub-Bass 32' in the pedal; the three measures of transition were to be taken on the *Plenum* (probably of the *Oberwerk*). The last movement shows *"Rückpositiv"* instead of *Brustwerk*, but this is actually only an inaccuracy in naming, for in the general heading this concerto, like the other four (VIII, 1-4), is described as being for two manuals and pedal *(a 2 Clav. e Pedale)*.

In 1714 Bach declined an appointment in Halle as organist of the Church of Our Lady (a position offered him and virtually accepted by him) as successor to Zachow. Here he would have had "a really large and really fine organ for his regular use"—it had 65 stops[47]—had he not preferred becoming concert-master in Weimar in the hope of rising to the post of conductor. It was a fateful decision, which now led the course of his life farther and farther away from the organ.

When the prospect of his appointment as conductor was not realized, Bach went to Cöthen (December, 1717) after spending four weeks under arrest "because of his stubborn insistence on a release."[48] In Cöthen he became chamber composer and conductor to the music-loving Prince Leopold. Since the court was Reformed [i.e., Calvinistic], there was virtually nothing to be done in the way of church music. However, if we quite rightly associate the F Major Toccata with the organ of the Church of St. Agnus in Cöthen, since its pedal extended to f', we may conclude that even there, where his official duties were of another kind, Bach did not neglect the organ.

Once more, in the year 1720, Bach considered returning to the organ. He applied for the vacant post of organist at St. James's Church in Hamburg. On the 28th of November eight candidates, among them Bach, were called for a test of their playing. Bach had already visited Hamburg in advance in order to inform himself about the conditions, and he withdrew when he learned that the candidate chosen would have to contribute a large sum of money to the church treasury as a token of gratitude. (The organist Johann Joachim Heitmann, chosen instead of Bach, paid 4,000 marks current.) During his stay, however, as the obituary relates, "he played for more than two hours

47. 16 in the *Hauptwerk*, 16 in the *Oberwerk*, 15 in the *Brustwerk*, and 18 in the *Pedal;* Löffler sees in it actually the "ideal of Bach's period." See Adlung, *op. cit.*, pp. 239f. for its stop list.

48. That is, from his position.

on the fine organ of St. Catherine's Church before the Magistrate and many other distinguished persons of the town, to the general astonishment of all.

"The aged organist of this church, Johann Adam Reinken, who was at that time nearly a hundred years old,[49] listened to Bach with special pleasure. At the request of those present, Bach worked out the chorale 'An Wasserflüssen Babylon' extemporaneously and in different ways for almost half an hour, as formerly the better Hamburg organists had been accustomed to do at Saturday Vespers. Reinken paid Bach the following compliment, expressly on his treatment of the chorale: 'I thought that this art was dead, but I perceive that it lives on in you.' This verdict from Reinken was all the more unexpected since he himself, years before, had set this chorale in the way reported above. Our Bach was not ignorant of this fact nor, moreover, was he unaware that Reinken had always been somewhat envious. But Reinken then urged Bach to come over to him and was very courteous to him."

The organ had four manuals (*Rückpositiv, Hauptwerk, Oberwerk,* and *Brustwerk*) and 58 speaking stops, among them 16 reeds.[50] Possibly the five-part arrangement of the chorale (VI, 12a) had its origin in connection with this improvisation. Since Spitta,[51] the Great G Minor Fugue also has been associated, rightly, with the Hamburg journey.

On May 5, 1723, after long inglorious delays, Bach was chosen Cantor of the Thomas School and Director of Music for the two principal churches of Leipzig, St. Thomas' Church and St. Nicholas' Church. In this position his first responsibility was to the School and in the Church [St. Thomas'] to the direction of its music. Poets and novelists are in the habit of representing Bach at the Thomas organ, improvising with upturned glance; the fact is, that he played on it very rarely indeed: for one reason, that was not his position; for another, his relationship with the organist placed under his authority was not always sympathetic. St. Thomas' Church had a glorious choral tradition, but never organists of standing. A certain Christian Gräbner was organist there until 1730; from then on, Johann Gottlieb Görner.

The instrument was not a bad one but was somewhat out of order. It was a 3-manual organ of 35 stops. The Nicholas organ was new and of about the same size. Both were far surpassed by the organ in the University Church of St. Paul, which had been constructed by Johann Scheibe and tested and approved by Bach in 1717. It had 3 manuals and 53 voices, among them only four reeds, however.[52]

49. He lived from 1623 to 1722!

50. A list of the stops on this organ is given in Klotz, *op. cit.*, pp. 155-156.

51. Spitta, *op. cit.*, II, 22-25.

52. Its specifications may be seen in Klotz, *op. cit.*, pp. 230-231.

As an organist, Bach played mainly on the occasions of his approval of an organ or privately for friends and pupils. For example, he was called to Kassel in September of 1732 to test the rebuilt organ of St. Martin's Church and in connection with this examination gave an organ recital. The newspaper issued an invitation to hear "the celebrated organist and music director, Herr Bach of Leipzig." Bach received 26 thaler for traveling expenses, 50 thaler as honorarium, 2 thaler for the sedan-chair man, and one for his servant. Even without any motive such as the testing of an organ, Bach played a few times formally in recital. On September 14, 1731, he played at the Church of St. Sophia in Dresden, where he had gone to hear [the first performance of] Hasse's opera *Cleofide,* Hasse being among those present on that occasion. (Two years later Friedemann became organist of this church.) Again, on December 1, 1736, Bach played in Dresden on the recently built Silbermann organ in the Church of Our Lady, a few days after its dedication, "in the presence of Baron Kayserling and many distinguished persons." His playing lasted two hours and was received with "distinct admiration" by all those present.[53] On his visit to Potsdam he played on May 8, 1747, on the organ in the Church of the Holy Ghost, but no further particulars are known about this visit.

His artistry as a performer on the organ was highly praised by his contemporaries, though in those days even lesser talents received similar accolades. The obituary calls him "the best performer on the organ and clavier who ever lived. . . . With his two feet he could perform on the pedals passages which many a capable clavier player would find it hard enough to play with five fingers. . . . How strange, how new, and how expressive were his fancies while improvising! How perfectly he brought them forth!" In Gerber's *Lexikon* it is reported that "His feet had to play on the pedals (following his hands which preceded) every theme and every passage most exactly. No appoggiatura, no mordent, no *Pralltriller* could be missing or sound any the less neat or clear. He performed long double-trills with both feet even while his hands were no less active at the same time."[54] For the last sentence it might prove difficult to find illustrative examples in Bach's organ works, yet Bach's pedal technique must have seemed unbelievable to a generation that was gradually giving up playing on the pedals; after all, Philipp Emanuel in Hamburg could say of himself that he had not played a pedal for years!

"Bach's way of registering," says Forkel, "was so unusual that many organists and organ builders were startled when they watched him registering. It seemed to them that such a combination of stops could not possibly sound well, and they were greatly surprised when

53. Flade, *op. cit.*, p. 86.
54. Quoted after Frotscher, *op. cit.*, p. 953.

they noticed afterwards that the organ sounded best exactly this way and had now achieved something strange and unusual in sound that could not be brought forth by their manner of registering."

Forkel wrote this at a time when the organ and the art of registration along with it were in a sharp decline, a decline that was already impending at the beginning of the eighteenth century. How else could it have been possible that the order of service at St. Mary's Church in Halle in 1713 was obliged to dictate to the organist how he should register the chorale?[55] The principles of registration of the outgoing seventeenth century were still alive in Bach, principles which now threatened to disappear in the eighteenth. Of course Forkel, as a child of his time, also had too narrow an idea of true organ style. Everything should be "grand and solemn"; "a reverential awe" should overcome the listener. For this reason the employment of the organ for "rapid movements" was disapproved of. The D Major Fugue or the C Major Toccata would scarcely have met with Forkel's approval!

Bach was both admired and feared as an expert on organs. As the obituary states, "He not only understood the art of playing the organ . . . to the greatest perfection, but he also knew the construction of the organ thoroughly. . . . No one could draw up or judge specifications for new organs better than he." "His tests of organs were very stiff but always fair," says Forkel. "The first thing he did in trying out an organ was to pull out all the speaking stops and then, using the whole organ, play as loudly as possible. He used to say as a joke that he had to know first of all whether the organ had good lungs. He then began to test its individual parts. . . . After the examination was over, and if the instrument was in good condition and had his approval, he ordinarily made use of the skills mentioned above for a little while, for his own pleasure as well as that of those who were present, and demonstrated anew each time that he was really 'the prince of all performers on the clavier and organ'. . . ."

Of these skills Forkel reports: "When Johann Sebastian Bach seated himself at the organ on occasions other than church services, as he was very often requested to do by visitors, he used to select a theme and then work it out in all the forms used in organ music in such a way that it remained his material continuously even if he played without interruption for two hours or more. First, he used this theme for a prelude and fugue with the full organ. Then his skill in registration appeared in a trio, a work in four parts, etc., always on the same theme. Then followed a chorale, in which the original theme reappeared to play about the chorale melody in three or four different voices in the greatest variety of ways. At length came the

55. Frotscher, *op. cit.*, pp. 954ff.

conclusion in the form of a fugue on the full organ, in which either another treatment of the first subject alone prevailed or, depending on its character, one or two others were combined with it. This is in reality that skill on the organ that the aged Reinken of Hamburg had considered already lost in his day but which, as he afterwards discovered, not only lived on in Johann Sebastian Bach but through him had attained its highest perfection."

CHAPTER 4

THE ORGAN MUSIC OF THE BAROQUE

The literature proper to the organs of the Baroque was as rich and varied as were the instruments and, similarly, was subject to a continuing development. The secular music flourishing throughout the sixteenth century vanished in the seventeenth, Scheidt's secular variations being its last offshoots. The sacred music for organ, however, took over unscrupulously the expressive resources of the new secular music and became "concert music." In close comparison with the ecclesiastical architecture of the Baroque, the sacred music was more strongly secularized than—with a glance at Bach's Passions, perhaps—we are usually ready to admit. At the price of this vast tolerance, the Baroque still had the capacity to create a unified art—as its last period—and Bach as its last composer gave this union its final, highest formulation in his music.

At the beginning of the seventeenth century, German organ music received decisive stimulation from two directions: from the South through Frescobaldi, whose influence extended over the Catholic South of Germany especially, and from the North through Sweelinck, whose many pupils were scattered among the Hanseatic towns and as far south as Halle (Scheidt). In Central Germany, from the time of Michael Praetorius, a separate and distinct school was maintained by a number of lesser masters. These were connected through Scheidt with the North German tradition, and through Pachelbel, who was active for several years in Thuringia, with the South German tradition.

A table, limited to the most important names and divided into three parts according to both period and region, may illustrate this line of descent:

Period	Style-Epoch	South Germany	Central Germany	North Germany
1600 to 1660	Early Baroque	(Frescobaldi) Froberger (Vienna)	M. Praetorius (Wolfenbüttel)	(Sweelinck) *S. Scheidt* (Halle) H. Scheidemann (Hamburg) M. Weckmann (Hamburg)
1660 to 1710	High Baroque	Kerll (Munich) Muffat (Passau) *Pachelbel*	Joh. Christoph Bach (Eisenach) (Nuremberg, Erfurt)	J. A. Reinken (Hamburg) F. Tunder (Lübeck) *D. Buxtehude* (Lübeck) *N. Bruhns* (Husum)
1710 to 1750	Late Baroque	J. K. F. Fischer (Rastatt)	J. G. Walther (Weimar) JOH. SEB. BACH	*Vinc. Lübeck* (Stade, Hamburg) G. Böhm (Lüneburg)

The most important works of these masters are available today in numerous convenient modern editions: for the works of Scheidt, Buxtehude, and Lübeck I should like to refer to my editions published by Peters; Pachelbel appeared in a Bärenreiter publication edited by Matthäi; J. C. F. Fischer was published by Schott *(Liber Organi)*; the others, especially the North Germans, in the collection *Organum* (Kistner & Siegel) edited by Seiffert; in addition there are the anthologies such as those edited by Straube, *Alte Meister* and *Choralvorspiele alter Meister* (Peters), my edition of the *Achtzig Choralvorspiele* (Peters), and many others.

Instead of an historical survey of this epoch, which can be studied best in Frotscher, another method of consideration will be adopted here. The essence and form of this art will be illustrated by four contrasting pairs: by the contrast between forms comprising many sections and the duality of prelude and fugue, by the contrast between vocal and instrumental styles of writing, by the contrast between Catholic and Protestant, and finally, by the separation of clavier and organ styles.

At the beginning of the seventeenth century, the free organ music, not involving a chorale, still claimed a large number of forms of its own, such as the canzona, fantasy, ricercar, toccata, preamble, prelude, and fugue. A hundred years later the prelude and fugue were almost the only ones remaining. This process involved at first consolidation and clarification, but later—atrophy: around 1700 it was necessary for organ music to borrow from the sonata and suite.

The large compound forms of Buxtehude and his pupils, in which elements of the toccata and the canzona were combined, represented the climax in structural development shortly before 1700. An essential feature of the instrumental canzona was the fugal development of the subject more than once, at first in binary and then in ternary meter; if these fugal sections were surrounded by toccata-like sections, a form resulted which was usually in five sections, though occasionally in seven: a short toccata-like prelude, a fugue in binary meter, a toccata- or recitative-like interlude, a second fugue in ternary meter, and a concluding toccata. The improvisatory character of this form was shown in that all these parts passed over into one another without any fixed limits, and in that the fugue subject usually grew spontaneously from motives of the introductory toccata. Bach himself wrote one more work in this form, the E Major Toccata. A feature that may be traced for a still longer period in his works, and that has its roots here, is the thematic relationship between prelude and fugue.

From the beginning of the eighteenth century a smaller modification of this five-part form was preferred, namely, the three-part form: toccata, fugue, toccata. From this the path led to the duality of prelude and fugue: at first the virtuoso concluding toccata was repressed, and then finally was omitted altogether, a process we can trace easily in Bach's early works. The introductory prelude acquired greater independence, and its form was also contrasted clearly with that of the fugue; with this final development the thematic relationship between prelude and fugue was given up.

The variation forms of passacaglia and chaconne also died out rapidly after 1700. Again Bach created one more immense work in each of these two forms; Walther, Telemann, and others, however, did nothing further. As if in compensation for this impoverishment, the forms of the Italian instrumental concerto and the chamber sonata were transferred to the organ. Even Bach gave his large organ preludes the form of a *concerto grosso* movement. A final decline set in only when the forms of the new sonata of C. P. E. Bach and the Mannheim School automatically eliminated the organ, so to speak.

The contrast between vocal and instrumental styles of writing traverses the entire history of music. "In the beginning was melody." This means that every instrumental melody, no matter how free, may be traced back to an original line *(Urlinie)* of the vocal kind; the fugal forms of instrumental music around 1600, especially, all had vocal prototypes. In opposition thereto, however, each instrument had an "instrumental" style peculiar to it alone; only the organ among all instruments was able to sustain harmonies in several parts without change in volume, and the fingers could pass swiftly over the keys. Hence, series of widely-spaced chords, intermingled with running passages, produced the building-stones of the toccata as a form of improvisation (*toccate un poco* = "prelude a little"). The runs, at first clumsy, as for example in Leonhard Kleber's *Tabulaturbuch* of 1524, were refined in Merulo's works into virtuoso passages. Simple chord progressions became in Frescobaldi intertwined chains of bold dissonances *(toccate di durezze e ligature)*. Soon the toccata was interspersed with small movements in fugal style which retained their vocal character for a long time yet, so that, until far into the seventeenth century, vocal and instrumental styles of writing often existed side by side.

One may look, for example, at Christian Ritter's Toccata in D Minor (he calls it "Sonatina"), the opening and closing sections of which are kept instrumental, the fugal middle section, however, purely vocal. Another example is Buxtehude's Prelude and Fugue in F♯ Minor,[56] in which measures 1-13 of the Prelude are instrumental in style, but measures 14-26, vocal; and similarly in the Fugue, the first part *(Grave)* is treated as vocal, the following *(Vivace)* as instrumental. Occasionally even the fugue subject is broken up into figures; for example, in the Toccata in G Major of Reinken. This contrast is most effectively utilized in the literature of the chorale preludes, where repeatedly the unornamented c. f. retains its vocal, communal style but is embellished by parts that are kept instrumental; that is, they are kept individual.

Even in Bach the two styles stood for some time independently side by side. When Bach began writing, his music was strictly "instrumental" under North German influence. Then, in Weimar, he turned to the study of the more recent as well as the older Italians, his style undergoing a clarification vocally as a result. He thus attained a unique synthesis of the two, which, from about the end of the Weimar period on, permitted him to conduct choral parts with the freedom of an instrumental part and instrumental parts with the singableness of a choral part. In this way originated the intellectualization of his polyphony which Forkel described so enthusiastically: "In all the works which he composed from about the year 1720, or from his 35th year, till his death, Johann Sebastian Bach's harmony consisted of an interweaving of melodies of this kind, which are all so singable that each may, and actually does, appear in its turn as the top voice. In this he excels all the composers in the world."

---

56. Dietrich Buxtehude, *Ausgewählte Orgelwerke*, ed. Hermann Keller. 2 Vols. (Peters No. 4449), Vol. 1, No. 8, pp. 37ff.

The contrast between the Confessions had immediate significance for organ music to the extent that the differing religious services in the Catholic and Protestant Churches assigned quite different tasks to the organ. Since the Catholic celebration of the Mass nowhere permits the independent display of the organ to any great extent, the larger forms of organ music could be developed neither in France and Italy nor in the Catholic South of Germany. One will hardly find a single piece among the old French masters of the organ edited by Guilmant[57] which exceeds the duration of two or three minutes. Still less did the Reformed [i.e., the Calvinistic] worship give the organ opportunity for display. Thus, the flourishing of music for the organ was limited to the Lutheran sections of Germany. In other respects, however, music often bridged over the stark contrast between the Confessions: Sweelinck was influenced by the Catholic Merulo and, a hundred years later, Bach received stimulation from Frescobaldi and the French composers.

A further line of demarcation, that between the styles of writing for clavier and for organ, was drawn more sharply for the first time toward the end of the seventeenth century; till then there was a common literature for the two instruments. Of course, arrangements of chorales were destined all along for the church and for the organ, dance pieces for the stringed keyboard instruments; but for a large part of the free works of Scheidt, Pachelbel, Reinken, and others, no strict co-ordination can be found. Works with obbligato pedal, like the large preludes and fugues of the North Germans, could be performed only on the organ, of course, but the dividing line was not more clearly defined till a more distinct style of its own was worked out for the clavier—in Germany with Kuhnau's sonatas. One may still remain in doubt about a number of Bach's early works, but from the *Little Organ Book* (1717) and particularly from the *Well-Tempered Clavier* (1722) on, the separation of the styles of writing for organ and for clavier was finally accomplished.

57. *Archives des maîtres de l'orgue* (10 vols., ed. Alexandre Guilmant, 1898-1910).

CHAPTER 5

AUTHENTICITY AND CHRONOLOGY OF THE ORGAN WORKS OF BACH

We shall now pass on to the organ works of Bach and inquire first about their authenticity and afterwards about the chronology of their origin.

As for their authenticity, we must differentiate various degrees of certainty. Unquestionably authentic, of course, are those works published by Bach himself and those extant in the autograph.

1. Bach brought out in print: the *Third Part of the Clavierübung* (see pp. 268-286), the *Six Chorales* (pp. 262-268), and (through the Mizler Society) the *Canonic Variations on "Vom Himmel hoch, da komm ich her"* (pp. 286-291).

2. In Bach's autograph have come down to us (including a few autographs missing today):

Vol. I: the Six Sonatas and the Passacaglia.
Vol. II: the Preludes and Fugues in C Major (No. 1), G Major (No. 2), A Major (No. 3), E Minor (No. 9), and B Minor (No. 10).
Vol. III: Prelude and Fugue in G Minor (No. 5; 1st version) and Fugue (only) in E Minor (No. 10).
Vol. IV: Prelude and Fugue in C Major (No. 1), Fugue in C Minor (No. 6), and Fantasy in C Minor (No. 12).
Vol. V: the *Little Organ Book* (see p. 197).
Vols. VI and VII: the *Eighteen Chorales* (Nos. 36, 37, 12b, 49, 27, 48, 43, 56, 45-47, 9, 8, 7, 31, 32, 35, and 58).
Vol. VIII: –
Vol. IX: *Pedalexercitium* (No. 11).

3. We may be almost equally certain about the following works, which are adequately authenticated by good contemporary copies and by tradition:

Vol. I: Pastorale in F Major.
Vol. II: the Preludes and Fugues in F Minor (No. 5), C Minor (No. 6), C Major (No. 7), A Minor (No. 8), and the Fantasy and Fugue in G Minor (No. 4).

Vol. III: the Toccatas and Fugues in F Major (No. 2) and in D Dorian (No. 3), the Prelude and Fugue in D Minor (No. 4), the Fantasy and Fugue in C Minor (No. 6), and the Toccatas in E Major (No. 7 and the Appendix) and C Major (No. 8).

Vol. IV: the Preludes and Fugues in G Major (No. 2) and D Major (No. 3), the Toccata and Fugue in D Minor (No. 4), the Fugues in G Minor (No. 7) and B Minor (No. 8), the Canzona in D Minor (No. 10), and the Fantasy in G Major (No. 11)

Vol. V: Nos. 7, 18, 20, 23, 26, 27, 36, 39, 43, 53, and the three Partitas.

Vols. VI and VII: Nos. 4, 11, 12a, 15, 16, 22, 26, 29, 34, 41, 44, 50, 51, 53, 54, and 62.

Vol. VIII: the Concertos in G Major (No. 1), A Minor (No. 2), and C Major (No. 4), and the *Allabreve* (No. 6).

Vol. IX: the *Fantasia con imitazione* (No. 1), the Fugue in G Major (No. 2), the Trio in G Major (No. 3), the Fantasy in G Major (No. 4), the "Little Harmonic Labyrinth" (No. 9), No. 12, and No. 25.

4. For the following works Bach's authorship remains probable:

Vol. III: the Prelude and Fugue in A Minor (No. 9).

Vol. IV: the Prelude and Fugue in C Minor (No. 5), the Fugue in C Minor (No. 9), the Prelude in A Minor (No. 13), and the Trio in D Minor (No. 14).

Vol. V: Appendix, Nos. 1, 3, 6, and 7.

Vols. VI and VII: Nos. 3, 23, 25, and 55.

Vol. VIII: the Concerto in C Major (No. 3), the Preludes in C Major (No. 7) and G Major (No. 11), the Fantasy in C Major (No. 9), and the Fugues in C Major (No. 10) and G Minor (No. 12).

Vol. IX: Nos. 14, 18, 22, 23, 24, and 26.

5. The following must be considered doubtful:

Vol. V: Appendix, Nos. 4 and 5.

Vol. VI: Nos. 21 and 28.

Vol. VIII: the "Eight Little Preludes and Fugues" (No. 5) and the Prelude in C Major (No. 8).

Vol. IX: the Fantasy and Fugue in A Minor (No. 6), the Fugue in G Major (No. 7), the Trio in C Minor (No. 10), No. 13, Nos. 15-17, and Nos. 19-21.

6. The following have been proved not to be genuine:

Vol. VI: "Ach Gott und Herr" (No. 1) and "Gott der Vater wohn uns bei" (No. 24); their composer is J. G. Walther.

Vol. IX: The Aria in F Major (No. 5) is a composition by Couperin (see p. 141) and the Trio in G Major (No. 8) a composition by Telemann.[58]

The criticism of Johannes Schreyer[59] went very much farther, for he wished to have everything except the *Allabreve* deleted from Vols. VIII and IX; moreover, out of Vol. II, Nos. 2 and 3; out of Vol. III, Nos. 4 and 9; and out of Vol. IV, Nos. 1, 2, 5, 6, 9, 12, 13, and 14. In the *Bach-Jahrbuch* for 1912 Schering refuted Schreyer.

The complete picture of Bach's production for the organ, therefore, may experience a little retouching in the future, but should undergo no further important changes.

If we bear in mind how great the uncertainty of even excellent judges was when formerly a work by Beethoven (for example, the *Rondo a capriccio:* "Fury over a lost groschen") was handed down without an opus number, then a reliable chronological order for Bach will appear impossible, since external evidence is almost completely lacking. But even if the problem can be solved today in only an approximate fashion, every attempt leads us somewhat nearer the truth.

From a comparison of its paper with that of cantata scores, Spitta ascertained that the hand-written copy of the Prelude and Fugue in G Major (II, 2) was made in the year 1725, that of the Prelude and Fugue in C Major (II, 1) in 1730,[60] but we do not know that the composition of these works was not begun at an earlier date, perhaps. From similar evidence Spitta dated the E Minor Fugue (II, 9), probably correctly, within the years 1727-1736.[61]

We would have further objective criteria if a manual- or pedal-range required by Bach enabled us to connect a certain work with an organ which showed this compass. By this means the date of origin of the work would be determined with fair accuracy. The ranges required by Bach differ at the top: the manual range usually extends only to c^3, but twice to d^3; the pedal often ranges only to c^1, but repeatedly to d^1, and several times to e^1 and f^1. In spite of many at-

58. In my revision of Vol. IX in 1940 I deleted from the previous contents (1904): the Fugue in D Major (No. 5), the Concerto in E♭ Major (No. 7), and 7 chorale-preludes (Nos. 3-5, 13-15, and 17). In the BG edition the following works, not included in the Peters edition, must also be considered spurious: the Fugue in C Major (XXXVIII, p. 213) and the chorale-works "Erbarm dich mein, o Herre Gott" (XL, p. 60), "O Vater, o allmächtiger Gott" (XL, p. 179), and "Allein Gott in der Höh sei Ehr," a partita with 17 variations (XL, p. 195).

59. *Beiträge zur Bach-Kritik*, 1911 and 1912.

60. Spitta, *op. cit.*, III, 208.

61. *Ibid.*, III, 210.

tempts, however, I have been unable to find any satisfactory bases for this way of dating.[62]

For none of Bach's organs do we know the top of the manual compass; we know only that during the course of the eighteenth century it was extended from c^3 to d^3. (Adlung demanded d^3 and apparently did not yet [1758][63] regard it as a matter of course.) Bach required d^3 only in the G Minor Fantasy (II, 4) and in the C Major Toccata (III, 8). He avoided it elsewhere, however, sometimes in so striking a manner as in the F Major Toccata (III, 2)[64] and, extraordinarily, also in the works of the later period. From this evidence shouldn't we be permitted at least to place together the two works just mentioned?

The pedal compass of Bach's organs in Arnstadt and Mühlhausen extended up to d^1; the d^1 is required in most of the early works of Bach, but also again in those of his last period. On the other hand, it is striking that a few of the large works, like the Fugue in F Major (III, 2) and the Passacaglia, and the Prelude and Fugue in E♭ Major as well, forego using d^1, while the chorale arrangements of the *Third Part of the Clavierübung* require it. The Concerto in A Minor after Vivaldi calls for e^1. Since this transcription almost certainly falls within the Weimar period, and since J. G. Walther never goes beyond d^1 in his works intended for the organ of the City Church, might it not be possible that the compass of the organ in the palace chapel, about which nothing is known, ranged to e^1 or, more probably, up to f^1?

In the chorale "Gottes Sohn ist kommen" from the *Little Organ Book* Bach takes the pedal up to f^1 with the Trumpet 8'; this he surely would not have done had his Weimar organ not permitted. Under these circumstances, other compositions that require e^1 in the pedal should be dated in the Weimar period: the Prelude and Fugue in A Major (II, 3)—in the earlier version of which e^1 is still avoided—the Prelude and Fugue in G Major (IV, 2), and then, probably, also the F Major Toccata with its f^1. Even the G Major Fugue (IX, 2), then, belongs in this period if one more correctly assigns the entry of the theme, p. 6, 3, 5, to the pedal.

The Aria in F Major after Couperin also requires e^1, but since Couperin's composition that Bach transcribed was not published till 1726, this transcription falls in Bach's Leipzig period. Once, in the organ chorale "In dulci jubilo" of the *Little Organ Book,* Bach seems to be requiring $f\sharp^1$ of the pedal, but one may assume here that he played

62. Hans Klotz investigated this matter thoroughly in *Musikforschung,* 1950, Nos. 3-4, and reached conclusions that are to a certain extent new. David, *op. cit.*, p. 7, also reproduces Klotz's chart.

63. This is the date of Adlung's preface. The book was published posthumously in 1768. See also Vol. I, p. 23.

64. See p. 117.

the c.f. an octave lower with 4'. The Arnstadt organ lacked C♯ and D♯ in the pedal; these notes were avoided in the Preludes and Fugues in A Minor (III, 9), E Minor (III, 10), and C Major (IV, 1) and in the Toccata in D Minor (IV, 4), all of which were probably composed in Arnstadt. On the other hand, these pitches are not avoided in a few works which by their style may be judged to be about contemporary, such as the Toccata in E Major (III, 7), the Prelude and Fugue in C Minor (IV, 5), the Fugue in C Minor (IV, 6), and the *Pedalexercitium* (IX, 11). No definite clues, then, can be obtained from this information, so that we must try to obtain a clearer picture on the basis of Bach's inner development from his first beginnings to his mastery.

Bach laid the foundation of his stupendous pedal technique in Arnstadt. Works which presuppose only a modest ability on the pedals, therefore, originated either in the very earliest Arnstadt period or earlier, in Lüneburg; for example, the Preludes and Fugues in A Minor (III, 9) and C Minor (IV, 5). Even the first pedal entry of the subject in the C Major Fugue (IV, 1), curtailed for technical reasons, suggests the very early origin of this work. However, the development of the young Bach in compositional technique stands out even more clearly and in a greater variety of ways.

By "compositional technique" is meant here what one needs to know to be able to compose according to the scholastic rules. There was, of course, no instruction in composition at that time; as a pupil at St. Michael's in Lüneburg, Bach probably learned the fundamentals of thorough-bass from Niedt's *Musicalische Handleitung* (1700), which he himself later took as the basis for his teaching at the Thomas School, and he was then directed to "perfect himself" further by imitating other composers' works.

As Forkel asserts, "The common practice for all beginners is to run riot up and down the keyboard, to play as many notes as the five fingers of each hand can manage, and to continue in this wild course until some point of rest is reached by chance." The Prelude in G Major (VIII, 11), the Prelude and Fugue in C Minor (IV, 5), and the first movement of the E Major Toccata (III, 7) show indiscriminate doublings of this sort. Gradually, however, a type of composition much more substantial makes its appearance. We still see carefree parallel octaves occasionally in the Preludes and Fugues in E Minor (III, 10), C Major (IV, 1), A Minor (III, 9), and others. Later we find doublings of this kind at climactic points only: in the D Major Fugue (IV, 3), in the F Minor Fugue (II, 5), and in the D Minor Toccata (IV, 4; p. 29, 1, 2).

Then we see Bach trying hard to present this full-chorus effect in "real" part-writing: at the end of the *Adagio* of the C Major Toccata (III, 8),[65] for example, where the part-writing is still not quite "real."

65. The short section marked *Grave*.

In contrast, the close of the Prelude and Fugue in G Minor (III, 5) and, similarly, the *Grave* of the G Major Fantasy (IV, 11) show five real parts, while in the detached chords of the F Major Toccata (III, 2) and in those at the end of the Dorian Fugue (III, 3) Bach achieved writing in seven real parts. The setting in four real parts was the normal one, however, and from his Weimar years on, Bach took pains to avoid parallel octaves and fifths for the sake of the eye, even if they were inaudible, as in two passages in the Passacaglia (I, p. 82, 3, 3, and p. 86, 3, 3).

At first the contrapuntal ability of the young organist was quite as modest as was his compositional technique; the voice-leading in the first fugues was frequently awkward and usually did not go beyond two- or three-part writing. The pedal often made an unthematic entry (even in the G Minor Fugue, IV, 7); frequent cadences interrupted the flow of the fugues, and even the fugue subjects themselves cadenced more than once (IV, 5); the counterpoints were modest and changed often; in the C Major Fugue (IV, 1) the answer was constructed irregularly.

Soon, however, the path led upward: the voice-leading became freer, countersubjects became more frequent, and sequences, which were used to excess in the early works (III, 7), were gradually reduced to the classical number of three. The subjects became more compact and unified (sometimes still with separation of the head of the subject from its continuation, as in the D Major Fugue, IV, 3); cadences at the ends of fugue sections were now usually bridged over, and a motion once established was maintained, which was in contrast to the frequent change of motion found in the North Germans, Bruhns in particular.

To this increase in professional ability, which we may follow step by step, corresponded a like increase in Bach's artistic independence. It was only natural that at first he should try to imitate his models. We find "trilled" chords like those found in Buxtehude (IV, 3 and III, 10); a long dwelling on the subdominant just before the end, a procedure usual among the North Germans (III, 9); passages for both hands in sixths and tenths as found in Pachelbel and Lübeck; double pedalling as in Tunder and Bruhns; repeated notes in fugue subjects, found particularly in Lübeck; etc. In spite of these really obvious influences, the young Bach tried even in his first works to speak his own language—still unskillfully, to be sure, but yet *his* language. In this respect he is in marked contrast to Mozart, who as a child prodigy appropriated the language of his many models with the greatest of ease,[66] and only relatively late attained his own distinct style. For this reason we have mainly a biographical interest in the youthful

66. Théodore de Wyzewa and Georges de Saint-Foix, *W. A. Mozart: Sa vie musicale. . . .* (Paris, 1912).

works of Mozart, but an immediate, lively interest in those of Bach. Even an unfinished work like the Prelude and Fugue in C Minor (IV, 5) still makes a deep impression today.

Forkel says: "As soon as an artist becomes distinguished, every one wants to possess something by him. Before he can fully complete his career, however, the curiosity of the public is usually satisfied; especially so if, by unusual perfection, he deviates too greatly from their ideas. This seems to have been the situation with respect to Bach. It is for this reason that his most perfect works are far less widely disseminated than are his early preparatory exercises." These principles are still valid today; perhaps because "Storm and Stress" works of a man of genius appeal to us more directly, and in their conflict between form and content can be appreciated by us today more easily than can his more mature, more perfect creations.

As for form generally, it has already been mentioned (p. 28) that Bach contributed only one early, incomplete experiment (III, 9) and one fully developed piece (III, 7) in the five-part form of the toccata cultivated by Buxtehude; his formal development was connected with the three-part form with built-in fugue. At the outset the concluding toccata was still equivalent to the prelude (IV, 5, and IV, 4); the Fugue in C Minor (IV, 6) even had an appended concluding toccata without the counterweight of a prelude, as had also the Fugue in C Minor (IV, 9); but the "signs of the times"[67] caused these virtuoso endings to become less and less important. They were now bound up organically with the fugue, but they still gave a special brilliance to the fugue endings of the Preludes and Fugues in C Major (IV, 1), D Major (IV, 3), G Minor (III, 5), and A Minor (II, 8), as well as the C-Major Toccata (III, 8).

The thematic relationship between prelude and fugue may still be seen clearly in the Preludes and Fugues in C Minor (IV, 5), E Minor (III, 10), G Minor (III, 5), and E Major (III, 7); in addition, in the Toccata in D Minor (IV, 4) and, less clearly, in those in A Minor (II, 8) and F Minor (II, 5)—here at the end. It was gradually given up, however, and there are even preludes and fugues combined with each other which originated separately, as did the Prelude and Fugue in D Major (IV, 3), the Fantasy and Fugue in G Minor (II, 4), the Toccata and Fugue in F Major (III, 2), and the Prelude and Fugue in C Minor (II, 6).

Along with this treatment larger structures resulted from short preludes which were frequently developed from a single propelling motive—for example, those in C Minor (IV, 5), G Major (IV, 2), and A Major (II, 3): either by an interpolation of an improvisatory kind, as in the Prelude in G Minor (III, 5); by a beginning in the form of a

67. It is my conviction that no changes in style of this kind were devised by the artist but were dictated to him by his "period."

pedal point, as in the toccatas with pedal of Pachelbel[68] and Kerll, in the Preludes in F Minor (II, 5) and A Minor (II, 8), and both Fantasies in C Minor (III, 6, and IV, 12); or by arrangement in a kind of three-part song-form (VIII, 11).

A few preludes are in themselves so multiform that they do not require completion by a fugue at all; for example, the Fantasy in G Minor (II, 4) and the Prelude in D Major (IV, 3). For some time the preludes—in the form of a *concerto grosso* movement—surpass the fugues; the Prelude in C Minor (II, 6) and the Toccata in F Major are examples. In the large works of the last years in Leipzig, which cannot be brought under any formula, they stand again side by side, on an equal footing.

Several chronologies of Bach's organ works have been drawn up which take into account all these aspects. In the first four volumes of their edition, Widor and Schweitzer attempted to arrange the free works in this way. The Englishmen Harvey Grace[69] and Charles Sanford Terry[70] worked out chronologies of this kind, as did Hans Klotz[71] and Gotthold Frotscher[72] quite recently in Germany. The latter emphasized, however, that he attached more importance to stylistic relationships than to stylistic development. For the early works only, Ernst Isler[73] set up a chronology in which he had Bach begin with small manual pieces (VIII, 9 and 10).

CHAPTER 6

ON THE PERFORMANCE OF BACH'S ORGAN WORKS

Every musical performance consists of two components, an objective one supplied by the work of art and a subjective one conditional on the interpreter. The ideal situation, in which both coincide, probably never occurs, not even when the composer himself performs his own works. However, both factors must be brought so close to each other that a certain fusion may take place. The goal, therefore,

68. See *Johann Pachelbel: Ausgewählte Orgelwerke*, ed. Karl Matthäi (4 vols.; Kassel and Basel: Bärenreiter, 1929; 2nd ed. 1931). Vol. I contains five Toccatas as Nos. 3-7.
69. *The Organ Works of Bach*, 1922.
70. *Bach: A Biography*.
71. *Orgelkunst der Gotik. . .*, pp. 247ff.
72. *Op. cit.*, pp. 854ff.
73. *Schweizerische Musikzeitung*, 1930, No. 22.

is not (as is often supposed) to suppress the subjective factor but to bring it as close as possible to the objective one.

With the older music, to which Bach of course belongs, this is difficult for two reasons: first, because a distance of more than two centuries must be bridged; secondly, because the "objective factor" has come down to us in a very indefinite state. For us this means that the music has been handed down without assignment of tone-color or registration, without markings for articulation, tempo, or dynamics, but only in the "pure" musical symbols.

Inevitably this freedom with respect to the old music must at first result in arbitrariness and uncertainty. Every young musician "expresses himself" at first in the old masters. "As I see it" was the motto Karl Straube inscribed on his first edition of the *Alte Meister* (1904). Then, during the course of a long life, every performer conscious of his responsibility strives to achieve a style as objective as possible.

In the following presentation the objective factors valid for all Bach's works will be clarified as far as is possible considering the scarcity of tradition. Of the subjective factor there can and need not be any discussion here.

REGISTRATION

This is really the most delicate and most controversial question, with which we have not progressed much beyond the experimental stage. How often indeed have we discarded registrations which were still pleasing to us yesterday, and done so with the feeling that today's also would not be the final one!

Of Bach's original registrations virtually none exists: the beginning of the D Minor Concerto after Vivaldi (see p. 22); the preparation (reconstructed by Spitta) of the fantasy "Ein feste Burg" for the rebuilt organ in Mühlhausen (see pp. 20-21); in the *Little Organ Book* the instruction that "Gottes Sohn ist kommen" should be played with the Principal 8' on the manual and the Trumpet 8' (see p. 34) on the pedal (c.f.); in addition, *forte* and *piano* a few times for echoes (III, 1, and IX, 2); and in the *Six Chorales* specification of pitch (8', 4', or 16').

Many times, however, one finds the marking *In Organo pleno*, the meaning of which has been discussed on pp. 14ff. This is in Bach's autograph on the Preludes and Fugues in C Major (II, 1), B Minor (II, 10), and E♭ Major (III, 1), as well as over the measures introductory to the first *Allegro* of the D Minor Concerto. In addition, it appears with the following organ chorales in which the c.f. lies in the pedal: "Komm, heiliger Geist, Herre Gott" (VII, 36), "Nun komm, der Heiden Heiland" (VII, 47), and "Komm Gott Schöpfer, heiliger Geist"

(VII, 35)—these three from the *Eighteen Chorales*; from the *Third Part of the Clavierübung*, "Kyrie Gott, heiliger Geist" (VII, 39c), "Aus tiefer Not" (VI, 13), and the fugue on "Wir glauben all an einen Gott" (VII, 60), but, curiously, not with "Jesus Christus, unser Heiland" (VI, 31), although it does appear with an earlier version of this work (VI, p. 112).

It is significant that no early work is among these pieces marked *Organo Pleno*. Since, *ca.* 1730, the change in the meaning of *Organum Plenum* into "Full Organ" was already brewing, we may conclude that where Bach especially prescribed it, he was requiring a "full" sound, *forte*, most certainly with strong reeds in the pedal for the organ chorales with the c.f. in the bass. In the preludes and fugues, however, this direction does not mean an indiscriminate *ff* (a meaning which the markings *forte* and *piano* in the E♭ Major Prelude contradict) but the *Plenum* of the *Hauptwerk*, while the *Rückpositiv* and *Brustwerk* may have a lighter registration.

The marking "*Pleno*," which appears three times in the A Minor Concerto after Vivaldi (VIII, 2: p. 12, 3, 3; p. 13, 2, 5; and p. 14, 4, 4) is striking. (These are not autograph, of course.) Here the person helping with the registration (for without an assistant it cannot be done) has only the time of an eighth in which to increase the *Oberwerk* from a *mf* or *f* to a *Plenum*, or to reduce it again. Bach's conception of *Plenum*, then, was certainly narrower than that of the seventeenth century, which used a *Plenum* as a matter of course for all large pieces—especially preludes, toccatas, and fugues—and consequently did not specify it.

For conveying an unornamented c.f., particularly in the bass or inner parts, Bach preferred reed tone ("Gottes Sohn ist kommen"). For an ornamented c.f. in the soprano, in organ chorales or in the middle movements of the concertos or of the C Major Toccata, one may also use a combination of flue stops with 2 2/3' or the Sesquialtera (which Bach particularly liked—to judge by his suggestions for his organ in Mühlhausen), or something similar. But then one should perform the entire movement with this combination without change—just as in an aria Bach does not vary the obbligato instrument. For combinations of foundation stops (see p. 15) there will be opportunities, particularly in the chorale partitas and in the *Little Organ Book*.

May the registration be changed within a prelude or fugue without change of manual? On this question, which the nineteenth century had answered "Yes" quite readily, and which today usually is answered categorically "No," it is not easy to reach a decision. In six places in Vincent Lübeck's Prelude and Fugue in D Minor are found marks (x) which Gottlieb Harms interpreted as directing the registrant to add or subtract stops at these points.[74] If this be correct, one may proceed similarly in Bach without hesitation. Yet it is very probable that in principle Bach did not commit himself on this point, but, whenever he had a fine, large organ and one or two clever registrants at his disposal, he played with greater differentiation than when alone at a smaller instrument. Nevertheless, this remark gives no authorization for reckless procedure in the matter of style!

During the Baroque, the most important technique used in registration, and the one of greatest assistance, was not change of stops but

CHANGE OF MANUAL

If we disregard the situations in which it is obvious that we should play on two manuals—in the trio sonatas, for example, or in playing a c.f. with accompaniment—the most significant evidence of the use of two manuals exists in the Dorian Toccata (III, 3) and in the organ transcriptions of the five concertos (the D Minor Concerto and VIII, 1-4). In this matter the Toccata, as an original work, takes precedence over the transcriptions; we can indeed learn a great deal from this one admirable example. We observe that Bach regularly made use of breaks in the rhythm for passing from one manual to another. Consequently the more or less imperceptible (and more or less makeshift) manual changes in most of the more modern editions (of Straube in particular but also of Schweitzer in his suggestions for the A Minor Fugue, for example) are musically possible, of course, but, strictly speaking, are not Bachian. In the Great G Minor Fugue (II, 4) the following transitions from *Hauptwerk* to *Positiv* and back would be possible, if we were to take the Dorian Toccata as a model:

- mm. 1-36: *Hauptwerk* (HW);
- m. 36 (p. 24, 4, 1): l.h. to the *Positiv;* r.h. following in m. 39 on the 6th eighth;
- m. 57 (p. 25, 4, 3): on the 6th eighth, l.h. to the HW; r.h. a half measure later;
- m. 93 (p. 27, 4, 2): r.h. to the *Positiv* on the last eighth; l.h. one measure later;
- m. 110 (p. 28, 3, 5): on the last eighth both hands again on the HW.

There are a number of passages, however, in which places for transition as evident as these do not exist. On this point the con-

74. In my edition of the organ works of Lübeck, Peters No. 4437, an account of these places is given in some concluding remarks. Lübeck's organ works were first published in 1921 (Ugrino Verlag) and edited by Gottlieb Harms.

certos, in which Bach was compelled to adapt to the organ pieces which were already finished, offer us good material for study. The places where either the end of one section coincides with the beginning of the next, or the caesura is bridged over, cause us the most trouble. If we are playing with manuals uncoupled, we can, when ending note and beginning note coincide, play this note with the same hand on both manuals.[75] Bach himself prescribes this procedure in m. 16 of the first movement of the A Minor Concerto (VIII, 2):

(The A is struck simultaneously with the third finger of the right hand on the OW and the thumb on the RP.)

However, Bach does not apply this principle consistently. In the first movement of the G Major Concerto (VIII, 1) at the return from the RP to the OW, he has this manual enter an eighth later:

When the transition is the reverse (i.e., from the OW to the RP) he suppresses the ending note:

In view of the rapid tempo of this movement, surely technical reasons were also a deciding factor.[76]

When there is a bridging-over of end and beginning, a "fusion of phrases," Bach most frequently has the new movement start up a

75. I found this technique carried out consistently for the first time in Krebs's *Orgelwerke*, edited by Walter Zöllner (Peters No. 4179), at the bottom of p. 22 and elsewhere.

76. The authority of the markings in the concertos is of course lessened by virtue of the fact that they have not been handed down in Bach's hand but only in copies.

sixteenth after the conclusion. Bach distributes the beginning of the C Major Concerto (VIII, 4):

Here he uses motivic segments for this organization. It would be incorrect, however, to take this as a model for the F Major Toccata (III, 2) and play, for example,—as is often done:

—rather, the transition to the OW should be made two measures earlier (on the 1st eighth) so as not to destroy the unity of the theme.

On the other hand, let us take as an example the transition in the B Minor Prelude (II, 10) from the episode (m. 17) to the principal section (m. 27), which is expressed by the change from an adjacent manual to the principal manual:

Performed in this way, the transition at B would bring out clearly the re-entry of the principal theme, but it would break up the line; it would be preferable, therefore, to change over to the HW at A.

It has been said with some justice that Bach "registers" in his orchestral works, that he adds flutes and oboes, trumpets and timpani to the strings as though they were stops; conclusions applicable to the organ, therefore, may also be drawn from his handling of the orchestra. There, too, we find runs like that at A above, which are used to prepare entries that are important because thematic.

In the late works of Bach, transitions from secondary to principal sections are sometimes so closely knit that it is almost impossible to unravel the texture. Consequently, nearly all players make a transition from the secondary to the principal manual on the 2nd eighth of m. 70 (p. 38, 4, 3) in the C Minor Prelude (II, 6):

This is always heard as an ugly break; it would be better to make the transition with the l.h. on the 2nd eighth in m. 75 and with the r.h. on the last quarter of m. 77.

The old rule followed by organists, that in preludes and fugues one should play the episodes for manuals alone on a secondary manual and should then return to the principal manual at the next entry of the pedals, has validity for the majority of Bach's early works but no longer for the large works of his late period.

An important question concerns the couplers. A two-manual organ in Bach's day did not yet have as many as three couplers but at most one manual-coupler and sometimes a second coupler from the *Oberwerk* to the *Pedal*. That most of Bach's works count on there being no pedal coupler is shown by many passages in which the tenor has to strike a note already being held by the pedal, as for example in the Dorian Toccata (III, 3):

For this reason the modern performer, even though he does not have at his disposal a pedal as well supplied as Bach's, should nevertheless not couple the principal manual to the pedal, but as a substitute, if necessary, couple down an adjacent manual which is not in use. Of course Bach was also thinking of the manuals as uncoupled wherever the voices cross each other (as in the Dorian Toccata).

When works have several sections and these movements are to be distributed over the various divisions of the organ, Klotz proposes that the last section be played with manuals coupled. Matthäi assumes that Bach added the manual slide-coupler[77] during the general rest just before the end of a work, as for example in the Fugue that follows the Passacaglia.[78]

The Dorian Toccata and the concertos also show us, however, that Bach not only clarified large-scale organization through contrast of manuals but often used alternation on a small scale. For example, the detached chords in the A Minor Concerto (VIII, 2) were to be played in turn on the OW and the RP:

Accordingly, extensive alternation is perfectly justified in the *Alla-breve* movement of the D Major Prelude, in the first movement of the C Major Toccata, in the F Major Toccata (for the second theme, p. 19, 4, 5), and in similar passages.

BACH ON MODERN ORGANS

The most difficult question concerns how these principles are to be put into effect on modern organs; i.e., on those under nineteenth-century influence. The conditions here are more unfavorable than when, for example, the *Well-Tempered Clavier* is played on a modern grand piano, which occurs daily (and will continue to occur in spite of the renaissance of the harpsichord and the clavichord), for it is the modern organ that must be dealt with, not a first-rate instrument on a par with the grand piano. Despite this fact, it would be thought

77. "Manualschiebekoppel." This was one of the simplest and earliest devices for coupling two manuals. The organist grasped small knobs found at each side of a manual and pulled this manual forward. It then locked with a second manual (either above or below it). When a key was struck, it simply activated the corresponding key on the coupled manual.
78. Matthäi, *Vom Orgelspiel*, p. 206, fn. 1.

too severe if one were to characterize a performance under these conditions as stylistically impossible.

It has already been pointed out above (p. 16) that Bach's music is more independent of sound than is that of Buxtehude and the rest of the North Germans. The more Bach deepened and universalized his style with increasing maturity, the more independent of the instrument his inspiration became. To a certain extent this is also true of performance of his music. Matthäi is right in pointing out that "Bach did not always compose for the instrument currently at his disposal, but often—and the later works of greatest maturity show this especially—he created his finest music in contemplating an ideal instrument. Only too frequently we experience something almost incomprehensible: that effects which lay hold of heart and soul can yet be achieved with a 'box of whistles' which is sometimes wretched. The factory organ of the last generation, which is today outmoded, is all too capable of colorless and superficial effects; yet even it can be sharpened in some measure with the powerfully radiating vigor of Bach's genius."[79]

Klotz[80] gives a number of directions for "playing classical music on a romantic organ" which are interesting—particularly for registration. We cannot agree, however, with his proposals for manual transitions in the F Major Toccata, for example,[81] or for the Great G Minor Fugue.[82] Even on a romantic organ it is not necessary to play the beginning of the G Minor Fugue by having the soprano and alto go from one manual to another after their subject-entries have come to an end, in order that the tenor may play its entry prominently on the first manual, etc. Instead, by omitting any stops that are too thick, heavy, or harsh, one must try to obtain a *forte* tolerable for Bach, with which the whole first section of the fugue may then be played without change of manual. On a 3-manual organ of 50 stops, 15-20 will often suffice for the attainment of a clear, transparent *forte*. The saying holds true here, also, that "to outline means to leave out."

An inappropriate modernization is wrong, but equally wrong would be an organist's attempt to force at any cost a "baroque" tone from an organ that is not adapted for it. Anyone who tries to register in opposition to his organ will soon have a fiasco.

Where the line of compromise is to be drawn (for compromise it will remain in any event) must be left to the performer in each individual situation. The right speed, steady rhythm, vital articula-

---

79. Matthäi, *Vom Orgelspiel*, p. 204.
80. Klotz, *op. cit.*, pp. 322-338.
81. *Ibid.*, pp. 331 and 337.
82. *Ibid.*, p. 333.

tion, and correct phrasing can and must help the listener to forget the defective tone-quality of the organ.

Yet a few practical suggestions may be made. The organist who plays on an organ built around 1900 should not use pre-set combinations or the *sforzando*. By experimenting he should try to bring together stops which will produce a usable *Plenum;* similarly, a usable combination of principals. If the subordinate manuals are too poorly stocked, the use of adjustable combination-pistons (which are usually available) will have to take the place of manual changes. If the pedal division is too weak, a subordinate rather than the principal manual should be coupled down; if the organ has three manuals, one of these that the organist can do without may be coupled down and then has only the task of making the pedal line come out more clearly. Expression- and *crescendo*-pedals should be dispensed with altogether.

Even the experienced modern organist, who knows how to handle his various mechanical aids to registration, may prefer, in Bach, to have additional registration done for him. He will thus not be forced into even more compromises, for the sake of his independence, than he is already obliged to make. When playing with manuals coupled, instead of going over to the weaker manual, one may remain on the stronger one, but take off the coupler. Technically this is sometimes considerably easier and often will prove equally effective. But these few suggestions will have to suffice, for this subject, after all, is inexhaustible.

DYNAMICS

Actually, in a book on the organ there should be no mention of dynamics at all, for they result spontaneously—a by-product, as it were, of the registration. Bach's generation, however, was already on the road to granting them an importance of their own, along with "color" (registration), even in organ music. Eventually, during the period of the organ's decline, it was no longer color that mattered, but only intensity. Consider the "*crescendo*-pedal style" after 1900!) It was only logical that, along with this preference for intensity, the principle of intensification, the Beethovenian *crescendo*, also should be applied to organ music. For a long time this style misled even good organists into playing no fugue without the familiar "large-scale final intensification." This is an effect that the overwhelming majority of the public still expects from the player even today. At the end it must roar, so that one is "simply overcome." We must first educate our listeners gradually to understand that a piece does not have merely the two possibilities—of ending either *ff* or *pp* (somewhat as in Czerny's edition of the *Well-Tempered Clavier*)—but that it may end just as it began, in its own characteristic sound.

The dynamics of the organ are terrace dynamics and, as in Bach's choral and orchestral music, terracings on the organ are produced by the addition or subtraction of tonal groups. When, for any piece by Bach, we seek the color suitable to it (and usually to it alone), we find the right intensity at the same time. With this, everything has been said on dynamics in Bach's organ music!

Bach was not acquainted with the venetian-blind swell, which was invented in England during his lifetime. His compositions, therefore, have no need for it—at any rate the large free works do not, although the French school and Schweitzer permit its use even for these. If the swell is used at all, it should be reserved for controlling a voice containing an ornamented c.f., on condition that the accompanying foundation-stops stand outside the swell. Where Bach calls for echo effects, and no suitable manual is available, the echo may be performed on the same manual with swell-box closed; if this is done, the opening and closing of the swell should take place quickly and unnoticeably during the pause.

TEMPO

The right choice of tempo has greater significance for our ears than it had in Bach's day, for the Viennese classicists have so refined our feeling for nuances of tempo that a very small metronomic change gives quite a different complexion to a Mozart *Allegro,* for example; and this effect is even more pronounced in Beethoven. In contrast, for Bach as for Handel, the right time, the *tempo ordinario,* was self-evident and assumed, yet its own peculiar aesthetic value was relatively limited.

If we read the old theorists, we notice that each maintains that earlier tempi were slower; that what had earlier been *allegro* was now at most *andante,* etc. This is obviously self-deception, since in old age one always feels the tempo of the young generation to be faster than that in the time of one's own youth. Yet there were also set standards: there was an *allegro* of the Baroque which resulted from an attitude toward life different from ours. It is often wrongly interpreted, especially in Handel's works (as, for example, in his organ concertos and violin sonatas) to the point of spoiling the overall impression; that is to say, it is taken too fast and without sufficient solidity.

Concerning Bach's tempo we have reliable information in the words of the obituary notice: "In conducting he had a very accurate and extremely steady tempo, which he commonly took at a very lively pace." This means that as conductor he maintained a beat once established without slackening. That he took it at a lively pace is accounted for by his choleric temperament; his superior technique also enabled him as a performer to play his own pieces faster than could his pupils or contemporaries. In Bach, therefore, there can be no talk of the freedoms in tempo that Frescobaldi considered indispensable to the correct performance of a toccata and still less of the freedoms which the generation of C. P. E. Bach introduced immediately after Bach.

Only the six trio sonatas, which are closely related to the chamber music, bear indications of tempo, as of course among Bach's instrumental works only the chamber-music works are provided with markings for articulation. A few scattered markings may be added to these: *Vivace* for the Prelude in G Major (II, 2); *Largo* once in the *Little Organ Book* (with "Jesu, meine Freude") and a few times *Adagio* and *Adagio assai* ("O Mensch, bewein dein Sünde gross"). Whether or not the markings of the D Minor Toccata and the G Major Fantasy ("*Très vitement*") are original can no longer be determined. It might be added that Bach's *andante* is closer to *allegro* than to *adagio;* generally it means *allegro molto moderato*.

Widor and Schweitzer make a suggestion well worth heeding:[83] "The player should have in mind the listener who is perhaps hearing the piece for the first time, and who may not be able to absorb and understand it in the tempo that seems unobjectionable to the player himself. The player must recall the tempo that seemed the appropriate one when he began to study the work. As a rule, this will also be the right one for the listener. In his treatment of the tempo, as in everything else, he must be guided by the immediacy of the first impression. Also, he must counteract with all his might the deadening effect of the factors of attrition and routine which he cannot escape when practicing." (All this is very true.) "The vivacity demanded by Bach is different, is spiritual; it is an inner vivacity corresponding to that of the choleric Bach, but which must also do justice to the structure of his works. Moreover, since the range of ideas in these works is above that of our daily thoughts, we shall do well to call to mind again and again the following: if so many organists choose the wrong tempo and cannot escape giving an impression of haste and unrest, the fault lies not in a lack of artistic insight but in the fact that they have not attained that profound inner composure without which they remain strangers in the sublime world to which the preludes and fugues belong."

ORNAMENTATION

The subject of ornamentation is undoubtedly the most disputed department of the older music. If, from the beginning, we limit our-

83. See the Widor-Schweitzer edition of Bach's organ works, Vol. I, pp. v-vi.

selves to Bach and to his organ music, it may be said that he uses ornaments more sparingly and with greater meaning than do his contemporaries (J. G. Walther, for example) and that he often deprives the performer of the exercise of his discretion by writing them out. In the organ works are found the following signs for ornaments:[84]

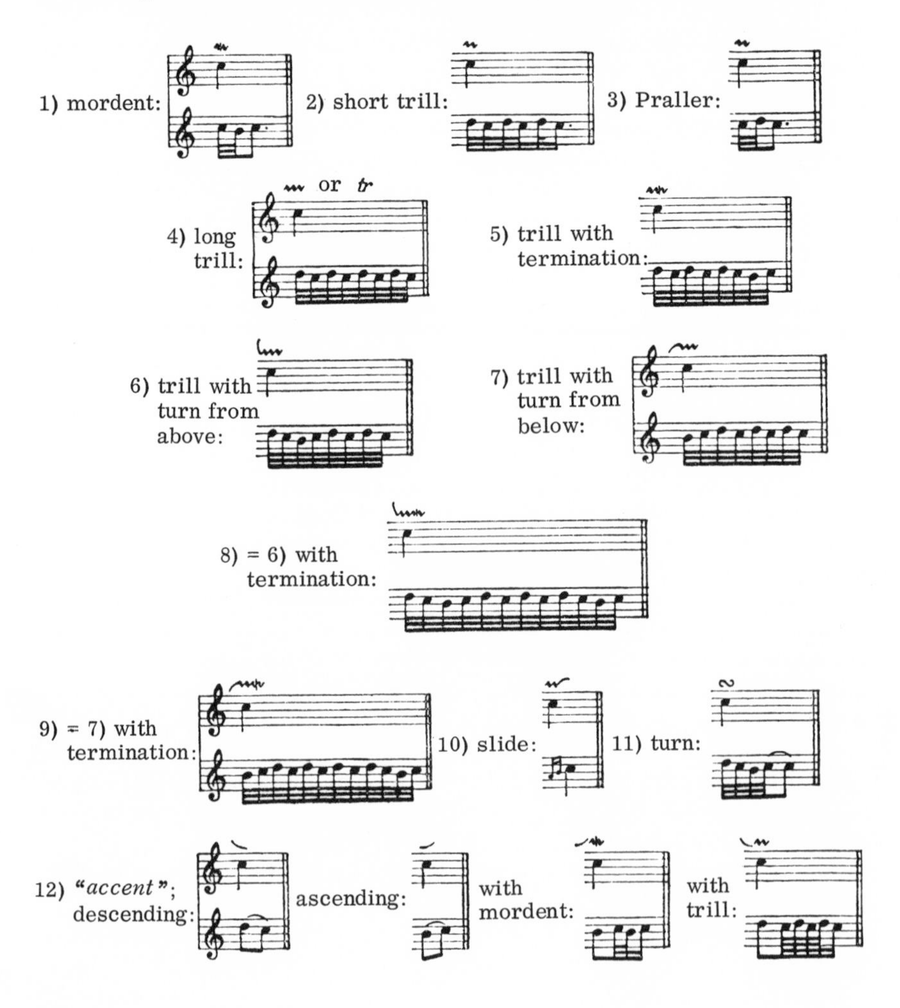

84. Nos. 1, 2, 5-9, 11, and 12 are from the table in the *Klavierbüchlein für Friedemann Bach* (modern edition by Hermann Keller, Kassel & Basel, Bärenreiter-Verlag, 1927). Two other recent books dealing with ornamentation are the following: Walter Emery, *Bach's Ornaments* (London: Novello and Co., Ltd., 1953); and Putnam Aldrich, *Ornamentation in J. S. Bach's Organ Works* (New York: Coleman-Ross Company, Inc., 1950).

(Sonata in G Major, I, 6)

Obscurity prevails most of all in connection with the trill. I should be glad if the following explanations could help to clarify this matter.[85]

Since the trill has the meaning of an oft-repeated suspension from above, it is clear that as a rule it should begin with the note above. This should be done especially when a repetition would otherwise occur between the first note of the trill and the preceding note—which should never happen. Therefore:

(Sonata in C Minor, I, 2)

But how should the trill be performed if a repetition or a leap would result from following this rule of starting from above—for example, the trill in the subject of the Great E Minor Fugue (II, 9)? Straube begins this trill with the principal note; Matthäi[86] begins it with the upper neighboring-note. It is correct to begin it with the principal note in order to avoid the leap of a third, but to dwell on it somewhat so as not to deprive the trill of its quality of retardation, thus:

also the trill at the end of the fugue of the C Major Toccata (III, 8):

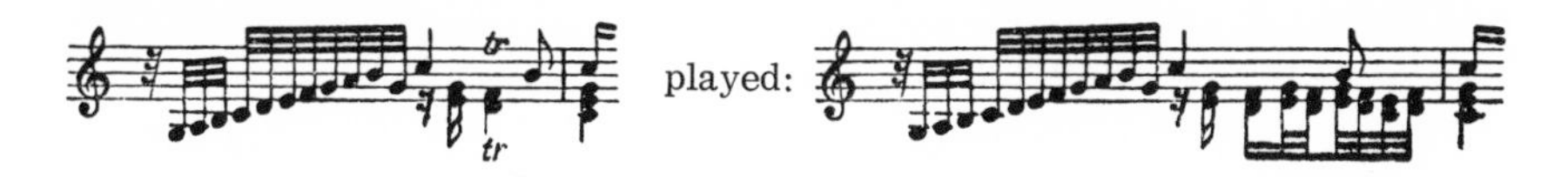

85. For this section I am indebted to my friend and colleague Alfred Kreutz for valuable suggestions.

86. *Vom Orgelspiel*, p. 84.

or again, the trill in the subject of the Dorian Fugue (III, 3):

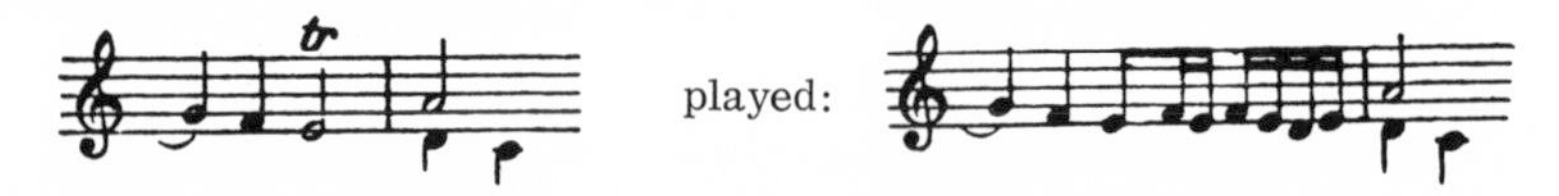

The same is true when a characteristic interval would be destroyed by beginning a trill from above; for example, in the subject of the F Minor Fugue (II, 5), the diminished seventh:

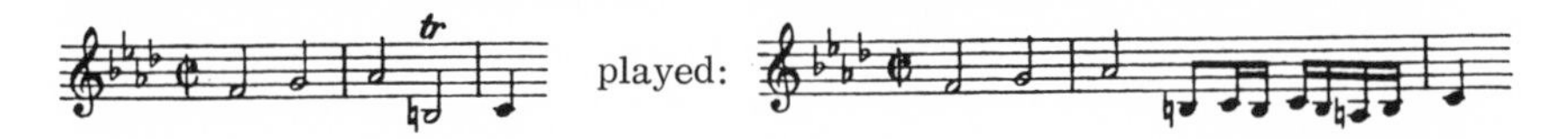

Occasionally Bach writes the sign ∽∿∿ instead; for example, VII, 37, m. 17.

The trill begins with the principal note when it has the function of a pedal point. Bach himself demonstrated this in the Dorian Fugue (III, 3):

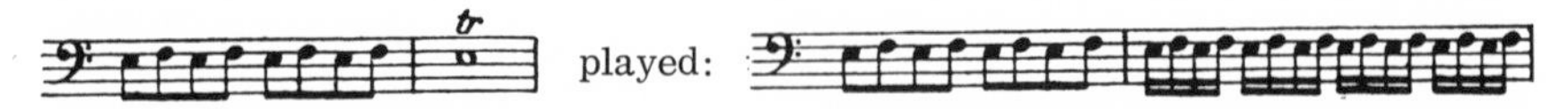

Even when it occurs in the soprano, as in the C Minor Sonata (I, 2) it should be performed in the same way:

With these three rules the player should be able easily to find a stylistically correct performance for every trill he encounters.

Further, every trill will normally receive a termination, even though none is specified. If the end of the trill is linked with an anticipation, a termination is still made, but the anticipatory note shortened correspondingly:

The division of the trill into triplets, which is particularly favored in the more recent piano technique, was not known to the old theorists.

The sign ∿ is ambiguous in Bach. It frequently stands for a long trill in place of ∿∿. Particularly where a termination is written out, a trill should always be made:

(Passacaglia I, 7)

But it can also mean a short trill, as Bach wrote it out in the table in the *Little Clavier-Book for Friedemann* (see No. 2). Yet Bach's organ music offers little opportunity of performing it in this way. The sign has its present meaning of inverted mordent in Bach only where it appears on a short note.

The mordents with which several of the large organ works begin (the E♭ Major Prelude, the G Minor Fantasy, etc.) may be taken broadly; a monumental style requires just such ornaments.

Many sins are committed in the performance of the appoggiatura. When Bach wrote four eighth-notes, not beamed together as eighths but like this:

(Fantasy in C Minor, IV, 12)

he certainly must have meant something by this notation. The player must make the appoggiatura audible as such; that is, he must emphasize the appoggiatura-note by detaching the note of resolution, so that a very small rest results; both notes are thereby imperceptibly lessened in value: about like this

It is a matter here of fine points which the notation cannot express but which were self-evident in that day.

Double-dotting was not yet known in Bach's period, but it is to be used wherever the resolution of a suspension would clash with an anticipation. Passages like:

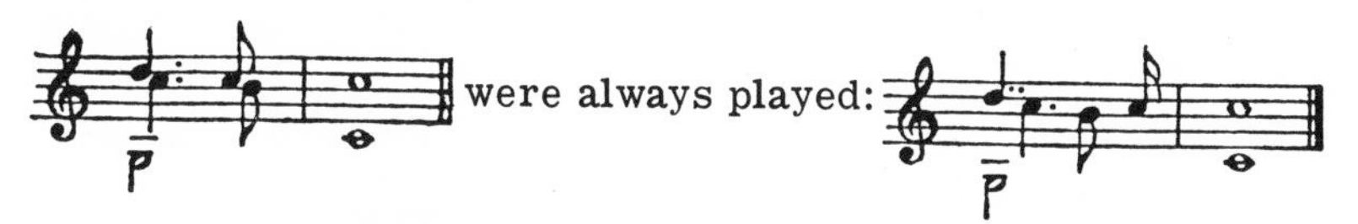

The formations (so frequent, particularly in Handel) are always to be performed: .

Sometimes we notice that the subject of a fugue appears with ornaments which it later discards. This is not carelessness of notation. The subject has need of its embellishment only on its first appearance, in order not to stand there "denuded"; later, the contrapuntal voices take over the task of decorating it. To be sure, it would suit us better, in some situations, to omit the ornaments from the very beginning; for example, in the subject of the F Major Fugue (III, 2).

No domain tolerates dogmatism of any kind as little as does ornamentation; no matter how much a performer may study—and he must study—in the end, his taste must be the basis of decision.

PHRASING AND ARTICULATION

These two departments, which are of the greatest practical importance for the organist, and more especially for the one who plays Bach, must be treated briefly here, as was the subject of ornamentation. For a fuller discussion I venture to refer the reader to my study *Die musikalische Artikulation, besonders bei J. S. Bach,* which appeared in 1925.[87]

First of all, the two departments should be kept clearly apart, even though they may often be confused with each other in the everyday speech of the musician. "Phrasing is the analysis of a melodic line; its function is the same as that of punctuation in language (comma, semicolon, etc.), namely, to set off clearly from each other the musical sentences called phrases, or parts of these sentences called motives. As a rule, phrasing is not indicated by the composer, but it is sometimes marked by a comma or short vertical line in teaching editions."[88]

The difference between language and music, then, is that hardly any uncertainty can arise concerning the meaning of a connected series of words. If a short story, for example, were issued entirely without punctuation, anyone could insert the correct marks of punctuation without any great trouble.

The large sections in homophonic music, like those in the sonatas and symphonies of Beethoven, are presented with almost equal clarity; in the main, they are made quite as obvious to the performer by the insertion of rests or other equally recognizable caesuras in the musical text as are the divisions in a verbal text by periods, question marks, or exclamation marks. But just as in the written language the placement or non-placement of a comma may often be debatable, in homophonic music the smaller homogeneous segments are no more obvious and have often led to the most curious interpretations, as for example in Riemann's "phrased editions."

---

87. (Diss.) *Veröffentlichungen des Musik-Instituts der Universität Tübingen. Heft II.* (Augsburg: Bärenreiter-Verlag). A 2nd, enlarged edition of the book appeared under the title *Phrasierung und Artikulation* (Kassel & Basel: Bärenreiter, 1955).

88. From my *Kunst des Orgelspiels* (Peters No. 4517), p. 70.

The conditions are still more difficult in the field of polyphonic music, where the overlapping and entwining of phrases and motives are so frequent that a clear separation is often not possible at all. A simple example may make this clear. Not even in such an apparently simple subject as that of the first fugue in the *Well-Tempered Clavier* can one say where it ends, since it passes over into the counterpoint imperceptibly. The point at which this occurs remains unknown to the listener, and a "phrase mark," wherever it might stand, would be wrong, since it would produce a separation that the composer did not want at all:

In many other situations, and these are in the majority, a decision can be reached with a certain plausibility, yet without any assurance that it is the correct interpretation. The theme of the Little G Minor Fugue (IV, 7) might read either:

Therefore, if I may make a frank confession, I should remove from my editions of the works of Buxtehude, Scheidt, and Lübeck a number of phrasing marks put there by me—not because they are "wrong," but because today I see in these passages other possibilities for separations as well. Riemann, as is well known, coined the concept of the "dead interval"; i.e., an interval that, cut up by the phrasing, is no longer felt as an interval. There are many of these in the works of the Viennese classicists, but few in those of Bach.

Articulation does not concern itself with the intellectual context, but assumes it as fact; or it can even go in opposition to it, as for example, when articulation is to make the musical expression abundant, exuberant, and vital. To this end, all degrees of slurring and detaching of notes are available to it: *legatissimo,* normal *legato, legato-portamento* , *portato, non legato, staccato,* and *staccatissimo.* "In a perfect *legato* the stream of the melody flows through the individual tones without encountering any resistance and without losing any of its flowing power; the tones receive it and direct it onward; consequently, *legato* is the only expression of the melodic line without conflict; it is a symbol of composure, of stability, of preservation, of union, even of perfection, or rather, of humility inspired by it. . . .

"The *staccato* mark, as it is usually found toward the end of the seventeenth century, the sharp, diagonal line slanting down toward the note, symbolizes the touch with which the individual tone is placed outside the continuous line. . . . The range of expression of *staccato* is far greater than that of *legato*, for many types of 'lack of restraint' may be contrasted with the one concept of restraint."[89]

Intervals, tempo, and dynamics all have influence on articulation: small intervals (scale steps) are normally connected; large ones ("leaps," as they are termed), detached. The intellectual context, the "connected" quality of a theme, however, can also maintain the connection over a large interval. The subject of the F Major Fugue (III, 2) would be torn into two meaningless parts and would lose its inner calm and unity if the sixth were interrupted:

The subject of the F Minor Fugue (II, 5) would suffer in the same way.

Naturally, stepwise progressions may also be played *staccato*, when a special expression is to be attached to it; thus the "spread-out" character of the second countersubject of the G Minor Fugue (II, 4) can best be expressed by *staccato:*

For the organist, a knowledge and mastery of the various types of articulation are of special importance, because for him articulation must replace the accent lacking on the organ. The more a tone is shortened, the less accented is its effect in comparison with that of tones held their full length. In order to accent a strong part of the measure, which the pianist achieves by means of dynamics, the organist must shorten the upbeat. If, in the C Major Prelude (II, 1), the highest voice, in mm. 8-10:

89. Cf. *Phrasierung und Artikulation*, pp. 32 and 33.

is to come out rhythmically distinct and accented, it should be articulated something like this:

But naturally this is not to say that every upbeat is to be detached.

In articulation, as in phrasing, the player is advised to do too little rather than too much. We know from experience how easy it is for beginners to exaggerate articulation, and this gives an impression of affectation. On the organ quite small separations are sufficient; it would be wrong to transfer the articulation of the piano directly to the organ. Broad outlines, in particular, should not be torn apart by articulation, but undergo only an imperceptible organization and relaxation. For the beginning of the Dorian Toccata (III, 3) for example, Schweitzer's proposal was:

This is certainly not tenable today, since it is falsely "phrased"; but neither would a *staccato:*

be in keeping with the grandeur of this music. The best rendition would probably be:

Thus the listener would realize only indirectly that the *legato* of the first three notes is strict in comparison with the relaxed *legato* of the next five sixteenths. He would hear the subject firmly fitted together and clearly accented at the same time. The same would be true in the F Major Toccata.

From the very beginning, a fine, clean *legato* has been considered the very heart of organ playing. But not till Bach's generation—when passing the thumb underneath was introduced—could *legato* be carried out generally. Frescobaldi still wrote in the Preface to his *Fiori Musicali* that the *cantus firmi* should be played well connected, but where that was too difficult, one could let go! By no means, however, may one conclude from this that, because in Bach all parts *can* be played connected, they always *must* be played connected. Perhaps one may say that the more nearly polyphony approaches strict counterpoint, the more *legato* should prevail in it. In Bach this is the situation in the *Allabreve* (VIII, 6), for example.

The more clearly perceptible the influences of violin style on organ style are, the more abundant may be the articulation; consequently, the *Six Sonatas*, being closest to chamber music, should be the most fully articulated, and—this is important—were marked to some extent in this way by Bach himself.[90] Toccatas and fugues require a less differentiated articulation, particularly Bach's early works not yet influenced by the Italian violin style. The close texture of a fugue becomes animated only when the player articulates each individual part throughout. Mediocre performers often content themselves with articulating the subject only.

As a rule, there will be *one* correct phrasing, but several possibilities for articulation. Since articulation is one branch of the expression of music (not a constituent part of its grammar), and since the expression of a theme may change during the course of a composition (for example, the character of the principal subject of the E♭ Major Fugue in the second and third sections of the Fugue), the articulation may change also. Nevertheless, this situation would seem to be rare in Bach.

Recently Hugo Distler[91] attacked the concept that the *legato* of the organ represents the norm; in exchange for it he wished to put playing in a *portamento* style, which he considered better suited to the old music. To be sure, there is a viscous, sticky *legato* which can be ugly, especially on organs with pneumatic action, but the whole wealth of articulation in Bach is not to be comprehended without a *legato* consciously cultivated and meaningful.

I am aware that these short explanations by no means treat all the problems connected with the performance of Bach's works for the organ. A number of other questions will be raised in the discussion of the individual works, which will form the second and chief part of my task.

---

90. See also the original rich articulation of "Vater unser im Himmelreich" (VII, 52).
91. In *Musik und Kirche*, 1940, No. 3.

PART II

THE WORKS

A. FREE WORKS

Preludes, Fugues, Toccatas, etc.

CHAPTER 7

YOUTHFUL WORKS

(Lüneburg, Arnstadt I, *ca.* 1700-1705)

From earliest childhood Bach lived in a world of music. "As Cantors and organists in how many churches the name Bach was familiar! . . . What a fund of inherited experience informed Sebastian's young fingers as they spread over the keyboard of organ and clavier or clasped the viol's finger-board!"[92] or—we are adding to this idea—when he covered with childish characters music paper he had ruled himself! His father, Ambrosius Bach, was "Stadt-Haussmann";[93] i.e., he was a town musician; Johann Christoph Bach, the famous organist of St. George's Church in Eisenach, was Sebastian's father's first cousin.

In 1677 Pachelbel made a short visit in Eisenach on his way to Erfurt. In Erfurt he became the teacher of Sebastian's older brother who, in 1695, took the orphaned boy to Ohrdruf and into his own home, and gave him his first regular instruction in music. The legend is told of the young Bach, as of Handel, that he copied out secretly "at night by moonlight. . . a book filled with clavier pieces by the most famous masters of that day—Froberger, Kerll, and Pachelbel—" a book his brother had withheld from him. Perhaps his

92. Terry, *op. cit.*, p. 17.
93. Geiringer, *op. cit.*, p. 71, fn. 2, states: "Rollberg. . . claims that the expression *Hausmann* frequently used for the town musician points to his duties in the city house, i.e. the town hall. He was sometimes also called *Haustaube*, house-pigeon, because of his domicile in the city tower."

first experiments with composition, three small chorale fughettas (see p. 190) and a clavier fugue in E minor (BG XXXVI, No. 29), fall in this period. Quite certainly, however, he began to prove himself as a composer on the organ in Lüneburg under the influence of Böhm and the Hamburg organists; he may also have worked out sketches from the Lüneburg years in Arnstadt. The visit to Buxtehude (1705-1706) was a landmark in his artistic development; the pieces which, according to their workmanship, originated before this journey will be called here, in the strict sense of the words, "youthful works." They are the following:

Prelude and Fugue in A Minor (III, 9; BWV 551)

This is probably the earliest, but certainly the most imperfect and hence the most rarely played, of all Bach's free organ works. It would indeed have found its place more suitably in the eighth than in the "classical" third volume of the Peters edition. It is in five sections—prelude, *fugato*, interlude, double fugue, and concluding toccata—but lacks thematic unity. It was Seiffert[94] who ascertained that the double subject of the fugue

could be traced to a Fantasy by Sweelinck:[95]

Since the young composer as yet lacked skill in composition, the Fugue seldom goes beyond two- or three-part writing; the motive

94. *Geschichte der Klaviermusik* (Berlin, 1899-1901), p. 149.
95. *Werke,* (Amsterdam: Alsbach, 1943), I, 38.

with which the Fugue is prolonged after the somewhat odd modulation to C minor, emerges later in the D Major Fugue, as is well-known. The downward leap

in the concluding toccata is also curious, yet ultimately it has an uplifting effect on the piece. The

Prelude and Fugue in C Minor (IV, 5; BWV 549)[96]

is a three-part toccata with built-in fugue, the subject of which grows thematically from the Prelude:

The Prelude, clearly separated from the Fugue, manages with only the opening motive and a few improvisatory extensions. In the Fugue Bach tries to pile up five entries of the subject in ascending order, as he does later in the C♯ Minor Fugue of the *Well-Tempered Clavier;* the pedal does not enter till near the end where, after two modest developments, the fugue merges with the toccata's flood of tone. Here Bach is in his element. In this conclusion, as Spitta observed, "there is much more than mere striving after executive brilliancy. . . the true fire of youth burns throughout the piece with a bright flame."[97] The subject of the Fugue, a complete period of two phrases, is longer than any other of the period. Compared with the often aphoristic subjects of Buxtehude, these first subjects of Bach are already significantly effective.

The authentic text of the piece can hardly be determined any longer from the unreliable copies in which it has come down to us. In m. 14 of the Prelude, the sixteenth notes should be in the pedal.

Performance: the Prelude (♩ = 58) with the *Plenum* of a subordinate manual; the Fugue (♩ = 76) on the *Hauptwerk* with the *Plenum,* increased toward the end.

---

96. According to Klotz ("Bachs Orgeln," pp. 196f.) D minor, not C minor, would have been the original tonality.

97. Spitta, *op. cit.*, I, 251.

Possibly the first draft of the

Prelude and Fugue in C Major (IV, 1; BWV 531)

should be included in this earliest group; it may have been revised later. An incomplete autograph omits the very part of the Fugue (mm. 26-54) which brings the only thematic pedal entry, so that these measures probably must be considered a later addition, while the schoolboy-like mutilation of the subject when the pedals first enter has to be appraised as a sign of a very early origin. Even the pedal solo in the Prelude is simpler than any other in Bach. Spitta and most scholars after him do the piece too much honor when they place it in the Weimar period. At that time Bach would no longer have written parallel octaves as impudent as those in mm. 13/14 of the Prelude.

Nevertheless, Spitta is right when he says, "With a good performance and a correspondingly strong organ the effect of this composition is an extraordinary one; something like a spring storm on a March night rages through it, and one feels that such power will achieve wonders."[98] But it is a promise only, not yet a fulfillment.

Its stylistic dependence on Böhm's work in the same tonality is unmistakable.[99] This is one more reason to believe that it originated in Lüneburg. There is even a certain relationship to Vincent Lübeck's Prelude and Fugue in C Major. In our own time Max Reger plainly refers to this early Bach in his first work for the organ (Op. 7, No. 1).

In mm. 3 and 9 the entries of the answer follow in the subdominant, contrary to rule. For a tonal answer of the subject, however, this was the only possible expedient. Bach already shows here, as later in the first fugue of the *Well-Tempered Clavier*—in which two dominant entries of the theme occur in succession—that he regards himself as master, not slave, of the scholastic rules.

Its *performance* should be brilliant and exuberant: the Prelude (♩ = 84) with the *Plenum* of the HW throughout; the Fugue (♩ = 80) affords opportunity for a change of manuals for mm. 14-23 (1st eighth) and again for mm. 26 (2nd half) to 36 (1st quarter).

In connection with these three preludes and fugues we may consider three individual fugues which, like Bach's separate clavier

98. *Op. cit.*, I, 402.

99. *Georg Böhm: Sämtliche Werke*, ed. Johannes Wolgast (2 vols.; Leipzig, Breitkopf & Härtel, 1927-1932), Vol. I, No. 1.

fugues, are typical studies. The

Fugue in G Major (IX, 7; BWV 576)

has come down to us in a single manuscript only, and this is missing today. The fugue betrays its early origin in several careless parallel octaves (mm. 19/20, for example) and in the small amount of thematic work that becomes lost time and again in improvisatory figures. But here also it is the melodic beauty and charm of the subject that transport us beyond these weaknesses. It is related to one of Pachelbel's subjects,

but is longer; the extension at the end is found similarly, later on, in the B-Major Fugue of the *Well-Tempered Clavier*,

so that I am inclined to believe in Bach's authorship, after all—contrary to my doubts expressed in the Preface to Vol. IX.

The

Fugue in C Minor (IV, 6; BWV 574)

("Thema Legrenzianum elaboratum cum subjecto pedaliter ab J. S. Bach")

has been placed in the Weimar period by most scholars. It is written on a theme of Giovanni Legrenzi (1626-1690, Venice) and it would be quite natural, in fact, to include it with the rest of Bach's studies on Italian themes. But the bombastic concluding toccata, which is attached to the fugue without any inner connection, and the type of thematic treatment, "the frequent recurrence of a perfect cadence before a new entry of the theme, a feature making it seem somewhat fragmentary and short-breathed,"[100] make it impossible to place the

100. Spitta, *op. cit.*, I, 423.

fugue on a level with the works of Bach's first master-period. In short, it is boring.

From which work of Legrenzi's this subject was borrowed is not known as yet. Bach combined it with another theme of his own. Consequently, the subjects are developed separately at first, and then together; but that inner tension, which needs to be vital in this pretentious form, is lacking. It was Bach's first attempt in a form to which he later contributed masterpieces in the F Major Fugue (III, 2) and the C Minor Fugue (II, 6).

The artistic value of a second

Fugue in C Minor (IV, 9; BWV 575)

is much higher. This is perhaps the most charming of all Bach's early fugues.[101] Its florid subject, which is related to the theme of the E Minor Toccata for clavier, suggests the pedal-harpsichord rather than the organ. Bach's beginning the subject on the sixth degree of the scale and the vague, swaying rhythm are bold and unusual. On the other hand, if Spitta is of the opinion that, "since the organ has no power of accentuation,"[102] the listener is obliged to hear the beginning like this,

it may be contended that correct accentuation can be produced quite well from the very beginning by means of articulation:

It is obvious that with this subject collaboration of the pedal was out of the question. It enters only in the closing toccata as support and has the final word in the form of a long solo-passage ranging through two octaves.

Spitta describes this work admiringly: "what a vague indefiniteness in rhythm and harmony. . . . From the theme onwards the work

101. A conjecture by Grace (*op. cit.*, p. 19) that Philipp Emanuel Bach might be its composer is untenable.

102. Spitta, *op. cit.*, I, 253.

is pervaded by a feeling of tension and an expression of longing for a blissfulness as yet but dimly anticipated."[103] Perhaps he read too much of Schumann's "piano poetry" into the little piece. Nevertheless, any organist who has a desire to play this fugue must first of all be an excellent pianist if he is to lure its charm from the obstinate organ.

Probably also the isolated

Prelude in G Major (VIII, 11; BWV 568)

was intended for the pedal-harpsichord rather than for the organ; it betrays an early origin particularly in its careless doublings within the chords. Spitta feels that "a sort of thematic development is indeed perceptible, but the chief motivating idea was the releasing of a tumultuous flood of sound, in which the impetuous spirit of the young composer revels with delight."[104]

The strongly pianistic style suggests Reinken and Böhm; the rolled chord in measure six, French models; but what deters us from listing the work among the earliest compositions is its excellent, formally balanced layout in three sections. Possibly completion by a fugue was never intended; one could follow it, however, with the G Major Fugue in the same meter (IX, 7) or the one in 12/8 (IX, 2). Isn't it curious that a number of Bach's compositions in G major start out similarly from g^2: the Preludes II, 2, and IV, 2; the Fantasy IV, 11; and the clavier Toccata?

For the *performance* of this Prelude I should like to refer the reader to my *Kunst des Orgelspiels;* there I have taken the soprano of the diverging outer parts in mm. 16-22 up to e^3:[105]

Two short, easy pieces which Bach labeled *Fantasia* no longer have any connection with the fantasy of the Sweelinck period. Probably their ambiguous titles have reference to Pachelbel, who so named a few quiet, meditative pieces lacking the preparatory quality

103. *Op. cit.*, I, 253f.
104. *Ibid.*, I, 398.
105. Peters No. 4517, pp. 53-57.

of a prelude.[106] In the

Fantasy in C Major (VIII, 9; BWV 570)

(notated in the Peters edition as a manual piece but in the BG with pedal throughout) Bach does not quite come up to his model. After a fine beginning he never escapes from the rhythm: ♪ ♫. The

Fantasia con imitazione in B Minor (IX, 1; BWV 563)

is also animated by this rhythm. Originally it was among the clavier works in the Peters edition, but the more correct place for it is among the organ works. The *Imitatio* takes its modest subject from mm. 20 and 21; perhaps Bach decided upon this title, rather than "Fughetta," because of the irregular construction of the answer (a♯ instead of a). The development of the subject is also modest: enlivening counterpoints are wanting, and harmonically it hardly leaves B minor and D major.

In the second half of m. 13 the soprano seems corrupt; it probably would have read like this:

In connection with these individual preludes and fugues, two works may be dealt with which hardly admit of a definitive classification, since they display such a variety of stylistic features.

The isolated

Prelude in A Minor (IV, 13; BWV 569)

106. See, for example, *Orgelwerke*, ed. Matthäi, Vol. 1, No. 2, p. 12.

exhibits a marked contrast between careful composition and limited inspiration, so that it is almost unique among Bach's organ works. Frotscher comments (pp. 861-862) that "the whole piece is developed from a four-note motive and indeed—most admirably—without true imitative work. . . . At the same time Bach creates distinctly idiomatic techniques that remain permanent artistic resources for him from then on. The very beginning is characteristic; although others would have written the passage as a run, he distributes it among the voices and thereby makes it important."

If the double pedal and elaboration of the subdominant at the end were not signs of a fairly early period, one would be tempted to see in this work a study in the style of the chaconne from the mature period; but the later Bach would have known how to avoid the monotony that mars the piece. Something similar is found in an early Fantasy in A Minor for clavier (BG XXXVI, pp. 140ff.):

Thus, in spite of everything, both performer and listener are left disappointed by this curious work.

Similarly disappointing, on the whole, is a

Fantasy in G Major (IX, 4; BWV 571)

In one manuscript it is labeled "Concerto," probably because of its being in three parts: Fantasy, *Adagio*, and Chaconne. Here the *Adagio* replaces the fugue, and a *Ciacona* the concluding toccata of Buxtehude's model. The theme of the *Adagio* is an inversion of the theme of the Fantasy,[107] which in turn may have been borrowed from Kuhnau's *Clavierübung*.[108] The descending bass was then derived by extending the theme of the *Adagio*.

The unevenness of invention in this Fantasy is remarkable: it is quite weak in the first part, much better in the second (notice the daring chromatic ending), while the Chaconne is excellently done.

---

107. See Seiffert, *Geschichte der Klaviermusik*, pp. 253-254.

108. In 2 parts (Leipzig, 1689 and [?] 1692). Modern edition of *Ausgewählte Klavierwerke*, ed. K. Schubert (Mainz; Schott, 1938).

The

Fugue in G Major (IX, 2; BWV 577)

is also an isolated piece. Quite unjustly it is seldom played. (Is this because it appears in Vol. IX?) It deserves more attention, however, in part because of its style, which—within the organ works—is unique. In addition, it makes an excellent study for coordination of hands and feet in rapid tempo. It is also good practice for quick and sure changes of manual. It has the rhythm and meter of a *gigue* and was probably intended for the pedal-harpsichord rather than for the organ. Buxtehude furnished a model in his separate C Major Fugue, but Pachelbel also wrote several fugues in similar style; for example,

etc.,

Bach, however, was the first and only composer to venture to write a fugue with obbligato pedal in such a tempo. (The concluding sections of Buxtehude's large preludes and fugues in 12/8 meter are quite different in style.) The use of echo, specifically indicated, suggests French prototypes, but the adaptation of the pedal entry of the subject for the use of alternate toes is genuinely Bachian:

Later we shall encounter even more frequently ingenious modifications of this kind. Aside from the passages marked *f* and *p*, the following ought also to employ changes of manual:

The tempo should be *presto* (♩. = 116 or more), the articulation a prevailing *leggiero,* and the tone bright and clear.

The

Pedalexercitium in G Minor (IX, 11; BWV 598)

holds unusual interest for us, if indeed it is the only extant technical exercise that the young organist contrived for perfecting himself in pedal-playing. The sixteenth notes develop agility and evenness in the use of alternate toes. The eighth notes, however, produce bold leaps. It must be left undecided whether Bach also played these alternately; that is to say, with the left foot on the 3rd and 7th eighth notes, or two in succession with each foot. With the most unusual downward leap one could suppose that he wished to avoid the low C♯ that the organ perhaps lacked, if this were not called for in m. 26. The study is incomplete; Bach probably sketched it hastily while practicing. I wrote the last two measures, yet I doubt that Bach would have stopped there. In m. 17 one quarter of the measure is lacking; the other editions repeat the first quarter, a solution that did not seem plausible to me. The modern player, to whom the study of this excellent *étude* may be highly recommended, can also use it as a study in precise and rapid registration while playing, if he registers mm. 2, 5, etc. as echoes.

CHAPTER 8

DOUBTFUL WORKS

There are doubts about a few pieces, whether they should be associated with Bach's clavier music or with his organ music; of a number of others, Bach's authorship has not yet been settled definitely.

A little three-part

Prelude in C Major (VIII, 7; BWV 943)

as a preparatory study for the Inventions, probably should be numbered among the clavier works rather than the organ works, also the

Fugue in C Major (VIII, 10; BWV 946)

a study in "tied" style on the ascending and descending hexachord (a favorite subject in the older organ music). It is probably one of Bach's earliest experiments in the form of the fugue and, in spite of its use of pedal at the end, appears in the BG more correctly among the clavier works.

The

Little Harmonic Labyrinth (IX, 9; BWV 591)

Spitta[109] includes among the clavier works, and he questions Bach's authorship; he names Johann David Heinichen as its possible composer, and Günter Hausswald[110] does the same. But the extant manuscripts speak in favor of Bach and, as regards internal evidence, particularly the four recitative-like measures preceding the *Centrum* lead one to decide on Bach (the Chromatic Fantasy!) rather than on Heinichen. Whether it is by chance that the notes B A C H occur in the wrong order in the fugue subject of the *Centrum* may be left undecided.

Music took over the "maze" of baroque horticulture; we have several by Caldara, Locatelli, and others, but none approaches the Little Harmonic Labyrinth. As in a maze, we are misled by genuine enharmonic changes, in the Center find ourselves again near the exit,

109. *Op. cit.*, II, 43.

110. In *Johann David Heinichens Instrumental-Werke* (diss., Leipzig) (Wolfenbüttel: Kallmeyer, 1937).

and, after a few shifts corresponding to those of the *Introitus*, the sun of pure harmony shines again in the *Exitus*. Thus, over and above the documentary evidence, this well-thought-out plan, even the *fugato* in the *Centrum*, seems to me to speak in Bach's favor. Here he set foot on new harmonic territory of which he finally took possession in the G Minor Fantasy and in the Chromatic Fantasy for clavier.

The following works, on the other hand, are probably not genuine:

Prelude in C Major (VIII, 8; BWV 567)

In m. 26 it contains an augmented six-five chord, elaborated in a way not found elsewhere in Bach's organ works; also, Bach would not have labeled such a small work *pro Organo pleno*. Probably one of Bach's pupils (Kittel, perhaps?) was its composer.

The

Fantasy and Fugue in A Minor (IX, 6; BWV 561)

sounds like Bach in many details, to be sure, but they seem rather to be reminiscences of Bach, especially of the Prelude and Fugue in A Minor (II, 8), that we hear. Several organ works by Krebs, in which he copied his master, sound quite as Bachian. But what unmistakably differentiates a pedal solo by Krebs, for example, from one by Bach is that in Bach the virtuosity is justified and occasioned musically, while in Krebs it seems superficial and set down almost as an end in itself. Consequently, the virtuoso manual-part here is also ostentatious and colorless (particularly in its harmony) as never in Bach. It is also not entirely clear why the pedal was limited to a few supporting tones only. In one of the two extant manuscripts the piece is marked expressly *"per il Cembalo,"* so that in no event does it belong among the organ works. I do not believe that Krebs was its composer, but rather Kittel, particularly because of the abrupt transition of the motion from sixteenths to thirty-seconds, which is found from time to time in Kittel, for example in his C Major Prelude.[111]

111. See *Orgelkompositionen aus alter und neuerer Zeit*, ed. Otto Gauss. 4 vols. (Zürich, 1909-1913). Vol. I, p. 432.

The

Eight Little Preludes and Fugues (VIII, 5; BWV 553-560)[112]

I take to be a work by Johann Ludwig Krebs from the period when he was a pupil of Bach in Leipzig, as I explained in detail in the *Bach-Jahrbuch* for 1937. If one accepts this hypothesis, which gains in probability owing to a few striking reminiscences of works by Krebs, the difficulties which these compositions have posed for critical evaluation and which have led to such divergent appraisals by Bach scholars are automatically overcome.

On the one hand, there are the many immature errors in composition, especially the many parallel octaves between tenor and bass; and on the other hand, the fine thematic invention and the many features reminding one of Bach, which indeed are still found in abundance even in the later large works of Krebs. The whole style of these works bears the stamp of Telemann's period. That they should be youthful works of Bach is therefore out of the question. Similarly, it appears out of the question that Bach should have written compositions so immature and so filled with errors in Leipzig.

In spite of these statements they need not lose their popularity for the instruction of beginners. Yet for this purpose one should use the modern edition by Karl Straube (Peters No. 4442). There, weak passages and those containing errors have been improved cleverly and unhesitatingly—even if many of Straube's changes in the text have overstepped the bounds of necessity.

The

Trio in C Minor (IX, 10; BWV 585)

is very probably a composition by Johann Ludwig Krebs. "No pupil of Bach approached so near his master as did Krebs, especially in his trios, among which are found pieces of great beauty. The family resemblance between our trio and several others by Krebs in the

---

112. See also Walter Emery, *Notes on Bach's Organ Works. . . Book I. Eight Short Preludes and Fugues* (London: Novello & Co., 1952). Emery gives a summary of the opinions of various authors on the authenticity of the "Little Eight," pp. 31-42.

same tonality is striking. One may compare, for example, the beginning of No. 22 in the Heinrichshofen edition:

Even the characteristic combination of a slow movement with an *Allegro* in a two-part form is found repeatedly in Krebs but nowhere in Bach."[113]

CHAPTER 9

ARNSTADT II AND MÜHLHAUSEN

(1706-1708)

Bach's stay of several months in Lübeck (October, 1705, to February, 1706) fell in the middle of his Arnstadt period.

As the obituary notice relates, "Here in Arnstadt he was once moved by a particularly strong desire to hear as many good organists as he could. He therefore set out on a trip to Lübeck—on foot, that is—to listen to the distinguished organist at St. Mary's Church there, Diedrich Buxtehude." Probably the journey was not so romantic or original as it is often represented; at that time journeys to famous centers of art and to famous masters formed part of the education of a musician. Bach may have felt that Arnstadt and Thuringia in general no longer offered him a standard by which he could measure himself. The great masters of the organ were located in Hamburg and Lübeck. Despite the fact that we know no further details about Bach's stay in Lübeck, we may assume that he returned home with a vast increase in self-assurance.

He was now 21 years of age and fully conscious of a youthful strength in his art, for which his Arnstadt position soon seemed to him too limited. In the very next year he competed successfully for the position of organist at the Church of St. Blasius in the Imperial Free City of Mühlhausen in Thuringia. He moved there in September, 1708, and in October married his cousin Maria Barbara in Gehren.

In the organ pieces of this period the influence of Pachelbel recedes, and individual stylistic features, especially the great demands

113. Hermann Keller, "Unechte Orgelwerke Bachs," *Bach-Jahrbuch*, 1937, pp. 59-82.

on virtuosity, show the influence of Buxtehude. On the whole, however, Bach achieves a certain liberation from the North German style. He is trying to get from all sides what he needs for his development. These works are distinguished especially by their youthful ardor. They have a directness which still makes them favorites of organists today.

We shall mention first the

Toccata in E Major (III, 7, and Appendix; BWV 566)

Perhaps this was begun earlier and now completed. It is a curious fact that it has been handed down in two keys, E major and C major. In the BG it appears in the former key; in the Peters edition, unfortunately, in the latter, but with the first two movements in E major also in the Appendix (pp. 94ff.). There can be no doubt that E major was the original key; no one would have transposed a C major piece to E major, but the reverse might have been done: either to avoid keys that were too high (perhaps on organs with unequal temperament); or to make somewhat easier the first pedal solo,[114] which is really difficult in E major—and harder than the big solo in the F Major Toccata. Possibly Bach himself transposed the work to C major in Weimar, since his organ there was tuned a third higher than normal. At all events, it sounds incomparably better in E major than in C major.[115]

A second uncertainty relates to its title: *Präludium concertatum, Preludio con fantasia, et al.* The eighteenth century no longer had a uniform designation for the form of the five-part toccata with two fugues, a form which was dying out. Buxtehude's influence on the form is particularly evident here: the subject of the first fugue is developed from thematic material of the introductory toccata; i.e.,

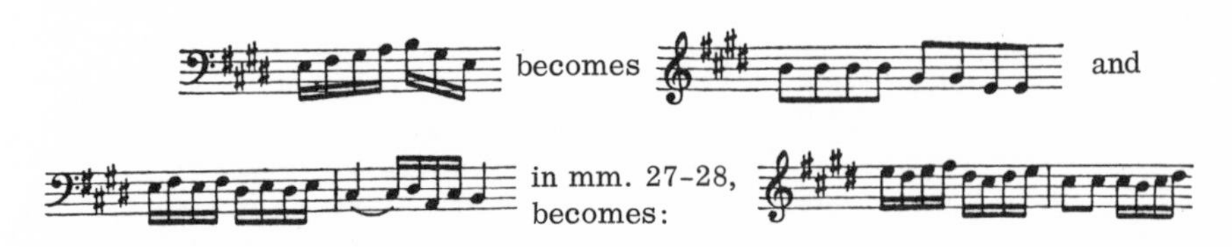

114. It is related to a pedal solo in the G Major Prelude by Bruhns. See *Bruhns: Orgelwerke*, ed. Fritz Stein (Peters 4855), No. 1.

115. The Capriccio in E Major for clavier also occurs in one manuscript transposed to F major.

After a barren interlude, which shows how far beneath his models Bach still stood at this point, follows the second fugue in 3/4 meter. Its subject is a transformation of the beginning of the subject of the first fugue. This second fugue flows into a toccata-like close.

One of the most brilliant inspirations of the young Bach is the first movement, which one could very well play alone as a short festive prelude. The introductory monophonic passage is divided between the two hands in the manner, characteristic of Bach, that he had already used in the C Minor Fugue (IV, 5), and was to use later at the beginning of the E Minor Prelude (III, 10), in the C Major Toccata (III, 8), and in the G Minor Fantasy (II, 4). Originally the reason for this division was merely to avoid turning the thumb underneath, but with Bach it became an important means of motivic organization. The organist who carries out this division as he directed, actually feels Bach, as player, near enough to touch.

The first fugue is no masterpiece; it suffers, very much as does the fugue of the Toccata in C Minor for clavier, from an excess of sequences which also spread to the counterpoints. The repetition of notes in the subject is a stylistic device *(repercussio)* taken over from violin music by the keyboard instruments around 1700. Although this was in fashion, so to speak, for a short time, it contributed just as little to the subject in the way of ornament. The crown of the work is the second fugue, of which Widor said, "It begins like a fugue, becomes a chorale, and ends like a concerto." It is to be interpreted with solemnity and deliberateness and with an imperceptible increase in volume from the polyphonic to the chordal writing at the end.

Performance: 1st movement: (♩ = 96) mm. 1-4 on the RP, brilliant; then the full *Hauptwerk;* 1st fugue (♩ = 104): bright principal-combination; interlude on the RP; 2nd fugue (♩ = 112): HW, begin with a moderate *forte,* gradually increase in mm. 39, 49, 73, and 82, to the *Plenum.* In m. 5 of the interlude[116] the first pedal entry may be played an octave lower (Bach was avoiding the low C♯). For the last pedal solo (15th m. from the end) Widor and Schweitzer propose as an improvement (analogous to the measures to follow in the manual):

116. This and the following sentence refer to the E major version which is in the BG, XV, 283.

The so-called

"Little" Prelude and Fugue in E Minor (III, 10; BWV 533)

is one of the best known and most widely played of the early works of Bach. Spitta thought it worthy of a searching, affectionately poetic discussion; Widor and Schweitzer assigned it to the very last, most mature, creative period; whereas Schreyer found the Prelude so full of clumsy errors in composition that it could not be by Bach at all. A number of stylistic features prove that we are dealing with an early work: the careless doublings and the resulting parallel octaves, the Buxtehudian "trilled" chords in the Prelude, and the thematic relationship between Prelude and Fugue. The motive 𝄾♪♩ gains more and more control of the situation from m. 12 of the Prelude to the end, which, like the close of the *Actus Tragicus*, composed in 1707, is to be interpreted in echo fashion:

The introductory passage is related to that of the Toccata in E Major (III, 7) but is still more akin to the expressive *passagio* which opens the Prelude of the Suite in E Minor for lute:[117]

The decisive factor here, however, is not that of form. It is the unusually strong spirit of the work which permits us to overlook the problematic nature and immaturity of the form. Moods which we do not find again, perhaps, till Mozart's D Minor Fantasy, appear to be anticipated here. As Spitta observed,[118] "In the Prelude sullen

117. H. D. Bruger, *Bachs Kompositionen für die Laute* (Wolfenbüttel: J. Zwisslers Verlag, 1925), p. 6.

118. *Op. cit.*, I, 402-403.

haughtiness struggles against a deep-seated melancholy, which prevails generally in the Fugue. . . . The Prelude begins with broad rolling passages. . . but from the eleventh measure on, shows a quieter development from which the earnestly meditative countenance of the composer peers unveiled. . . . Like a deep sigh [a four-note motive] moves through the various parts, accompanied by chords which come in reluctantly after the tones of the melody. The pedal indeed ascends with mighty strides, at the last even in tenths, but in vain—it is obliged to yield. Then the fugue comes in;[119] its meaning as a whole is at once intelligible to every one, but in detail it is full of expression which is quite indescribable, and which yet seems to crave for interpretation. . . ." Thus may someone speak who loves a piece because he has a profound comprehension of it.

In the Prelude the readings differ from each other to some extent. Measure 18:

is wanting in the BG, even though it is present in most of the manuscripts; some parallel octaves are also eliminated in the BG (perhaps an unnecessary discretion on the part of later copyists). The mordent in the subject of the Fugue is to be performed diatonically in the tonality of the moment; i.e., at the beginning, B A B; but in mm. 3 and 10, E D♯ E; in mm. 24 and 25, on the other hand, E D E.

Performance: Prelude (♩ = 69): mm. 1-5, *Plenum* of the RP; from there on, the *Plenum* of the HW. The Fugue (♩ = 76): foundation stops; it is customary, but not necessary, to go to an adjacent manual for mm. 15-19 (beginning) and from the entrance of the subject on, in mm. 27-33 (3rd quarter).

The

Prelude and Fugue in G Minor (III, 5; BWV 535)[120]

119. Significantly, this fugue refrains from closing with a toccata.

120. A shorter variant of only 21 measures appears in Bach's hand in the Möller MS.

throws the contour of the subject of the Fugue into bold relief in the pedal (mm. 10-11) in the midst of some apparently aimless improvisation over an implied pedal point. Then, breaking off, it flows through some monophonic passages into a chromatic sequence which descends through all twelve (!) half-steps of the scale only to rise magnificently again to an ending in five real parts. Here and in the "Harmonic Labyrinth" Bach makes his first voyages of discovery into the mazes of chromaticism and enharmonic spelling. Examine the notation of the sequence in the second measure, for example,

to perceive how new and strange this chromaticism must have seemed to the young composer. Unfortunately, these harmonic sequences, long since worn threadbare, no longer hold the same fascination for us. The sequential section, therefore, will always have a tiresome effect, even with an artful registration.

The Fugue vigorously unites the scattered elements of the Prelude. Its subject, like a woodcut with its repeated notes, still shows clearly features of Buxtehude's style; the rhythmical movement of the trills in the fourth measure is reminiscent of the "Amen" Fugue of Cantata 21, *Ich hatte viel Bekümmernis*. Even though the cadences of the individual sections are still brought about somewhat deliberately, nevertheless each new section brings an enhancement in accordance with the familiar rule of fugue-writing: in the first section a fugue must be good; in the second, better; but in the third it must be excellent.[121] Spitta quite properly calls it "a vigorous idea, carried out with power, depth, and great mastery,"[122] and he mentions with praise "how with each new entry of the theme a fresher and greater life is brought into the counterpoint."[123] The rise of the pedal at the end, with the simultaneous change of harmony to the Neapolitan sixth chord, is magnificent; the following passages and the five-part close make reference to the Prelude, with which the Fugue forms a union of an unusual kind.

Performance: Prelude (♩ = 69): mm. 1-14, foundation stops, then a combination with mixtures of an adjacent manual; from m. 32, again on the HW; the end on the *Plenum*. The Fugue (♩ = 96): mm. 1-24, HW; mm. 25-55, adjacent manual; from the alto entry in m. 55, again HW; broaden and increase the volume in mm. 64 and 72 to full organ.

---

121. Cf. Schweitzer, *op. cit.*, I, 270.
122. *Op. cit.*, I, 406.
123. *Op. cit.*, I, 407.

The

Prelude and Fugue in D Major (IV, 3; BWV 532)

in Spitta's words, "one of the most dazzlingly beautiful of all the master's organ works,"[124] is not only a virtuoso piece of the first rank, but is sustained from beginning to end by a youthful enthusiasm that communicates itself to player and listener alike. Even though only two of the four manuscripts in which the work occurs contain Prelude and Fugue together (the Prelude entitled *Pièce d'orgue*, and, in another manuscript, *concertato*), the sequences of the *Allegro* in the Prelude and those of the Fugue are nevertheless closely related, as Fritz Dietrich has pointed out.[125] The closing section of the Fugue and the beginning of the Prelude are also similar in style. Formally, however, each is complete in itself. Properly speaking, the Prelude is a three-part toccata, in which the *Allabreve* acts as substitute for the built-in fugue.

Its moods are as abundant and various as its form is daring: after the victorious beginning, which is like a fanfare, comes the vehement B-minor passage over the pedal point on F#. From this, the triumphal scale, as an intensification of the pedal scale of the beginning, draws us back again into the brightness of the major mode. In this mode the following *Allabreve* moves in truly southern serenity and composure reminiscent of Corelli. The recitative-like closing section, with double pedal, transports us anew, by its sorrowful dissonances, into a passionate unrest from which only the Fugue finally sets us free.

Prelude and Fugue alike utilize partly the familiar melodic resources of the time, partly material from Bach's own works. Thus, the beginning of the Prelude goes back to the Toccata in D Major for clavier:

where it is marked *Presto*. This marking, however, one must not carry over literally to the pedal-beginning of the Prelude. The motive

124. *Op. cit.*, I, 405.
125. *Bach-Jahrbuch* for 1931, p. 60.

in eighth notes used in the *Allabreve* is found similarly in Corelli, and was used later by Handel in his Suite in F# Minor:

The outline of the fugue subject is clearly foreshadowed in a fugue by Pachelbel:[126]

The head of the subject, separated from its continuation by a "daring pause,"[127] is related to the opening of the fugue from the Toccata for clavier, as the beginning of the Prelude was also related to this work. Spitta has already alluded to the connection between the counterpoint which breaks into the rest and Buxtehude's Fugues in F Major and F# Minor.[128] The ascending scale at the beginning of the Prelude is probably unique in the literature; a descending scale is found only once, in the Prelude and Fugue in G Major of Bruhns.[129]

A comparison of the Fugue with the variant (BWV 532a) given in the Appendix in the Peters edition (IV, p. 79) is very instructive. It will not do to see in this variant merely an earlier, less complete form of the Fugue. Spitta even conjectured that this was a later revision in which Bach had "clipped the too luxuriant growth of brilliant executive passages, and greatly condensed the whole. . ."[130](The variant is 39 measures shorter.) But since quite the most brilliant sections are lacking in the variant, it must be concluded that the situation is the reverse of that assumed by Spitta. It is a pity that it is never played, for among all the variants of Bach's organ works it is the most noteworthy.

Performance: Prelude (♩= 80, 𝅗𝅥= 69, ♩= 44): at the beginning the *Plenum* of the HW and *Pedal*. In the *Allabreve,* one should use two manuals for the dialogues (in the French manner) in mm. 16-21 and mm. 35-43 (though not in mm. 22-28). The exchange between soprano and alto in mm. 46-48:

126. See *Orgelwerke*, ed. Matthäi, Vol. I, No. 9, p. 34.
127. Spitta, *op. cit.*, I, 406.
128. *Ibid.*
129. See *Bruhns: Orgelwerke*, *op. cit.*, No. 1.
130. Spitta, *op. cit.*, I, 406.

one can also make significant only by change of manual. There are further dialogues in mm. 55-65 and 78-80.

The *Adagio* requires reed tone, though without strong 16' reeds in the pedal. The tempo of the Fugue is a relaxed, flowing, but not hurried, *allegro*. Griepenkerl's ♩ = 80 is too slow; ♩ = 104-108 would be better, though hardly any faster (even if one can play it faster—only to show that one can!). In the last section of the Fugue the tempo should be broadened to that of the Prelude (♩ = 80). The boldly sketched conclusion causes the greatest difficulty; one would like to play it just as boldly; if one does, however, one usually succeeds only in bewildering the audience.

In the reconstruction of the Fugue one should try to show the organization produced by the key scheme: after the first third, which is kept entirely in the major, the Fugue takes a decided turn toward the minor in m. 51, and then, ranging from B minor through F# minor, C# minor, and E major, turns back again toward D major; in m. 96 it rises to its dominant, A major; here the Fugue assumes the characteristics of a closing intensification. The disconnected style of the Fugue permits so many manual-transitions that it is unnecessary to make suggestions.

Generally speaking, the

Toccata and Fugue in D Minor (IV, 4; BWV 565)

is probably the best-known organ work of Bach. Its popularity began with Tausig's transcription for piano, and has continued to grow down to the present time, especially through recordings of the orchestral arrangement by Stokowski. In its original form, also, it is almost never missing from an organ program, particularly abroad. As a counterpart to the Dorian Toccata, therefore, it has come to be known as "the epidemic." It is not always the most significant works of a great composer to which the fanatical love of a large public attaches itself. Yet these works must express in some measure the characteristics typical of their creator as the multitude imagines him. Surely Handel's *Largo* is not the most beautiful of his operatic arias, but it is the most "solemn" and the one going most immediately to the heart. The Toccata in D Minor has also won for itself, by virtue of its inherent characteristics, an exceptional position in Bach's collective work to which it has no right.

Doubtless there are greater fugues by Bach on more significant subjects. There is, however, no other example of a beginning as thrilling as that of the Toccata with its *unisono* descending like a flash of lightning, the rumbling thunder of the broken chords of the full organ, and the turbulently heaving triplets. ("Read *The Tempest* of Shakespeare!" said Beethoven in reference to his D Minor Sonata, Op. 31.)

For four measures Bach storms up and down on the diminished-seventh chord (recognized and used here for the first time in the history of music for its true harmonic expressiveness)—until the pedal becomes the spokesman with intense seriousness. The Toccata is important, in fact, for its unprecedented concentration and heightening of improvisatory elements of this type. In contrast, the Fugue brings relaxation, but the concluding toccata restores the tension of the beginning. Hence the Fugue does not form a central high-point of the work, but lies in a wave-trough between the peaks of the beginning and the end. The subject of the Fugue is contained in the very beginning of the Toccata (it took me thirty years to notice this):

This fact also shows the dependence of the Fugue on the Toccata.

Performance: The indications of tempo handed down—by copyists—make explicit what is in reality obvious; unfortunately, directions for manual changes are wanting. One does not need to count on three manuals, as Klotz thinks;[131] the many rests in the Toccata conveniently permit reduction of the HW for the two-manual passage beginning in m. 12; mm. 16-20, also, should be played in alternating fashion; whether the monophonic passages at the beginning should be handled similarly cannot be answered with certainty.

The Fugue (♩ = 88-92), which in itself is loosely constructed, takes on the characteristics of an episode from m. 57 (p. 30, 4, 3) to m. 85 (p. 32, 2, 3). The resources of our modern organs (such as adjustable combination-pistons) permit us to perform the echo passages in mm. 62-65 and 73-82 as "double echoes," in the course of which the finer shading may be achieved by change of manual, the more pronounced by means of pistons.

131. *Op. cit.*, p. 266.

The reading published in the BG shows that the arpeggio at the beginning of the Toccata should be taken very broadly:

Grace[132] considers the 7th eighth of the alto (e^1) on p. 33, 3, 1, a "slip of the pen" made by the composer and proposes g^1 as an emendation. This has much to be said for it:

The duplets in mm. 4 and 6 are probably to be interpreted in triplet rhythm in accordance with the style of the period.

CHAPTER 10

WEIMAR

(1708-1717)

In 1708 Bach made a formal request to the Council of the City of Mühlhausen for his dismissal. As he expressed himself in this written petition, he had "received the gracious admission of His Serene Highness of Saxe-Weimar into His Court Capelle and Chamber Music."[133] When he assumed his duties in Weimar, he took over the post of organist of the court chapel as well.

"The pleasure His Grace took in his playing inspired him to try to be as ingenious as he could in handling the organ. Here he also wrote most of his organ works," reports the obituary. But the court

132. *Op. cit.*, p. 63.
133. See *The Bach Reader*, p. 60.

household was frugal, and the Duke led a pious and secluded life. It is therefore not probable that he had any unusual understanding of the originality of his young court organist. The way in which Bach was passed over, in the succession of court conductors in 1717, and even more his "ill-humored discharge," which reminds one of the circumstances surrounding Mozart's departure from Salzburg, intimate that the Duke saw in Bach a clever and useful musical official—but no more than that.

Hence the encouragement Bach received in his composing for the organ was restricted mainly to the area of church music, to the writing of chorale preludes. In addition, he was stimulated particularly by the example of his colleague at the City Church, Johann Gottfried Walther. His Weimar position offered him something new in his practical occupation with Italian music for orchestra. The concertos of Vivaldi and his contemporaries were rapidly captivating German orchestras at that time, and were being imitated industriously. Even the young, highly gifted Prince Johann Ernst, a nephew of the reigning Duke, was among these imitators. Bach and Walther, eager to adopt this new style, transcribed a number of concertos for clavier and for organ. We have sixteen of these transcriptions for the organ by Walther, an equal number for the clavier and five for the organ by Bach.

All his life Bach transcribed works of other composers as well as his own with pleasure—almost with passion. "He liked other people's music in the most uncritical way," says Schweitzer, "simply because it stimulated his own creative activity."[134] But that was certainly not the only reason. Busoni, who was also a master of the art of transcription, expressed the opinion that every formation of a musical idea was already one kind of "arrangement," and that therefore a composer should not be prevented from recasting it into another form.[135] When Bach did that with his own works—when, for example, he recast the E Major Prelude for violin alone into the Overture of the Cantata for the Inauguration of the Council[136]—new creations of the highest order came into being.

Nevertheless, we must not yet apply this term to the Weimar concerto transcriptions. They are typical studies which are worked out partly with great care, but partly in a manner incredibly careless and superficial. Walther's transcriptions, for example, are more scholastic and neater than some of Bach's, and among Bach's transcriptions, those for the clavier rank higher than some of those for the organ. Yet even the latter cannot disclaim the title "transcrip-

134. *Op. cit.*, I, 195.
135. Ferruccio Busoni, *The Essence of Music: And Other Papers*. Tr. from the German by Rosamond Ley (London: Rockliff Pub. Corp., 1957), p. 87.
136. Cantata 29; see p. 164.

tion," not even the Concerto in D Minor, which is the most significant of them by far. Now that the original form of this concerto has again become generally known, we can no longer agree with the verdict of Hermann Roth[137] that in this transcription one does not think of Vivaldi but only of Bach. Our chief interest lies in Bach's specifications of the manuals to be used; from these we can draw certain conclusions about the performance of the original works (see pp. 41ff).

According to one manuscript the

Concerto in G Major (VIII, 1; BWV 592)

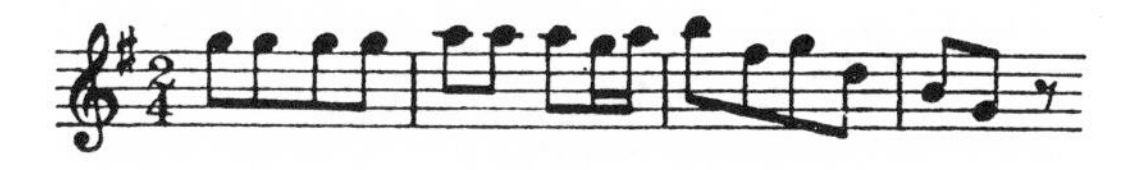

was composed by the young Prince Johann Ernst. Since Ernst died in 1715 at the age of nineteen, and since this work would hardly have been composed before his fifteenth year, one may infer that the origin of Bach's transcriptions probably should be set somewhere within the years 1711-1714. The young composer was a pupil of J. G. Walther and was esteemed by both Telemann and Mattheson. With its charming and natural melody, his concerto in fact shows more influence of Walther than of Vivaldi; the last movement is not much more than a joyful noise.

In the first movement Bach assigns the *tutti* passages to the *Oberwerk*, the *soli* to the *Rückpositiv*. In the second, the RP has the melody, marked *forte;* the OW has the accompaniment. The double pedalling called for in the first movement is rather unnecessary, since the left hand can take over the tenor quite comfortably. Perhaps this voice was written on the pedal staff only for convenience.

Performance: 1st movement, ♩ = 96; 2nd movement, ♩ = 76; 3rd movement, ♩ = 104. The first and last movements should be played with a light, bright *Plenum;* the second movement with a c.f.-registration composed of flue stops.

The

Concerto in A Minor (VIII, 2; BWV 593)

137. "Bach und Händel," in *Der Bär,* Leipzig, 1926.

was originally by Antonio Vivaldi (1678-1741) and was written for two solo violins, strings, and *basso continuo*.[138] In recent years it has also been heard in its original form: an attractive, spirited piece of music. Only the last movement is so weak in invention that in the past it has frequently been replaced by another Finale by Vivaldi.

Bach's transcription is almost "refined" in certain details. In the last movement, for example, the repeated notes are allotted to two manuals:

Again in the last movement, double pedalling is required, even though two manuals are being used. In the *Adagio* the duet for two melodic parts over a descending *ostinato* in the bass is both beautiful and well suited to the organ.

Performance: 1st movement, ♩ = 96; 2nd movement, ♩ = 58; 3rd movement, ♩ = 112. Concerning the marking "*Org. Pl.*" in the first movement, see p. 40.

The

Concerto in C Major (VIII, 3; BWV 594)

is a transcription of Vivaldi's Concerto in D Major for violin, Op. 7, Book II, No. 5. The composition is so weak and the arrangement so careless that Schreyer inquired scornfully, "Is Johann Sebastian Bach really supposed by the best authorities to have composed this musical monstrosity for organ, this wretched piping of a barrel-organ?" No, not composed, but arranged—and possibly this arrangement has reached us in an unfinished state. In any event, the passages left monophonic seem to support this assumption. These are not by Vivaldi, however; they are additions by Bach, just as he also substituted a recitative-like *Adagio* for Vivaldi's *Grave*. But even here one might inquire: Can this be by Bach?

---

138. The first movement is printed in the BG (XXXVIII, pp. 229-234) for comparison; the entire concerto has recently become available in miniature score (Philharmonia). See also Marc Pincherle, *Vivaldi: Genius of the Baroque*, tr. from the French by Christopher Hatch (New York: W. W. Norton & Company, 1957). The organ concertos are discussed on pp. 229-234.

The

Concerto-Movement in C Major (VIII, 4; BWV 595)

like the G Major Concerto, is a composition by the Prince Johann Ernst. Bach had already transcribed the whole concerto for clavier (No. 13 of the 16 concertos).[139] Then he re-arranged the first movement for the organ, at the same time lengthening it from 66 to 81 measures. The following passages correspond:

Clavier:	*Organ:*
mm. 1-9	mm. 1-15
mm. 10-18	mm. 16-24
mm. 19-29	mm. 25-43
mm. 30-66	mm. 44-81

Bach provided this movement with more manual-changes than he did any other (see p. 43). ♩ = 84.

The

Concerto in D Minor[140] *(BWV 596)*

has a truly romantic past. After Bach's death the manuscript of the organ transcription came into the possession of Friedemann, who wrote his name on it and, when he passed it on to Forkel, appended the memorandum "*manu patris mei descriptum*" ("written by the hand of my father"). Later owners, particularly Griepenkerl who edited it for Peters in 1844, concluded from this inscription that it concerned a composition by Friedemann, copied by his father in his own handwriting. Hence, in the nineteenth century, as an "organ concerto by Friedemann Bach," it contributed not a little to belief in the greatness of Friedemann's talent. Especially the effective transcriptions for piano by Stradal and Zadora were played a great deal.

139. BG, XLII, pp. 148-154.
140. Separate publication, Peters No. 3002.

In 1911, however, Max Schneider discovered the original:[141] the Concerto Grosso, Op. 3, No. 11, for two violins, cello, string orchestra, and *basso continuo*, by Vivaldi. This is a masterpiece that surpasses by far any composition by Friedemann! Since it may be heard frequently in its original form, the transcriptions are quite properly tending to retire into the background.

Bach's transcription is extraordinarily careful, and a comparison with the original is instructive in many respects. Vivaldi has an Introduction precede the first movement, a fugal *Allegro*. In this introductory passage the two solo violins begin alone (without any bass) and, overlapping each other, ascend to d^3:

Since the organ in Weimar had no d^3, however, Bach put this opening passage down an octave and directed that it be played on an *Oktav 4'*, dividing the two parts between the *Oberwerk* and the *Brustpositiv*. He also supported it by a pedal point in eighth notes on a *Prinzipal 8'*. Not till m. 21 was a *Subbass 32'* to be added in the *Pedal* and a *Prinzipal 8'* in the *Oberwerk*. According to the original, B♭ not B♮ should be played in the left hand, page 5, 3, 2 and 3. The three measures of the *Grave* are marked *spiccato e tutti* in the original.

It is curious that in the fugal *Allegro* Bach failed to reproduce the exchange between *tutti* and *soli* by means of manual-changes; nor did he take into account Vivaldi's dynamic markings. The *soli* are in mm. 20-29 and 45-52 of the fugue; p. 10, 2, 1 is marked *piano* in the original; p. 10, 2, 2, *forte;* similarly, p. 10, 2, 4, on the last sixteenth notes, *piano;* and p. 10, 3, 1, on the last three sixteenth notes, again *forte*. Organists today can carry out these instructions quite easily.

In the second movement, a *Siciliano,* Bach had to change the original reading from

to

141. See Schneider's article, "Das sogenannte 'Orgelkonzert d-moll von Friedemann Bach'," *Bach-Jahrbuch*, 1911, pp. 23-36.

in two places: mm. 4 and 12. Here, also, the modern player may follow the original.

In the third movement, dynamic marks should be added as follows: p. 16, 2, 2, *pianissimo;* p. 17, 1, 1, *forte;* p. 19, 3, 2, on the last quarter, *piano*—which is beautiful and unusual—and p. 19, 3, 4, on the second quarter, again *forte*. Bach transcribed a few passages (p. 17) all too faithfully in violin style and not sufficiently in organ style. The writer plays these passages as follows:

With this suggestion, however, he wishes only to stimulate the reader to make experiments of his own.

Performance: 1st movement, with introduction, ♩ = 96, 88; the Fugue on bright *Prinzipal*-tone. 2nd movement (♪= 116), light 8 solo stop with soft foundation stops 8 and 4 . 3rd movement, (♩= 104), *Plenum* on both manuals.

In this connection we might mention one other organ transcription from Bach's Weimar period, the

Fugue in G Minor (VIII, 12; BWV 131a)

This is taken from Cantata 131, *Aus der Tiefe rufe ich,* composed in Mühlhausen in 1708. The last movement of the cantata is a double fugue on the two following subjects:

Essentially, the transcription takes into account only the choral setting and includes little of the instrumental accompaniment. Spitta therefore formed the opinion that, "This meagre arrangement cannot possibly have come from the hand of the composer. . . ."[142] Yet one might recognize Bach's hand in the clever adaptation of the subject

142. *Op. cit.*, I, 456, fn. 152.

for the pedal, for example. Since the end of the cantata movement is lacking in the arrangement, Bach's intention was probably merely that of extracting the double fugue for study purposes. In the soprano, p. 86, 2, 6, one should read f^1 for g^1; p. 87, 1, 3, in the pedal, D for F.

STUDIES AFTER ITALIAN MODELS

At about the same time that Bach was making a study of contemporary Italian orchestral music, he was also pursuing studies in French music and in the older Italian music. He made a copy for himself of the *Livre d'Orgue* of de Grigny.[143] (Terry's conjecture[144] that this could have been done in Lüneburg is not tenable, since the *Livre d'Orgue* did not appear in print till 1712.) In about 1714 Bach also acquired the celebrated *Fiori Musicali* of Frescobaldi, which the latter had published in 1635 for the use of Catholic organists at the celebration of the Mass.[145]

We may consider the

Canzona in D Minor (IV, 10; BWV 588)

as the immediate fruit of these studies. Pirro[146] even suspected that Bach had had a specific model for his theme, the 5th Canzona of the *Fiori*, in which the bass entry of the theme reads as follows:

In Bach's time the canzona had already become an historic form. Of its construction it was still known that the same theme was treated fugally twice: at first in duple meter, and then in triple, with a short homophonic transition between these two sections. Bach held himself to this pattern; even the modest key scheme that he observed was "old-fashioned." On the other hand, the addition of a chromatic countersubject was modern and genuinely Bachian. Consequently, these two fugal sections show a charming blend of Bach's own and a foreign style.

---

143. *Archives des maîtres de l'orgue*, ed. Guilmant, Vol. 5.
144. Terry, *op. cit.*, p. 53.
145. See my edition: Peters No. 4514.
146. *Op. cit.*, p. 41.

The Canzona is not quite so easy to play as it looks. Beginners often founder on the syncopations in the subject; the player must "listen to himself" (to quote Widor) and ". . . let the piece flow on. . . in its contemplative, dreamlike loveliness. . . ."[147] Tempo of the first section, 𝅗𝅥 = 58; of the second, 𝅗𝅥 = 88; that is to say, so that the duration of the measure remains the same for both sections. The registration should sound "vocal"; that is, rather light foundation stops for the first section, somewhat stronger ones for the second. Seiffert published a version of the ending that was highly embellished (*Peters-Jahrbuch,* 1904) but of all places in the work, ornamentation is probably least appropriate at the very end.

Fantasy in C Minor (Anon.)

In the collection *Organum (Heft 10)* Max Seiffert published six pieces whose composers are unknown. Among these, as No. 6, was a Fantasy in C Minor from the *Andreas Bach Buch.*[148] Seiffert commented that "It must be one of the very great masters to whom we are indebted for this wondrous piece." If one compares this Fantasy with Bach's Canzona, the idea strikes one immediately that the two are very much alike in style; the chromatic counterpoint of the Fantasy, in particular, reminds one of the Canzona. Is it unreasonable, then, to surmise that we have before us a work by Bach—lost track of—from his Weimar period? It begins as follows:

The

Allabreve (VIII, 6; BWV 589)

pro Organo pleno may also have had Italian prototypes, perhaps the Concerto Grosso in D Major of Corelli[149] which appeared in 1713:

---

147. See Bach's *Organ Works*, ed. Widor and Schweitzer, Vol. II, p. xx.

148. Consult Spitta, *op. cit.*, I, 629f, for detailed information on this MS volume.

149. This beginning is heard again in the first choral movement of Cantata 29 (Cantata for the Inauguration of the Council), which also passed over into the *B Minor Mass* (the "Gratias" and the "Dona nobis pacem").

Here the marking *Allabreve* is not yet to be interpreted as an indication of tempo as Mattheson understood it (that is, "as when one says 'Giddap!' to a horse"), but as a generic term for a piece kept in the style of the old polyphonic music; i.e., notated in large note values. In Bach's music we have further examples in the E Major Fugue of the *Well-Tempered Clavier,* Bk. II, and in the second Kyrie Fugue of the *B Minor Mass.*

The piece is divided clearly into four parts, all of nearly the same length. The entries of the subject are prepared in a manner almost scholastic, mainly by letting rests precede them; even strettos, at intervals of one or two measures, are not wanting.

Of its structure Spitta writes: "Everything is calculated not so much to prove the vital and formative power of an individually characteristic idea. . . as to present a grand, organic whole, of which the fundamental principle is established only on broad lines. . . . Though we may call the Canzona a romantic child of German feeling and Italian mold, we must be reminded, in this *Allabreve,* of the bright blue heavens, whose image is reflected from the serene surface of a deep, clear sea."[150]

The purely diatonic style is abandoned eighteen measures from the end in order to make room for a chromatic condensation and compression in which the streams of tone become congested before they flow off, unimpeded, into the cadence. Bach also made use of this resource in the F Major Fugue (III, p. 28, 2, 6) and in the Dorian Fugue (III, p. 41, 2, 5).

Performance: 𝅗𝅥 = 88, with the *Plenum* of the HW, not shrill but like a full, vocal tone. No provision seems to have been made for changes of manual, but these are to be recommended because of the length of the piece: p. 72, 4, 1, to the second manual; p. 73, 4, 6, to the third; and p. 74, 2, 4, again to the second; on p. 75, 1, 2, the tenor will return to the HW, coupled meanwhile; 9 mm. later the alto, and then the soprano.

The

Fugue in B Minor (IV, 8; BWV 579)

150. Spitta, *op. cit.*, I, 423.

borrows its double subject from Corelli's 4th Church Sonata for two violins and *basso continuo,* Op. 3 (1689), the second movement of which begins thus:

There the two subjects appear three more times, always in stretto, thus giving the movement its terse and vigorous quality. Bach spins the Fugue out to 102 mm. (as against Corelli's 39) and makes it contemplative (according to Widor even "resigned") in mood. The Fugue has only one stretto, involving all four voices, and saved till the end. With this stretto Bach of course far surpassed Corelli, and himself surpassed it only once: in the five-part stretto at the end of the B♭ Minor Fugue in the *Well-Tempered Clavier.*

Corelli's double subject seems to have served in addition as model for the double subject of the A Major Fugue of Buxtehude.[151]

In compactness of form Bach's Fugue is inferior to both the Canzona and the *Allabreve.* Twice a sixteenth note rhythm is started and then given up again, a feature not found in any fugue of Bach's master period. His concealment of the entrance of the subject, p. 51, 2, 2, however, is excellently done.

Performance: ♩ = 76, moderately strong foundation stops. The passage from p. 51, 2, 6 (2nd half) to p. 52, 4, 4, may be played on a subordinate manual, but a larger number of subdivisions would break up the Fugue too greatly.

The isolated

Fugue in G Minor (IV, 7; BWV 578)

known as the "Little G Minor Fugue," tends to fill the layman with delight the very first time he hears it. Its subject, well organized and consisting of three phrases, reminds us of the subject of the

---

151. *Sämtliche Orgelwerke,* ed. Ph. Spitta (Leipzig: Breitkopf & Härtel, 1876-1877), 2 vols.; new ed. by Max Seiffert, 1903-1904; vol. III, ed. Max Seiffert, 1939 (supplementary volume), p. 21. Seiffert traces the genealogy still farther in his *Geschichte der Klaviermusik,* p. 107.

See also *Dietrich Buxtehude: Sämtliche Werke,* ed. Josef Hedar (4 vols.; Copenhagen: Wilhelm Hansen, Musik-Forlag, 1952).

C Minor Fugue (IV, 5); yet it seems equally to anticipate the subject of the Great G Minor Fugue (II, 4). The beauty of the Fugue as a whole rests on the beauty of its subject. Bach increases the compactness of the first phrase by reversing the first three notes (g d b♭) to give the last three (f♯ a d). From this ending, contracted, is derived the first motive of the next phrase; the last phrase, in turn, is but a variation of the second phrase.

For the sake of preserving the beauty of the subject, Bach refrains from making a tonal answer and from providing distinctive counterpoints. These are fairly florid and are always kept subordinate to the subject. The fact that the Fugue rarely goes beyond three-part writing does it no harm. Even the unthematic entry of the pedal in measure 26 and, in the same spot, the mere suggestion of stretto—to which Spitta objects[152]—scarcely injure it. Its musical merits are so great that it counts justly among the fugues of Bach most frequently played.

Its *performance* will depend for its success on a judicious phrasing and articulation of the subject and countersubject. In this connection it is debatable whether mm. 3 and 4 are to be interpreted as full measures or as beginning with an upbeat.[153] In order to be able to articulate subject and countersubject independently, a player must have considerable technique:

For the sake of the lively articulation the tempo (♩ = 80) ought not to be too fast. Bach does not appear to have intended any manual-changes; yet, in order to bring out m. 28 clearly, one might go to an uncoupled adjacent manual in m. 22 (2nd note) and then bring the parts back to the HW gradually: the tenor in m. 25, the alto in m. 33, with the soprano following in m. 40 (4th eighth). Use solid principals, *forte;* a *ff* ending, as is customary, is quite superfluous. In mm. 62 and 63 (p. 49, 3, 3) the reading of the BG is preferable to that of the Peters edition:

152. *Op. cit.*, I, 401.
153. See p. 55.

The

Fantasy in G Major (IV, 11; BWV 572)

presents us with puzzles. Where do the French terms come from?[154] They are not found elsewhere in Bach's organ music, although—which is equally remarkable—similar terms do appear in Cantata 61, *Nun komm, der Heiden Heiland,* composed in 1714. How ought the rollicking passages of the beginning to be connected with the ostentatious five-part writing of the *Grave,* and this with the closing section?

The second question concerns the inner homogeneity of the work. Possibly the answer is that the third section combines the stylistic features of the first and second sections. Behind the sparkling passages is hidden a movement in five real parts:

Looked at in this way, the formal unity of the work becomes credible. Its inner unity becomes so when the middle section is not interpreted in too stately a manner but, following other manuscripts, "*gayement*" (gaily) or *allegro;* hence, with animation and exuberance. Even then, the piece remains curious enough.

Spitta characterizes the middle section as typically Buxtehudian: "With insatiable enjoyment he repeats those doubled suspensions, chords of the ninth, diminished intervals, wide-spread harmonies, melodic phrases rapturously ascending and outsoaring one another—an entranced delight in the ocean of sound. . . . Towards the end. . . the expression rises gradually to an indescribable intensity and glow, which soars away far, far above the capabilities of the organ. The pedal slowly ascends with irresistible force from D, through two octaves in whole notes. . . until it is interrupted by the chord of the diminished seventh, and then, like a shower of rain in sunshine, down pour the glittering pearls of sound. . . ."[155]

---

154. Perhaps from his occupation with de Grigny (see p. 90)?
155. Spitta, *op. cit.*, I, 322.

What could one add to this sincere and poetic description other than to inquire where in the Northern organ music anything of the kind is to be found. Wasn't Bach stimulated far more by the South, by the polyphonic style of the Italian motet, to this intoxication by color and sound? In Bach there is only one other example of a similar manner of writing, the chorus "Ehre sei Gott in der Höhe" ("Praise to God in the Highest") from the Christmas Oratorio.[156]

Performance: Agreeing with Klotz,[157] I should like to propose playing the first section on a subordinate manual, or on two manuals if one wishes to play the echoes as such; the *Grave* with the *Plenum* of the *Hauptwerk;* the last section on the HW with manuals coupled. If one takes the first section on a light combination, *piano,* as is often heard, then no connection with the *Grave* results at all, and the listener is suddenly startled by a *ff* that finds him completely unprepared. One would like to do some shading in the *Grave,* but the close texture fails to break up anywhere; for this reason, as well, the tempo ought not to be slow. (1st section, ♩. = 88; 2nd section, 𝅗𝅥 = 76; 3rd section, ♪ = 72.)

Just a word about the B_1 in the pedal

which Bach calls for on p. 65, 3, 6: it is obviously unplayable. In a similarly abstract fashion Bach later wrote down a B_1 in the Ricercar for six voices from the *Musical Offering,* and both a B_1 and an A_1 in the *Art of Fugue.*

The

Pastorale in F Major (I, 8; BWV 590)

may also be included among the works that show Italian influence in their writing. The old Italian *pastorali* were not intended to express moods of nature, as in Beethoven's period, but to provide music of a pious and naive kind in honor of the Christ Child. Every year the shepherds of the *campagna* flocked into Rome during the Christmas season, following a beautiful and touching custom, for the purpose of playing on their shawms in the streets before the altars of the Virgin and the Child—a custom which still prevailed up to a few decades ago, when motor traffic made it impossible.

156. Schweitzer was the first to point this out (*op. cit.,* II, 305).
157. Klotz, *op. cit.,* p. 270.

Art music seized upon these tunes and refined them; thus originated the many "pastorales," of which probably that of Corelli (from No. 8 of the *Concerti Grossi*, Op. 6) has become the most famous. Frescobaldi, Pasquini, and Zipoli all wrote pieces of this type for the organ; these were usually in the sunny tonality of G major, while the colder North preferred F major. Bach's Pastorale conforms perfectly to these models. Curiously, however, after a cadence in A minor, Bach has three more small movements follow that are for manuals alone. Spitta had doubts about their relationship to the first movement, though hardly with justice.[158] Possibly some occasion unknown to us motivated Bach to write the four movements—as in similar fashion he inserted short movements characteristic of Christmas in the *Magnificat*.

The rather remote key of C minor used for the "Air" makes it seem improbable that he played all four movements in direct succession. The modern performer would also do well to separate them for playing in recital. Bach later took up the theme of the last movement again in the Finale of the 3rd Brandenburg Concerto.

Performance:[159] 1st movement, ♩. = 60 (Zipoli's Pastorale is marked *Largo*). In conformity with Italian directions for registration, the sound should be mellow principal- or flute-tone, 8' and 4'. Since one would often like to play the first movement alone, the custom was adopted quite early of playing mm. 1-9 as a *reprise* following the cadence in A minor and then of finishing something like this:

2nd movement, ♩ = 46, light foundation stops (flutes). 3rd movement, ♪ = 80; the c.f. with a mild reed or a c.f.-combination of flue stops. Widor proposed playing it on two manuals and pedal with a pedal part put underneath:

4th movement, ♩. = 63, bright foundation stops 8', 4', and 2'.

---

158. Spitta, *op. cit.*, III, 213, fn. 398.
159. Cf. also Ramin's edition published by Bärenreiter.

WORKS UNDER THE INFLUENCE OF THE ITALIAN CHANGE IN STYLE

In the following section are grouped those works which reveal Italian influence in their formal construction or in their style, yet which have not abandoned the traditional stylistic elements. Their individual sections, therefore, frequently make contradictory impressions.

This is especially true of the

Toccata in C Major (III, 8; BWV 564)

also frequently called the "Toccata, *Adagio,* and Fugue in C Major." This work is stylistically one of the most remarkable, and technically one of the most brilliant works by Bach. If we disregard his unsuccessful experiment with the Fantasy in G Major (IX, 4; see p. 67), it is obviously here that Bach makes his first and only attempt to transfer to the organ the forms contained in the three-movement Italian concerto. The *Adagio,* in particular, is quite clearly an imitation of the style of a slow movement from a violin concerto.

But also in the first movement, following the toccata-like passages for manuals and pedal, we find a concerto movement that is orchestral in type. We actually imagine that we see the first and second violins begin with vigorous strokes of the bow:[160]

Everything else, however, is suited to the organ and "German": the runs in the Toccata at the beginning, for example. It is from the improvisation in this Toccata, which seems to roam aimlessly, that the thematic material of the following concerto movement is derived. There is also the seven-part close of the *Adagio,* with its chains of dissonances in the manner of Frescobaldi's *toccate di ligature e durezze,* which is a sphinx after the human countenance of the Adagio.

160. Less convincing is the interpretation of Fritz Dietrich (*Bach-Jahrbuch,* 1931, p. 61) who professes to see in this passage a "duet" from a cantata.

The closing Fugue, with its delicious humor, is reminiscent of Kuhnau; in this, pedants are annoyed by the parallel fifths:

At the end the Fugue actually "flees," runs away, and leaves the listener behind, confused.

Perhaps the Fugue was the first part to be written. One could so infer from the really unlovely parallel octaves (p. 82, 4, 4) which the Bach of a later period would never have written.

The quadruple suspension of the first chord of the *Grave* following the *Adagio*-movement we encounter later in the "shout" with which Beethoven begins the Finale of the *Ninth Symphony*. Bach could have become acquainted with it in Bruhns, where it appears more than once.[161]

The echo passages in the pedal solo are also noteworthy. One has to assume that Bach took off a coupler or employed a ventil during the rest.

Equally noteworthy is the cadential chord, which is broken off short; significantly, this is changed to a chord with a *fermata* in another manuscript. Endings of this kind are very rarely found in the old literature, yet twice, nevertheless, in Buxtehude's works (Nos. 7 and 16 of Spitta's edition).[162] These could have served Bach as models for the abrupt endings of the C Minor Fugue (IV, 6) or the D Major Fugue (IV, 3) but the ending of the C Major Toccata seems completely original.

Performance: Just as the old composers almost always closed a piece on the strong part of the measure, they also frequently put a chord before a monophonic beginning (Böhm, for example, in his Prelude and Fugue in C Major).[163] It is advisable to follow this procedure with the C Major Toccata when it is to open a program. Otherwise it is very easy for the audience to miss the first few bars.

The manual passages require the silvery sound of the mixtures of a subordinate manual and a virtuoso tempo; on the old organs a fast tempo was not practicable at all on a principal manual because of the heavy key-action.[164] In the pedal solo one can easily manage the echo passages by taking off couplers or by using pedal pistons.

161. For example in the Prelude and Fugue in E Minor (*Organum IV*, No. 8, p. 6, or *Bruhns: Orgelwerke*, p. 14).
162. See the Spitta-Seiffert edition, *op. cit.*, I, p. 40, and II, p. 95.
163. *Alte Meister*, ed. Straube, No. 1, p. 7.
164. See Klotz, *op. cit.*, pp. 261ff.

The principal section which follows should be played with the festive sound of principals and fairly weak mixtures; it offers ample opportunity for alternation.

The *Adagio* is to be played without change of tone color: the melody with a light reed stop or a c.f. combination of flue stops, the accompaniment with very soft 8' and 4' stops, the pedal *quasi-pizzicato*, and the last two measures interpreted as echo. The connection with the *Grave* presents a problem. I don't consider it good either to take the two trasitional measures *piano* or to play them with a *crescendo*, but to begin immediately *forte:*

The *Fugue* (interpreted heroically by Busoni in his transcription for piano) is a little gem, which, as *allegretto vivace*, never needs to increase to a real *forte*. After the brief rise near the end, it may close in the color and strength with which it began.

With three manuals the following distribution may be recommended: mm. 1-43 on I; mm. 43-53 on II; mm. 53-75 on I, at the 6th eighth on II; m. 78 on III; m. 87, l.h. on II, with the r.h. following on the 5th eighth of m. 94; mm. 100-115 on I; mm. 115-123 on II; m. 123 to the end, again on I. Tempo: 1st movement, ♩ = 66; 2nd movement, ♪ = 76; *Grave*, ♪ = 58; 3rd movement, ♩. = 69.

The

Prelude and Fugue in G Major (IV, 2; BWV 550)

is also one of the works that make a stylistic classification difficult. Since it must be inferred from the A Minor Concerto that the pedal compass of Bach's organ in the palace at Weimar extended to e^1, and since the pedal range of our Prelude and Fugue extends to e^1, we have placed it in the series of Weimar works. We have done so despite the fact that the Prelude, which is developed from a single short motive, seems rather to belong to the Arnstadt period. The three measures connecting the Prelude with the Fugue could also have had their prototype in Buxtehude's Fantasy on "Wie schön leuchtet der Morgenstern."[165]

The incongruity between the long and brilliant pedal solo and the short Prelude is striking. Equally curious is the harmonic sim-

165. See the Spitta-Seiffert edition, Vol. III, No. 10, mm. 74-76.

plicity—not to say meagerness—of the Prelude and Fugue. This may be a transitional clarification under Italian influence. The Fugue is clearly related to the G Major Fugue in 12/8 meter (IX, 2)[166] and is marked *Alla breve e staccato* in the BG. Its subject, filled with sequences and to be interpreted in a half serious, half humorous manner, is developed correctly throughout some 148 measures. This subject is never absent, however, even from the episodes. The result is that, in spite of its flawless craftsmanship, the piece produces an effect as monotonous as that of the A Minor Prelude (IV, 13).

Bach needed a few years in which to make his own the new features that he encountered in the Italian chamber-style, so that he could achieve a synthesis of the two stylistic tendencies. These, German fantasy and Italian "singing" quality, merge in his writing in a unique way. The change is shown most clearly in the fugue subjects, which no longer bear the instrumental, florid stamp of the German school, but which are kept singable in the strictest sense of the word. "Their lack of showy effects is responsible for the fact that these works are not so popular with players and audiences as are the A Minor and G Minor Fugues," says Schweitzer.[167] Possibly an additional reason is that Bach could not yet express himself in the new style with the same assurance as in the earlier. At least *one* work shows such an uncertainty (in the Fugue) very clearly:

Prelude and Fugue in F Minor (II, 5; BWV 534)

It has been handed down in a single manuscript only (by Dröbs, a pupil of Kittel). Griepenkerl thought it worthy of finding acceptance in the "classical" second volume of the Peters edition. In the Prelude the two pedal points on the tonic and dominant, together with the canonic writing, refer back to the pedal toccatas of Pachelbel as well as forward to the F Major Toccata.[168] Its form is reminiscent of the two-part sonata-form of Scarlatti. (This feature is still more marked in the C Minor Fantasy, III, 6.) The classical symmetry of this form, however, is completely destroyed by the rapturous concluding toccata. After the echo-like passage in the manuals (above a dominant pedal point) comes an ascent to the diminished-seventh

166. Especially in the condensation of the movement at the end: in both fugues, about the last 9 measures.

167. *Op. cit.*, I, 274.

168. It is also closely related to the beginning of the E Minor Toccata for clavier.

chord, towering aloft, which is magnificent. Equally magnificent is the rest just before the final cadence. This rest is full of suspense, but the cadence brings release. How much more powerful are effects of this kind in Bach—in the G Major Fantasy, in the Passacaglia, and in a few other works—than are the traditional rests in all voices in Handel; for example, that at the end of the "Hallelujah Chorus" in the *Messiah*!

The Fugue, whose alto subject traverses the entire range of the [alto] clef:

has, as Spitta has already noticed, "a somewhat incoherent organization. Many new counterpoints appear. . . so that the subject is constantly obliged to look about for support. For this reason, despite great beauties, something of our full enjoyment is lacking."[169] Other features also spoil our pleasure: the lack of consistency in the writing for five parts; the doubled leading-tone in the 11th measure from the end,[170] which is far from beautiful; the parallel fifths in mm. 20-21; and the delayed consecutive octaves, p. 34, 4, 6-7. However, the way the subject changes its mood during the course of the Fugue is beautiful and, for Bach, unusual. Now it appears serious, now tender (in A♭ major), then heroic,[171] and again, entreating (in C minor). The interest in musical expressiveness in this Fugue is so great that its deficiencies in form and compositional technique are barely noticed. The close relationship between the end of the Prelude and that of the Fugue is striking; a certain relationship with the Prelude may also be traced in the curve of the fugue subject. The pedal point at the beginning becomes "*affettuoso*" owing to being circumscribed by the sixteenths, as Frotscher observed.[172] Bach transfers into the pedal the mordent with which the soprano begins, and from this, in turn, he derives the continuation of the melody (c b♭ c)—an astonishingly concentrated technique!

According to Mattheson the tonality of F minor had, for Bach's era, the quality of "anxiety and despair."[173] (It could indeed drive player and audience to despair on an organ tuned in unequal tempera-

---

169. *Op. cit.*, I, 592.
170. Deleted in the BG.
171. Moreover, this passage, p. 34, 1, 9, sounds completely un-Bachian; as does also the six-four chord, p. 34, 3, 4.
172. Frotscher, *op. cit.*, p. 876.
173. See Rudolf Wustmann, "Tonartensymbolik zu Bachs Zeit." *Bach-Jahrbuch*, 1911, pp. 60-74.

ment.) For us today it is the tonality of tragic emotion; in making this judgment we are thinking mainly of the large works in F minor by Beethoven and Brahms.

Despite this fact, the *performance* of the Prelude may not take a dark, Brahmsian *mf* as its model, as Straube claims, but must be played straight through on a characteristic *Plenum* without increase in volume. Only the manual passage, p. 31, 1, 2, permits a terracing. The thirty-second notes near the end should be taken on an adjacent manual only if it is registered more brilliantly than the principal manual; the conclusion may then be played with manuals coupled. Tempo: ♩ = 58-63 (according to Straube, ♪ = 80).

The Fugue (𝅗𝅥 = 60; Straube, ♩ = 88) begins on the HW with the grave tone color of the principals. It goes to an adjacent manual, p. 33, 1, 7, the f^1 of the alto being played simultaneously on the two manuals (see p. 42). The entry of the subject, p. 33, 2, 11, which is hard to reach, may be taken in the pedal with 4'. The return to the HW should not be made when the pedal makes its entrance, but preferably with the r.h. 3 1/2 measures before. At p. 34, 4, 1, again to an adjacent manual; here also a return to the HW with the r.h., p. 35, 2, 5 (2nd half), and with the l.h. simultaneously with the pedal. The reading of the BG, p. 35, 3, 9f., is preferable:

The

Prelude and Fugue in A Major (II, 3; BWV 536)

has come down to us in two versions: the one, evidently earlier and probably composed during the Arnstadt period, in the autograph;[174] the second, later, version only in copies. Since in this version the pedal is taken up to e^1, a pitch that the first version avoids, it seems highly probable that the revision was made in Weimar. In the revised version the Prelude shows small changes and improvements in nearly every measure. The Fugue has been rewritten from 3/8 to 3/4

174. See Vol. II, p. 89.

meter. Most remarkable of all, however, is the omission of the last three measures:

They are replaced by a casual ending in eighth notes:

It is instructive to study the different meanings Bach attaches to endings of this kind: an "exclamation mark" at the close of the C Major Toccata and the D Major Fugue (also, probably, in the early Fugue in C Minor, IV, 9); a "dash" in the A Major Fugue, as also in the B Minor Prelude. In the F Major Toccata and the C Major Fugue (II, 7), on the other hand, the expression in the measures preceding the final chord is so extremely rich that special emphasis can no longer fall on this chord itself.

All the brightness of a day in spring seems to have been cast over the Prelude.[175] Even the Fugue is a pastorale, in which the subject is displayed in ever new and charming lights; its figuration often reminds us of the Prelude. Spitta has already admired its "charming intimacy, its feminine character which is quite contradictory to the nature of the organ";[176] he links the subject with the instrumental introduction to Cantata 152, *Tritt auf die Glaubensbahn* (*Walk in the Way of Faith*), composed in 1715:

175. Cf. Buxtehude's Prelude in D Major. (Spitta-Seiffert ed., Vol. I, No. 11.)
176. *Op. cit.*, I, 590.

It is probable, however, that the first sketch of the Fugue should be assigned to an earlier period. Bach's extension of the last phrase of the Fugue subject to five measures is characteristic; in this way he destroyed the regularity of the cantata theme (2 + 2 + 4 measures) which was too great for a fugue subject. Actually the fugue subject may be taken as a model for phrasing and articulation: its phrase structure ought to be clarified by small breaks at the ends of the 2nd and 4th measures; the irregular rhythm in mm. 2, 4, 6, and 8 requires detaching the accented quarter note, which, however, must not be shortened too much:

Variants: p. 16, 3, 6, in the soprano $d^{\#2}$ is preferable to d^2; p. 19, 4, 3, the 2nd note in the soprano, e^2 would be better than d^2; in the passage for the pedals, p. 19, 4, 5ff.:

the BG edition shows the B of the 2nd measure an octave higher; this was probably a copyist's error. In a few other minor deviations the reading of the Peters edition is preferable to that of the BG.

Performance: the Prelude uniformly either in a clear *Organum Plenum,* or, corresponding to the intimacy of the work, with light but bright foundation-stops. Tempo: ♩ = 88 (Straube, 72-80). The Fugue also needs pastoral foundation stops, but with changes of manual as follows: p. 16, 4, 4, the r.h. goes to the RP, 2 mm. later, the l.h.; p. 17, 2, 4, the r.h. returns to the HW; p. 17, 3, 1, the l.h. to the HW; p. 17, 4, 2, the r.h. to the RP; p. 18, 1, 4, the alto with the l.h.; p. 18, 2, 7, all parts on the RP; from p. 18, 4, 7, everything again on the HW. Each performer will himself be able to discover differing transitions. Klotz (p. 334) proposes: mm. 1-49, HW, then RP; m. 65, BW; m. 77, RP; m. 89, BW; m. 97, RP; m. 115, BW; m. 123, RP; from m. 136, HW (*ibidem* suggestions for registration, also). Tempo: ♩ = 138 (Straube, 112-120); the marking *Allegro* is original.

The

Fantasy and Fugue in C Minor (III, 6; BWV 537)

like the Prelude and Fugue in F Minor, has reached us in a single manuscript only, from the literary remains of Johann Ludwig Krebs, "Soli Deo Gloria, den 10 Januarii 1751." (Of how many works, I wonder, may the only copy not have reached us.)

Possibly Bach had in mind Pachelbel's fantasies when he chose the title "Fantasy" to indicate its sober, contemplative mood.[177] (Cf. also the five-part Fantasy in C Minor, IV, 12.) Formally, both Fantasy and Fugue are more strongly influenced by the sonata form than are any others.

It is clear that the Fantasy has a second theme:

Its motive is found as the "motive of grief"[178] in Bach's vocabulary from the "Capriccio on the Absence of His Most Beloved Brother" to the *St. Matthew Passion*.

The Fugue is unique in that two new subjects[179] appear in a middle section,

which are never brought into conjunction with the main subject. Instead, the principal section is repeated in a note-for-note *reprise* so that a three-part form similar to the sonata form results. The plan of the Great E Minor Fugue is similar, but still larger and more daring.

The union of Fantasy and Fugue (required, of course, by the half-cadence and the marking *attacca*) is more intimate than that in most of Bach's other works. The expression of enduring sorrow in the Fantasy—grievous and great in the first subject, intimate and tender in the second—struggles through to defiant self-assertion in the Fugue. The symbol of this mood is the gallant, proud subject of the Fugue, which fights its way through night and doubt in the middle section, overcomes them, and finally triumphs. Compare the related basic mood in other works of Bach in C minor: the C Minor Fantasy for clavier, the Passacaglia, and the Prelude and Fugue (II, 6);

---

177. The BG gives "Prelude" instead.

178. See Schweitzer, *op. cit.*, II, 64f., where this motive is described as the "motive of noble lamentation. . . like a series of sighs from the depth of the soul."

179. The 8th-note subject is introduced 7 mm. earlier in masterly fashion.

even the final chorus of the *St. Matthew Passion* has something triumphal about it!

Performance: Fantasy, ♩ = 58-60; the two subjects expressed by change of manual: a grave, moderate *Organum Plenum* for the first subject; woodwind tone for the second. The Fugue, 𝅗𝅥 = 69, on the HW with *Organum Plenum;* the middle section on an adjacent manual, and the conclusion on the reinforced HW. Articulation: The upbeat of the Fugue subject, as well as those of the first and second themes of the Fantasy, should be connected with the downbeat (in this respect all three themes hang together); in contrast, the diminished seventh in the subject of the Fugue should be detached sharply.

CHAPTER 11

THE LARGE WORKS OF THE LAST YEARS AT WEIMAR AND THOSE AT CÖTHEN

(1717-1723)

A number of preludes and fugues, which may have originated in Weimar, later underwent revision at Bach's hands. In this group, for example, are the Preludes and Fugues in C Major, G Major, and C Minor (II, 1, 2, and 6). Since these have come down to us in Leipzig autographs, they will be discussed among the Leipzig works.

Other compositions were completed or reworked in Cöthen. Two probably originated there: the G Minor Fugue (II, 4) and the F Major Toccata (III, 2). The G Minor Fugue, in all probability, was composed for Bach's candidacy in Hamburg (1720). We assume that the Toccata, because of its pedal range (up to f^1), was written for the Church of St. Agnus in Cöthen, for the organ there was said to have had an f^1 in the pedal.

The Fugues in A Minor and G Minor are closely related, as are the Dorian and F Major Toccatas. Probably the A Minor is the earlier of the two fugues. Its final measures plainly refer to the detached chords of the F Major Toccata. It is striking that similar chords are found in a concerto by Marcello that Bach transcribed for clavier in Weimar. Hence, lines of communication which corroborate the stylistically intimate connection among these works also exist here.

The Passacaglia is also included in this group, for two reasons: it appears in a contemporary manuscript along with the F Major

Toccata; and the D Minor Chaconne for violin was also written in Cöthen.

Altogether, then, there exist five large, celebrated organ works that Bach produced when he was about 35 years of age. He had now attained the full height of his mastery, before he moved to Leipzig and before his official duties there first led him far away from the organ and from composition for the organ.

The first draft of the

Prelude and Fugue in A Minor (II, 8; BWV 543)

doubtless reaches back into a much earlier period. A variant of the Prelude,

shows the chromatic line still in its most concentrated form; in contrast, the form Bach later gave it produces a classical effect. The subject of the Fugue, clearly related to the Prelude in the line formed by its highest tones, has still other progenitors, however: the subject of a fugue by Pachelbel, although this is confined within narrower limits than is Bach's:

and, even more clearly, the theme of a concerto by Corelli which Bach had transcribed for clavier (No. 8):

One can imagine without difficulty that from this theme derived the subject of Bach's great Fugue in A Minor for clavier:

And then Bach must have conceived the idea of reworking this fugue into an organ fugue. First of all, the subject had to be made suitable for the pedals. The scale steps of the sequence were turned into zigzag steps and a few sixteenth notes near the beginning were bypassed, so that its final masterly form then read:

(Then J. L. Krebs probably imitated this great, famous subject for his "little" subject, that of the A Minor Fugue in the *Eight Little Preludes and Fugues* [see p. 72]).

A comparison of the clavier fugue with the organ fugue is instructive.[180] The former numbers 197 measures; the latter, 151; the first has longer episodes. Despite the far-reaching similarity in basic design, the two are independent of each other, and each has its own beauties. The clavier fugue has a greater wealth of harmony than the organ fugue, but is inferior to it in polyphonic workmanship.

The Prelude is significant, not in form but in its intensely emotional idiom. Never before had Bach put into a single line such suspense and intensity as he put into the first 23 measures of the Prelude. The accumulated energy then flows off into the dominant during the chordal trill and the pedal entry of the theme.

In contrast to the tremendous suspense of this beginning, the second part of the Prelude is merely episodic (or rhapsodic); yet the impressive ending builds up again to the height of the beginning. It would be quite unsatisfactory to play this Prelude alone, as one may do with other preludes of Bach; only the Fugue brings the resolution of the strong, powerful dissonances struck in the Prelude. In this respect, also, it is a counterpart of the Fantasy and Fugue in G Minor: the pent-up emotion becomes action, movement, but is not

180. See Reinhard Oppel, "Die grosse A Moll Fuge für Orgel und ihre Vorlage," *Bach-Jahrbuch*, 1906, pp. 74-78.

completely dissipated. This is proved by the gigantic "gesture" at the end, in which everything seems to collapse, and which leaves us in a state of shock. Seen from the point of view of the Fugue alone, this gesture would not be intelligible, but it reveals Prelude and Fugue together as a unit of the very highest order.

Performance of this work depends entirely on the mental image of it possessed by the player. In line with the interpretation given here, the first 24 measures of the Prelude should be played with great intensity in tone and in movement, but without increase; the following 22 measures in a more relaxed manner; the ending like the beginning. Tempo: ♩ = 76.

The Fugue also relaxes in the middle section; on p. 59, 3, 3, one should go to the RP; p. 61, 2, 6, back to the HW with the l.h., then p. 62, 1, 5, also with the r.h. Widor and Schweitzer are justifiably opposed to bringing the tenor, p. 62, 4, 6, into still greater prominence, and for that reason prefer reducing the other parts. After the return to the HW the Fugue should grow by three or four terraces to maximum intensity, and end thus. The tempo should be a controlled *allegro:* ♪ = 144.

One should also study the structural design of the Fugue as outlined by Schweitzer[181] and, above all, Straube's ingenious interpretation (in his edition, pp. 80-93) which differs completely from our own.

Readings. Page 55, 2, 3, in the BG

is better than the d^1 in the Peters edition; p. 62, 3, 4, the alto in the BG is ♩𝄾 instead of ♩., the tenor g♯ instead of g; p. 63, 3, 3, the penultimate note in the BG is g^2 instead of $g\sharp^2$.

Fantasy and Fugue in G Minor (II, 4; BWV 542)

This highly celebrated work—the Fantasy the most daring harmonically and the Fugue "the very best piece with pedals by Herr Johann Sebastian Bach," as one scribe called it—has been associated with Bach's application for the post of organist at St. James's Church in Hamburg, in 1720, ever since Spitta made his convincing interpretation (see p. 23).

The Fantasy and the Fugue occur separately in most of the manuscripts, and probably also were composed independently of each

181. *Op. cit.*, I, 306, fn.

other. Possibly the Fugue was written for Hamburg, the Fantasy even earlier, for, together with the first movement of the C Major Toccata (III, 8), it is the only organ work of Bach that requires d[3] in the manual. It is therefore probable that these two pieces have some connection with each other.

Bach used the ambiguous term "fantasy" here, neither in the meaning of the early seventeenth century nor in that of Pachelbel (see pp. 65f.) but for a toccata interspersed with two *fugato* sections. The improvisatory element of this form is replaced by a wonderful harmony among the sections and by motivic compactness: the motive in thirds of the *fugato*

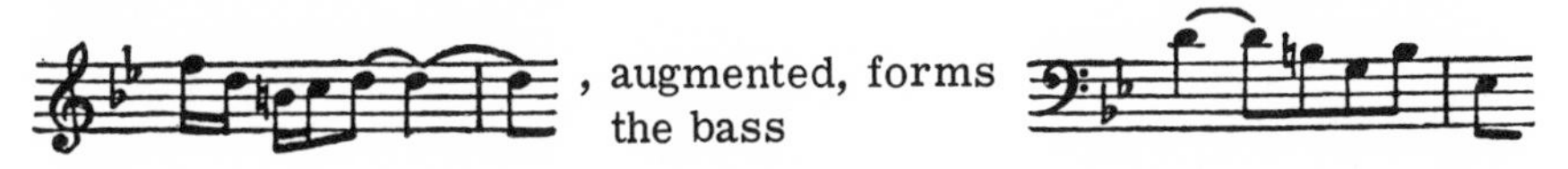

, augmented, forms the bass

Even the pedal scales are in reality filled in thirds:

and these emerge again in the pedal in the last section. The nucleus of this group of motives is contained in the very beginning of the Fantasy:

Without a compactness of this kind the superabundance of expression would act on this piece like an explosive.

In still another feature this work is unique: its harmony. A history of harmony has not yet been written; in this history the organ Fantasy in G Minor and the Chromatic Fantasy for clavier would have to be given a special place. As a rule, Bach's harmony is strictly tonal; that is to say, it is limited to triads and seventh chords elaborated within their own scale. The "precious spices of Bach's dissonances," which Liszt once preferred to Handel's triads, are in the main not the consequence of harmonic boldness, but of voice-leading both daring and also carefully calculated. In a few passages, however, there is a flash of lightning. Chromatic shifts and enharmonic confusion suddenly appear and indicate a departure on a new path which only later generations were to follow. Here Bach's daring is similar to that of the madrigalists of the outgoing sixteenth century.

Among the organ works we found passages of this kind in the G Minor Prelude (III, 5) and in the "Harmonic Labyrinth" (IX, 9, projected for this express purpose). But we find the first excellent employment of these new artistic resources in the G Minor Fantasy. It presupposes equal temperament; only in it is every enharmonic interval possible and justifiable.

Bach employs two harmonic resources here: chromatic inflection as a means of modulation and enharmonic spelling of the diminished-seventh chord. To Bach's generation chromaticism was perfectly familiar, but it was a new idea to make use of it for producing modulation. Measures 31ff. provide an example; with omission of the non-thematic voices these read:

The other resource, used in a later period to the point of boredom, was the effect of giving a new interpretation to the diminished-seventh chord enharmonically. In Bach (even in Mozart) this artistic resource was still strong and not yet worn out. The alteration of the diminished seventh chord into the augmented six-five chord (mm. 19-20) has a model in Buxtehude:

It is noteworthy that the Fantasy ends in the minor (only one manuscript shows an ending in the major). The relaxation of the tension should come only in the Fugue.

The subject of the Fugue, which captures the attention of the listener at once, and holds it, has a certain similarity to a theme of Reinken's from the fifth sonata of his *Hortus Musicus:*

182. After the corrected version of the supplementary volume, p. 56. (In the new edition by Max Seiffert, this passage is found in Vol. I, p. 30, mm. 45-47.)

Seiffert, however, established the true origin of this subject unequivocally—and surprisingly.[183] It is a Netherlands folksong:

Hence the Fugue paid homage to the venerable master Jan Adam Reinken, who was a Netherlander. At the same time we have an explanation for the melodic beauty and appealing quality of the subject: it is a folksong transformed by a few strokes of the pen!

As is well known, Mattheson was also acquainted with this theme. In 1725 he gave it at an audition of organists. "He knew very well with whom the idea originated and who formerly had worked it out with great skill."[184] He gave it in the following form:

together with the countersubject:

(It is probable that this truncation of the subject was intended to make it easier for the candidates; for, according to the scholastic rules, a subject was not supposed to exceed the range of an octave.)

To the first, syncopated, countersubject Bach adds still another one that is "spread out":

Solely by means of this addition such a wealth of rhythms and themes is generated that the Fugue could be animated by these alone.[186] During the episode, however, one more new motive is added:

183. *Zeitschrift für Musikwissenschaft*, 1924.

184. Spitta, *op. cit.*, II, 23.

185. Concerning the adaptation of this countersubject for the pedal, see p. 120.

186. For the technique of accompanying a fugue subject with two countersubjects Bach had models in the Fugue in D Minor of Buxtehude (Spitta-Seiffert edition, Vol. I, No. 10) and the E Minor of Bruhns (*Orgelwerke*, No. 2).

This and the note-for-note return of the episodes give the Fugue very nearly the form of a concerto movement. In this respect it is superior to the A Minor Fugue, which does not have this feature.

In the *performance* of the Fantasy one can hardly go astray: the toccata sections are played with the *Plenum* of the HW; the *fugato* sections on the *Positiv* with a penetrating combination of reeds, flues, and mutations. Tempo, ♪ = 63.

The *Fugue* requires of the performer an absolutely steady rhythm, a working-out of the various moods of the subject and two counter-subjects by means of articulation (see p. 56), a vigorously moving but not virtuoso or impassioned tempo (♩ = 84), a clear organization by means of manual changes (see p. 41), and a registration that sets forth the subject not in an easy-going, perfunctory way, but in a manly and vigorous fashion. Perhaps there are even organists today who should be told by Schweitzer that "It is actually painful to hear subjects that should enter proudly, like those of the A Minor and G Minor Fugues, given out softly on the third manual in a way that quite obscures their real character—all for the sake of the precious *crescendo*."[187] For all these reasons the G Minor Fugue has all along constituted a favorite and sure test of the technical proficiency of an organist.

Readings. In the Fantasy, p. 22, 2, 4, the c^3

is probably a copyist's error for a^2:

On p. 22, 3, 2, we probably should read (as in the BG) $c\#^1$ for c^1:

The Fugue has been preserved in two manuscripts which differ in a number of details. In 1913 I stated in the *Bach-Jahrbuch*[188] that I consider more authentic the version presented as a variant in the Appendix of the Peters edition (p. 93).

187. Schweitzer, *op. cit.*, I, 303.
188. In a short article, "Die Varianten der grossen G Moll-Fuge," pp. 59-62.

Intrinsically the Dorian and F Major Toccatas belong together, as do the A Minor and G Minor Fugues.

The

Toccata and Fugue in D Dorian (III, 3; BWV 538)

is less popular than the "youthfully dramatic" D Minor, and less magnificent than the F Major Toccata, but it is a masterpiece of homogeneity and compactness.

Pirro named a small composition by André Raison[189] as possibly having been the model for the principal subject of the Toccata:

One also hears reminders of Pachelbel; especially the passage p. 34, 4, 3, where the hands cross, sounds strikingly like the end of Pachelbel's well-known Prelude in D Minor:[190]

The only remaining vestige of the old conception of the toccata, however, is the "instrumental" figure in the subject. From it, without admitting any new idea—with the exception of the driving motive 𝄾♪♩—Bach constructs a concerto movement on the style of the Italian concerto grosso. The principal section appears four times: in D minor, A minor, G minor, and D minor. These principal sections are interspersed with three sections that are episodic, but even their themes are developed from the principal subject.

It is well known that the Dorian Toccata is the only original work by Bach in which Bach's own directions for change of manual have come down to us. Even though the autograph has not survived, no one

189. *Archives des maîtres de l'orgue*, ed. Guilmant, Vol. 2, p. 33.
190. See *Orgelwerke*, ed. Matthäi, Vol. 1, No. 1.

other than Bach himself can have specified these logical, convincing changes of manual. These, however, do not correspond to the divisions into principal and secondary sections; i.e., so that the main sections are performed on the main manual *(Oberwerk)* and the secondary sections on an adjacent manual *(Positiv)*. On the contrary, the two manuals oppose each other on an equal footing.

Bach produces intensification at the climaxes by increasing the number of parts to as many as seven. At these points he abandons the principle of strict part-writing. With only two manuals, one will hold strictly to Bach's markings; with three, the episodes may be divided between the second and third manuals, but—in doing so, take care! The "Dorian" is often performed on too small a scale and played in a belittling manner: hurriedly, too rapidly, and too "small" in tone. The grandeur and majesty of this architecture demand a broad, flowing tempo (♩ = 69), a big tone, and almost no articulation of the sixteenth notes[191] (see p. 57).

The Fugue derives the long, sweeping arch of its subject[192]

from the line formed by the top tones of the beginning of the Toccata:

As in the G Minor Fugue, two countersubjects are added. These, however,—a unique instance in Bach—have exactly the same length as the subject itself, and consequently quite obscure it:

The subject is thus not brought out into the light by these countersubjects, as in the G Minor Fugue, but is concealed. The entire Fugue is filled with this material and with an episode motive (a combination of elements of the subject and the first countersubject):

191. Cf. Distler in *Musik und Kirche*, 1940.

192. Marks for articulation are by the writer.

193. Entrance on the 2nd measure of the subject.

Consequently, no relaxation ever occurs; greater condensation results from the four strettos, all of which are formed at the same intervals (of one octave and of one measure):

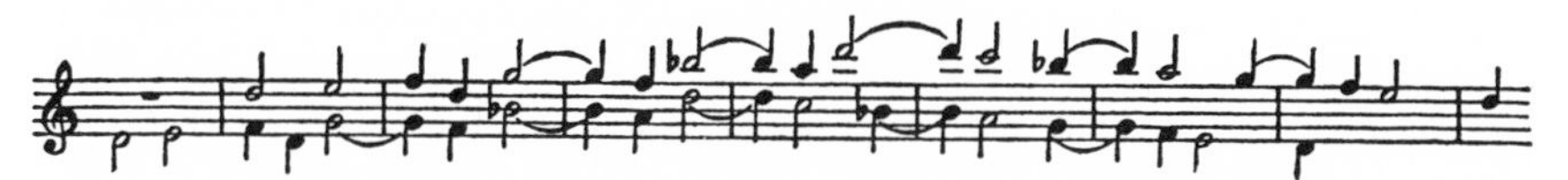

Thus, a parallel progression results, instead of a dovetailing, and the reason lies basically in the subject itself. But this parallelism makes it all the more difficult for the listener to follow both parts. Hence, this magnificent fugue, having one of the most magnificent subjects ever composed, is a favorite neither of audiences nor of players. For the latter, the uniformly close texture seems to offer no clues to its organization.

Performance: The Fugue has seven sections, of which four are principal and three subordinate, just as in the Toccata. The subordinate sections should be played on an adjacent manual; these three are the following: p. 37, last measure, the tenor (the other parts one measure later) to p. 38, 3, 10 (F major stretto); p. 39, 2, 8, r.h. (l.h. one measure later) to p. 40, 2, 7; p. 41, 1, 2, to p. 41, 2, 8. Tone quality: *Organum plenum*. Tempo, 𝅗𝅥 = 63.

Readings: A number of small discrepancies in the manuscripts of the Toccata are unimportant. On the other hand, in the sources and all the editions of the Fugue, the alto and tenor are interchanged in mm. 49 and 50. They should read like this:

The

Toccata and Fugue in F Major (III, 2; BWV 540)

does not constitute a unit internally, as does the Dorian, but consists of two parts, each magnificent in its own way. But these seem joined in a union not really convincing, and probably were not even placed together by the composer until later. Another argument against the simultaneous origin of the two pieces is that the pedal is taken only as high as c^1 in the Fugue.

In the last movement of the Concerto in F Major by Marcello, which Bach transcribed for clavier (No. 7), appear these measures:

It is possible, therefore, that one of Bach's most magnificent works was taken partly from someone else's store of ideas. As with many works by Bach and Handel, it is perhaps not the original idea but what these masters made of it that is decisive and great. It has already been mentioned (p. 107) that these detached chords (with the rest now on the accented part of the measure) also appear at the end of the Fugue in A Minor. According to a memorandum that can no longer be verified, the Church of St. Agnus in Cöthen had an f^1 in the pedal—one other reason, though not the crucial one, for dating the Toccata in the Cöthen period.

The gigantic form of the Toccata,[194] viewed as a whole, is to be understood as the combination of a pedal toccata,[195] with pedal-points on tonic and dominant and added long pedal solo, and a concerto movement on a new theme

This is fashioned from structural elements of the first theme:

194. The manuscripts that transmit both pieces together show *"Preludio"* instead.

195. Cf. Pachelbel's well-known Prelude in D Minor, his Toccata in C Major, Kerll's Toccata in F Major *per li pedali*, etc.

and the eighth-note theme: 𝄾 ♫. Within this concerto movement the three sections in the minor (with the principal theme) play the role of subordinate sections. The long dominant pedal point at the end serves to establish a balance with the beginning. The separation of the sections is accomplished by means of the motive with "spaced" eighth notes 𝄾 ♫, expanded to an eight-measure phrase.

Described schematically, all this sounds very prosaic, but what a profusion of riches this regal work spreads before us! The broad, expansive curves of the two voices treated canonically at the beginning, the stately calm of the pedal solos, the sharply detached chords, the spirited rise of the second theme, the daring modulatory shifts, the intimacy of the three passages in the minor, and the magnificence of the ending with its famous $\frac{4}{2}$-chord on C♭—who would not be inspired by all this?

How can one speak of a "grandiose monotony"[196] and even of "dryness"?[197] What a wealth of rhythmic formations within a 3/8 measure, what symmetry among the individual sections themselves;[198] and how ingeniously used here, for the first time in music history, are the secondary dominants of the second, third, and fourth degrees (and even of the Neapolitan sixth chord in major) of the scale!

For the detached chords in G minor Bach had to place two measures, p. 22, 2, 10, an octave lower, since his manual extended only to c^3; here we shall, of course, restore the original reading:

In this passage we may also see a proof that Bach wrote a d^3 in the manual, or an e^1 or f^1 in the pedal, only when his organ actually had this note within its compass. If anyone today still has no f^1 in his pedal, he will do well to omit the four measures of the pedal solo in question (not play them in octaves on the manual as Griepenkerl proposed) and play a few later passages an octave lower.

The zigzag passage in the pedal is curious:

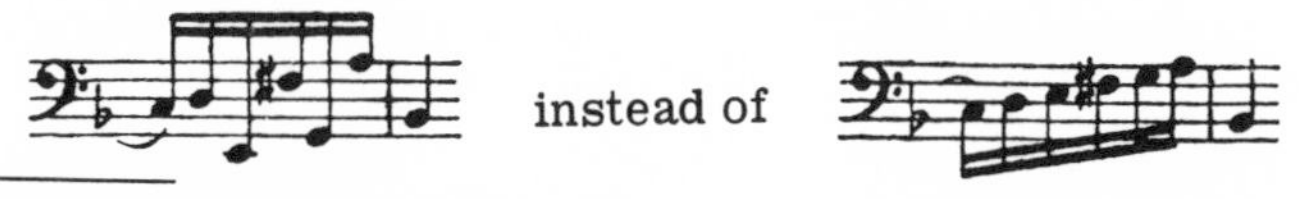

196. See the *Bach-Jahrbuch*, 1912, p. 34.
197. Pirro, *op. cit.*, p. 51.
198. The two pedal points are equal in length (54 mm.); the first pedal solo is exactly half as long; the three passages in the minor are, among themselves, of exactly the same length (each 21 mm.), etc.

We don't find arpeggios of this kind again until we reach Liszt.[199] Bach probably wrote the passage in this way because he wanted to avoid the scale in the pedal—although the beginning of the D Major Prelude is more difficult. But a motivic relationship does exist between the descending sevenths and those of the preceding measures, as Harvey Grace pointed out:[200]

In the G Minor Fugue, also, Bach had changed the step-wise progression of the second countersubject:

into one involving leaps:

We shall encounter these graceful adaptations to the natural pedal technique still more frequently from now on, up to the Prelude in E♭ Major (see p. 160).

First and foremost the *performance* should make clear to the listener the unusual formal structure of the Toccata. The organist needs one stop combination each for the canon, the pedal solo, the detached chords, the second theme, and the three passages in the minor. Since the sections are everywhere so dovetailed, a great deal of thought will be required. The beginning is usually played like a trio; the insertion of the third free voice, however, proves that Bach did not intend that. The second theme may be played by alternating manuals every four measures; but playing the detached chords also with a change of manual every two measures (which goes back to Homeyer) destroys the uniform curve of the eight measures. If one takes the minor passages on a third manual, a reinforcement of the pedal entry of the second theme is easy to manage; but the pedal may not be coupled to either of the alternating manuals.

---

199. In *St. Francis Walking on the Waves*, for example.
200. *Op. cit.*, p. 161.

As with the Dorian Toccata, a warning may be given not to cut up the long lines of the beginning by articulation that is too trivial. The tonal organization must be more restrained when the Fugue is to follow than when the Toccata is played alone—which is the usual practice.

Opinions vary as to tempo. A hundred years ago Griepenkerl considered ♪ = 76 suitable; double this tempo, ♪ = 152, might well be the correct one; in the United States I once heard it played at ♩. = 76 by a French virtuoso—Czerny instead of Bach!

The *Fugue*, whose subject

may be regarded as a remodelling and refinement of one of Pachelbel's,

is a double fugue of the second species—i.e., a "fugue with two subjects," according to Marc-André Souchay's definition[201]—in which the two subjects are developed at first individually and then together. The C Minor Fugue (IV, 6) had been an initial student effort in this form. In the C Minor Fugue (II, 6)—to be discussed later—we find the form again, though not fully defined. Consequently, the F Major Fugue is Bach's only genuine fugue for organ with two subjects. That it is far too little known and valued is due to the smothering proximity of the Toccata. The Fugue becomes most significant when played alone.

The first subject may be played without the ornaments; they are wanting in several manuscripts and, moreover, they seem to disfigure it by flourishes that conflict with its pure beauty. It should be played perfectly *legato*. The second subject:

enters, hovering lightly; this and the first subject together produce two-part writing which is actually ideal:

201. In "Das Thema in der Fuge Bachs," *Bach-Jahrbuch*, 1927, pp. 1-102; see especially p. 19.

In the third section of the Fugue the two subjects appear five times in combination,[202] the last time at an interval of over three octaves between bass and soprano, so that Bach had to deflect the second subject at the moment of its highest intensity:

The writer plays the soprano from here to the end doubled at the octave above:

Performance of the Fugue: 𝅗𝅥 = 69. First section, *Organum Plenum* of the HW; second section on an adjacent manual; p. 28, 2, 7, 3rd quarter, the r.h. and, in the next measure the l.h. also, on the HW.

Readings: Where the numerous small differences occur in both the Toccata and the Fugue, the readings in the Peters edition are always better than those in the BG, except on p. 22, 4, 8, where the *Praller*[203] probably belongs in the bass, not in the tenor.

The

Passacaglia in C Minor (I, 7; BWV 582)

deservedly concludes the series of Cöthen masterpieces. Why did Bach write only one large work each in the forms of the chaconne and the passacaglia: the D Minor Chaconne for violin alone and the Passacaglia for organ? Did he recognize, as Schweitzer thought, that "the incoherency of pieces of this kind is not productive of great organ music"?[204] But can there be any greater organ music than Bach's Passacaglia? Isn't it true that the passacaglia was a species of form that was dying out just after 1700 and that, for this reason, Bach did not revert to it again in Leipzig? One could more readily wonder that Bach did not cultivate this form in his early works under

---

202. Curiously, Frotscher failed to see the true state of affairs when he made the judgment (p. 893): "It does not reach an exposition of the two themes together."
203. See Example 3, p. 50.
204. *Op. cit.*, I, 280.

the influence of Pachelbel and Buxtehude. Significantly, however, almost all his works in the variation form—aside from the chorale partitas—had their origin in Cöthen or Leipzig.

Bach differentiates between chaconne and passacaglia. By passacaglia he means a work that is constructed above a ground bass that remains constant; the acknowledged instrument for it is the organ. The three passacaglias by Buxtehude[205] (he himself calls two of them *ciacona*) are of this description, as are, in addition, the two well-known works by Pachelbel in D Minor and F Minor (also called *ciacona*).[206] These all have a simple, four measure theme in the pedal. In the chaconne, according to Bach's terminology, the bass is felt rather than clearly stated. In Bach's Chaconne the descending tetrachord d—c—b♭—a is the ground theme; the top theme for the violin, which is felt by the listener as principal theme, is probably a variation of this bass.

Even in the theme of his Passacaglia Bach reaches out far beyond his models Pachelbel and Buxtehude: it is not a 4-measure but an 8-measure theme,[207] and is so significant melodically that it may appear alone at the beginning. The descending fifth at the end answers the ascending fifth at the beginning. The structure of the eight measures is 4 + 1 + 1 + 2. It has served as a model for all passacaglias of recent times, especially those of Reger, but without ever having been equalled in beauty.

Pirro[208] established that the first four measures go back to a little passacaglia (5 variations) by Raison:[209]

In the structure of the variations, references are found both to the C Minor Passacaglia (Chaconne) of Buxtehude and to that in F Minor of Pachelbel.[210] A number of scholars[211] have tried to analyze the construction of Bach's twenty variations, but the secret laws they obey are not to be fathomed by any purely rational method.

205. Spitta-Seiffert edition, Vol. 1, Nos. 1, 2, and 3.
206. Pachelbel, *Orgelwerke*, ed. Matthäi, Vol. I, Nos. 12 and 13.
207. Before Bach, Purcell wrote a Chaconne in F Major with an 8-measure theme.
208. *Op. cit.*, p. 46.
209. *Archives des maîtres de l'orgue*, ed. Guilmant, Vol. 2, p. 37.
210. See *Orgelwerke*, ed. Matthäi, Vol. I, No. 13, p. 54, "Ciacona in f."
211. See especially Frotscher (pp. 883-886), Hermann Roth (*Monatsschrift für Gottesdienst und kirchliche Kunst*, XX, pp. 18ff.), and Werner Tell (*Musik und Kirche*, 1938, p. 102).

The 1st and 2nd variations form a double variation in the manner of Pachelbel and Buxtehude; the ties settle over the theme like thick veils. Then imperceptibly it frees itself from this bondage during the next three variations: the 3rd is in flowing eighths but, in addition, is always in close imitative writing; the 4th introduces the invigorating rhythm ♩♫ ; the 5th extends this; and from the 6th on, the movement changes over into flowing sixteenths.

During the next three variations the movement becomes more and more powerful; especially the 8th, with its harsh dissonances clashing one against another, creates the effect of a violent eruption; in the 9th, the compelling motive

propels us forward toward the climax of the next three variations. In the 10th, the stream of tone flows along in great scale passages, freely and unrestrained; in the 11th, it carries on its back the theme, transferred to the soprano as a symbol of the victory that the concluding 12th variation emphatically confirms.

Here Bach stops short[212] at a climax attained in one single intensification, internal as well as external. The next three variations are like an intermezzo: the 13th conceals the theme in the alto; the next two break it up into two- and then one-voice figurations. Now the pedal takes up the theme again; once more, as at the beginning, dense suspension harmonies settle over it, yet no longer with an expression of melancholy, but with one of defiance. The most remarkable variation is the following 17th, in which the movement is whipped up to breathless triplets. In these two variations the development of the beginning is summarized briefly.

The next three variations are again intimately related; they restrain the raging movement ever more forcibly, while they fix the manual part more and more on a pedal point. The terrific congestion in the 20th variation presses toward release—into the appended Fugue.

In this Fugue, the "*thema fugatum*"—the first four measures of the theme—is modified, as in the G Minor Fugue, by two countersubjects: the hammering eighth-note motive,

212. In similar fashion as in the *Art of Fugue* after Contrapunctus XI.

and the quietly undulating sixteenth notes:

The intensification that continues to the end, together with the sudden cessation of movement during the rest after the Neapolitan sixth chord and the eventual turn toward the major, has no equal in the entire literature of music. It is "as if the eternal harmony were communing with itself." Goethe's well-known remark[213] about Bach may most readily be applied to such creations as the multiform and yet completely unified Passacaglia and Fugue.

For a registration of the twenty variations every organist will summon all his ability, so that general hints will be least appreciated here. Furthermore, the whole course of the work has been described above.

According to the manuscripts, the Passacaglia was composed for "*cembalo ossia organo*." Since today pedal-harpsichords are being built again, the work has also been played on one of these instruments a few times. The superiority of the organ is so great, however, that a performance on a harpsichord is still something of a curiosity. I myself transcribed the Passacaglia for two pianos a long time ago[214] in order to acquaint pianists with this piece. But even the sound of two pianos is a makeshift in comparison with the sound of the organ.

There is one small error in the Peters edition. The last note in the third measure from the end should read A♭, not c:

The four-part writing is scrupulously neat. One will notice, on p. 83, 3, 3/4 in the tenor, how parallel fifths have been avoided that would hardly have been audible. Again, p. 86, 3, 3, Bach eliminated parallel octaves—at least for the eye—by crossing the parts.

213. In a letter to Carl Zelter dated June 21, 1827. Quoted by Schweitzer, *op. cit.*, I, 240.

214. This is published by Steingräber.

CHAPTER 12

UNFINISHED WORKS AND TRANSCRIPTIONS

In its conception, the

Fantasy in C Minor (IV, 12; BWV 562)
with unfinished *Fugue* (BG XXXVIII, p. 209)

may perhaps go back to a Fugue by de Grigny:

In its expression of profound sorrow it shows a close connection with other works in C minor of Bach: the Fantasy (III, 6)—especially in the layout above the pedal points C and G—the large C Minor Prelude (II, 6), and the 6-part Ricercar in the *Musical Offering*. It has a still more compact structure than these, however, since the entire piece is developed from the one theme, without the supervention of further ideas. As in the F Minor Prelude, emotional disturbance breaks through the strict form at the end in the outcry of the diminished seventh chord, to which the resolution into the major brings relief.

The suspension in the theme must be set off distinctly by means of articulation, if it is to be made clear why Bach didn't write conventional eighth notes (see p. 53).

The four manual-parts at the beginning may be assigned—two each—to the HW and the RP. Tempo, ♩ = 69.

In m. 56 (p. 71, 2, 4) the suspension note should be restored in the pedal.

The *Fugue* (BG XXXVIII, p. 209)

of which only the first 27 measures were ever composed, is closely related inwardly to the Fantasy; its subject is the beginning of the Passacaglia theme, inverted. Since Bach introduces the subject in stretto at the very beginning, we may assume that he would have introduced a second subject later, and consequently have made a double fugue. Arnold Strebel of Stuttgart completed the Fugue following out this idea (MS).

Another five-part

Fantasy in C Major (BG XXXVIII, p. 209; BWV 573)

(in the first little clavier book of Anna Magdalena Bach) does not go beyond the 11th measure. The fragment is so sublimely beautiful, however, that I tried to complete it; consequently it now appears as the first piece in my *Orgelvorspiele alter Meister in allen Tonarten* (Bärenreiter).

As a final work connected with the Cöthen period we should like to mention the

Prelude and Fugue in D Minor (III, 4; BWV 539)

The Fugue is a transcription from the first Sonata in G Minor for unaccompanied violin.

The Six Sonatas and Partitas for violin alone, which originated in Cöthen, are among the finest works of Bach. That Bach himself thought highly of them may be judged from the fact that he transcribed several movements from them for other instruments: the A Minor Sonata and the first movement of the C Major Sonata (transposed a fourth lower) he transcribed for clavier; the Prelude of the E Major Partita, transposed to D major, he converted into the festive introductory Sinfonia of Cantata 29 (Cantata for the Inauguration of the Council) for orchestra and obbligato organ.

The Fugue from the first Sonata in G Minor he converted into an organ Fugue in D Minor and supplied with a Prelude of its own. Of this arrangement there exists a manuscript copy, which Spitta dated in 1725.[215] It must therefore remain uncertain whether Bach undertook the transcription for organ while still in Cöthen—or in Leipzig. Transpositi was necessary, since the original ranged up to f^3, while the compass of Bach's organ stopped at c^3. Moreover, Bach added one measure each at two points, mm. 5-6 and mm. 29-30, so that he could construct one more entry of the subject in the pedal. (The original version of the fugue is published in the Appendix of Vol. III of the Peters edition for convenience of comparison.)

The arrangement for organ ranks higher in artistic value than the clavier transcriptions, but is inferior to the Cantata for the Inauguration of the Council. When it is played on the same program with the original (an experiment I have tried occasionally), the result of the comparison is always in favor of the original version. The reason is that in the original work the violin is driven to its utmost limits in technique and capacity for expression, while in the transcription the organ does not pass beyond the medium area of its potentialities.

It is hard to understand why Bach didn't transcribe the magnificent and deeply emotional Prelude,[216] as well, but instead substituted a small, insignificant *Präambulum manualiter*. I have not been able to refrain from also transcribing for organ the G Minor Prelude (in content a second G Minor Fantasy) and transposing it to D minor, in order to be able to place in front of the Fugue a Prelude congenial to it.

Among the sonatas for violin alone, there is still another movement which so closely resembles organ music in its style that a transcription seems justified: the large Fugue in C Major on the subject:

In number of measures (354) it is the longest by Bach, and it surpasses even the Great E Minor Fugue (II, 9) in its structure: four principal movements separated by three monophonic episodes.

Its subject is the beginning of the chorale "Komm heiliger Geist, Herre Gott." Spitta thought[217] that it could have been conceived

215. *Op. cit.*, II, 81.
216. Was it perhaps not yet composed when Bach transcribed the Fugue?
217. *Op. cit.*, II, 82.

originally for the organ, and might perhaps have been taken along by Bach on his trip to Hamburg in 1720; for Mattheson also took this subject, together with its chromatic countersubject, as the basis of a test of organists in 1727, just as he had done with the subject of the Great G Minor Fugue.

A few passages in this fugue seem to overstep the bounds of the technical potentialities of the violin—and those acceptable to the audience. I have therefore tried to claim, or reclaim, this gigantic work for the organ.[218] The principal sections, in continuous four-part polyphony, created no very great difficulty—but the free monophonic episodes did!

I hear the obvious protest: after all, to what purpose arrangements of this type? Aren't there enough original works? No, there are not. There are not more than a dozen large works for the organ by Bach, and these are played again and again and again. And didn't Bach himself sanction transcriptions of this kind?

CHAPTER 13

LEIPZIG

1723-1730

There is no need to discuss here what it meant to Bach to exchange the freedom of court life in Cöthen for the varied duties of a Cantor at St. Thomas' and Director of Music at the two principal churches of Leipzig. That these duties kept him away from the organ for years, however, is certain. In addition, the townspeople attached no particular esteem to the position of organist either at the Church of St. Thomas or that of St. Nicholas. These posts were filled by second-rate musicians.

Even in the seventeenth century the position of organist at St. Thomas' Church had been of secondary importance. Except for Kuhnau, there was not a single organist of St. Thomas' whose fame could compare with that of the many cantors who preceded Bach. Before his term as Cantor, Kuhnau had been Organist of St. Thomas' Church from 1684 until 1701; significantly, however, he composed very little for the organ.

When Bach seated himself on an organ bench to play for friends, pupils, or patrons, it was probably at the organ of the University Church, which he had tested and approved in 1717 (see p. 23). It

218. The arrangement is still unpublished.

is very probable that he took along with him to Leipzig a number of older works started in Cöthen or Weimar; and that there, in occasional leisure hours, he completed or improved them. For this reason it is difficult to date a whole series of organ works, especially chorale preludes.

Not until after 1730, when he relaxed his efforts to improve and make secure his official position, did he devote himself again to the organ. In this period, with his last great organ works, he climaxed his writing for the organ.

The organ works we have received from the first five or ten years of his Leipzig period originated in part from pedagogical exigencies. To these belong particularly the

Six Sonatas for Two Manuals and Pedal
(I, 1-6; BWV 525-530)

Forkel states that "Bach composed them for his oldest son, Wilhelm Friedemann, who had to practice them to prepare himself to be the great organist that he afterwards became. One can hardly say enough of their beauty. They were composed when the author was at the height of his powers, and together may be considered his masterpiece in this style. Several separate ones,[219] still scattered here and there, may also be termed beautiful, although they do not attain the high level of the former."

The first drafts seem to reach back into the Cöthen period. The first movement of the Third Sonata appears among the variants of the *Well-Tempered Clavier*. The first movement of the Fourth Sonata is drawn from Cantata 76, *Die Himmel erzählen die Ehre Gottes (The heavens declare the glory of God)*, composed in 1723. Friedemann who, in addition to clavier and organ, also studied violin with J. G. Graun in Merseburg,[220] entered the university of Leipzig in 1729 as *studiosus juris* (law student) and in 1733 went to Dresden as Organist of the Church of St. Sophia. It is probable that his organ lessons with his father were taken during his schooldays; that is to say, before 1729.[221]

The sonatas have been handed down to us in two manuscripts: the first, autograph throughout; the second, written partly by Friedemann

219. This probably means separate trio movements, see p. 140.

220. Martin Falck, *Wilhelm Friedemann Bach: sein Leben und seine Werke* (Leipzig: C. F. Kahnt, 1913). Reprint with preface by Wilibald Gurlitt (Lindau/B.: C. F. Kahnt, 1956), p. 8.

221. Walter Emery, *Notes on Bach's Organ Works, Books IV-V, Six Sonatas for Two Manuals and Pedal* (London: Novello & Co., Ltd., 1957), p. 195. Emery refers to this suggestion.

(Sonatas 1-4), partly by his father (Sonatas 5 and 6).[222] Their neutral title leaves open the question as to whether they were conceived for a harpsichord (or clavichord) with pedal, or for the organ. Bach owned "3 claviers with pedal,"[223] so that the Sonatas were probably intended primarily for use in the home on a stringed instrument; the obituary, however, calls them "6 trios for the organ." That the Sonatas are so rarely heard, despite their acknowledged beauty, may be explained by their peculiar position between two styles. Side by side with themes suitable for the organ occur themes more suitable for chamber music; these present the organist with unusual difficulties of performance.

The strength of the link with chamber music arises from the fact that two movements (the 2nd movement of the Third Sonata and the 1st movement of the Fourth Sonata) are found also in the chamber music or in the cantatas. Hans Engel recently transcribed the First and Sixth Sonatas as trio sonatas for 2 violins, 'cello, and piano. I myself transcribed these two sonatas for 2 pianos.[224] On the other hand, Franz E. Thiele has tried, though unfortunately with less success, to obtain for the organ further trios of Bach's composition by transcribing for organ trio-movements from the chamber music.[225]

Bach gives the organ sonatas the three-movement form of the Italian violin concerto, not the four-movement form of the chamber sonata, but the forms of the individual movements are influenced by both species. Three slow movements (from the 1st, 3rd, and 6th Sonatas) and one Finale (from the 1st Sonata) are in two-part song form. Bach used this frequently in the chamber sonatas (for example, in the Flute Sonata in B Minor, the Violin Sonata in A Major, etc.) for slow movements as well as for fast concluding movements. On the other hand, he did not use this form anywhere in the concertos—except in the *Adagio e dolce* of the Triple Concerto in A Minor. In this movement, however, the recapitulation is both written out and varied.

In all other movements Bach obviously adapted to the keyboard instrument the familiar form-scheme of most of the movements of his chamber music and concertos. But he had to keep the music simpler, primarily the pedal part, for the pedals do not have the compass needed—nor are they sufficiently maneuverable or versatile technically—to perform a bass part written for a 'cello or harpsichord. Even the two upper parts are simpler than those of the chamber sonatas; this fact supports the view that Bach had thought of a performance on the organ from the very first.

---

222. Emery, *op. cit.*, pp. 8ff., discusses the writing of this second manuscript.
223. He bequeathed these to his son Johann Christian in his will.
224. Steingräber.
225. Steingräber.

Bach was the first and only composer to apply the style of the Italian trio sonata, for which Corelli had won classical recognition with his 48 Sonatas, to the sonata for one melodic instrument with required clavier. In his six sonatas for violin and *cembalo obbligato,* to which we may add three similar sonatas with flute and three with *gamba,* no less than 30 movements are written as follows: in sections of pure three-part writing the right hand of the harpsichordist adds a second solo part to that performed by the melody instrument, the left hand playing the bass line.

Bach wrote only four real trio sonatas, from which, significantly, one movement was also converted into an organ trio (see p. 141). It is from these works that an understanding of the organ sonatas—especially of their form—is to be derived.

Let us compare a movement that is formally one of the most elaborate in Bach's chamber music, the first movement of the Flute Sonata in B Minor, with a similar one from the organ sonatas, the first movement of the Second Sonata. The former numbers 119 measures, the latter 78. On the whole, the form-scheme is the same in both movements. The principal section is in the tonic (T) at the beginning and at the end; during the course of the movement, the principal theme appears twice more: in the dominant (D) and in either the relative major (RM) or the subdominant (S); these principal sections are separated by three episodes. Among these seven sections, however, clearly recognizable caesuras appear only twice: right after the first section and just before the last principal section. In the middle, the principal and subordinate sections are intermingled thematically as well as formally in such a variety of ways that it is never easy to determine where one ends and the next begins. These sections, of course, constitute a development of sorts. Presented schematically, the structure of the two movements is as follows:

	Flute Sonata in B Minor	Organ Sonata in C Minor
1st Principal Section	mm. 1-20/21 (T)	mm. 1-8 (T)
1st Subordinate Sec.	mm. 21-32/33 (T-D)	mm. 8-16/17 (T-RM)
2nd Principal Section	mm. 33-52/53 (D)	mm. 17-22 (RM-S)
2nd Subordinate Sec.	mm. 53-68/69 (D-S)	mm. 22-30/31 (S-D)
3rd Principal Section	mm. 69 and 70 (S)	mm. 31-38 (D)
3rd Subordinate Sec.	mm. 71-79/80 (S-T)	mm. 38-70 (D-T)
4th Principal Section	mm. 80-119 (T)	mm. 71-78 (T)

In playing this work, one should try to make this formal structure clear by changes of registration. As a rule, organists refrain from changing stops for reasons easily understandable; yet, with the help of one or two assistants, changes can be made quite easily. The registration should take into account the unusual nature of these sonatas.

For the slow movements one will contrast good solo stops (light reeds) with c.f. combinations of flue stops. For the outer movements Klotz[226] recommends that "stops ('from the first group')[227] be used that are rich in overtones ('brilliant'), and that the various overtone levels be amply filled (Principal or Quintadena, octaves, mixture, Scharf)." This suggestion may be followed, however, only when one has a good baroque organ. Usually mixtures will make the tone too cold and stiff, especially if they are used on both manuals. We may infer that Bach wanted a subtle registration from the fact that he himself not only supplied the sonatas (like the chamber music) with tempo markings, but also provided them with more marks for articulation than he did any of the other organ works.

This is also the place to speak of the modifications to which Bach subjected his themes when they were to appear in the pedal; not all the themes he composed, of course, were suitable for the pedal. We have already encountered simplifications of a few fugue subjects in the early works (for example, in the C Minor Fugue, IV, 6; in the E Major Toccata, etc.); later, in the Great G Minor Fugue (see p. 120) in particular. But now, in the Six Sonatas, we find that hardly any of the *allegro* themes could be put into the pedal without modification. Bach provides a solution either by having only the head of the theme appear in the pedal (1st Sonata), by making the continuation of the theme easier (Finale of the 4th Sonata), or by simplifying the entire theme significantly, as in the Finale of the 6th Sonata:

Or he even transforms it quite extensively, as in the 2nd movement of the 4th Sonata:

or he divests it of coloration, as in the 2nd movement of the 2nd Sonata:

226. *Op. cit.*, p. 290.
227. I.e., narrow-scaled.

Finally, Schweitzer's remarks about the sonatas may also find a place here: "Any organist who studies them thoroughly will find scarcely a single difficulty in the old or even in modern organ music that he has not met with there and learned how to overcome. Before all, he will have attained that absolute precision that is the chief essential of good organ-playing, since in this complicated trio-playing even the slightest unevenness in touch is heard with appalling clearness."[228] In fact, they are for the organist what the Chopin *Etudes* are for the pianist: the highest training for his art!

First Sonata in E-Flat Major (BWV 525)

This work, imbued with a truly Mozartian grace, requires a warm, pliant tone and rich articulation, but no changes of registration within any of its movements. In the 3rd movement an e♭¹ should be restored in the pedal in m. 9 of the second section:

The BG is incorrect in giving ₵ as meter signature of the 1st movement. This is the only movement without instruction as to tempo.

Performance:

228. *Op. cit.*, I, 279.
229. No faster; Bach specifies *allegro*, not *vivace*.

The

Second Sonata in C Minor (BWV 526)

begins in an unrestrained and spirited manner like a concerto for two violins. It is almost inexhaustible in its development of subordinate sections from which the main theme emerges only three times, and then only briefly: in E♭ major, G minor, and C minor. The tone quality should be changed for the subordinate sections: m. 8, 3rd quarter; m. 22, 3rd quarter; and m. 38, 3rd quarter. In Rust's opinion[230] the chains of trills were intended for the harpsichord and may be dispensed with on the organ.

The *Largo*, with its "motive of grief" ♪♩♪♩, is similar to the Fantasy in C Minor (III, 6) in its melancholy seriousness, and also in that both end with a half-cadence.

The Finale combines concerto form with fugal technique. Here the secondary theme, appearing at the bottom of p. 19, requires a different tone color which will correspond to the excitement it arouses. The return to the first tone color begins in the pedal, p. 20, 4, 3; in the soprano, with the last measure of p. 20; and in the alto, two measures later. The return after the second subordinate section is made in such a way as to bring out the stretto clearly: pedal, p. 22, 2, 6; alto, p. 22, 3, 3; and soprano, p. 22, 3, 4. The last 36 measures of the movement are a faithful *reprise* of mm. 23-58, except that the manual parts are exchanged.

Performance:

1st movement

Notice also the very unusual articulation at the bottom of p. 13.
2nd movement: ♪ = 84.

3rd movement

At the bottom of p. 19:

230. BG XV, p. XVIII.

Doubtless the

Third Sonata in D Minor (BWV 527)

was produced earlier than the other sonatas (see p. 130). Several features suggest this: its lesser technical difficulty, the small share the bass has in presenting the themes, and especially the lesser musical value of the last movement,[231] as well as the three-part form of the 1st movement, in which this sonata differs from the others.

The very beautiful *Adagio e dolce* was utilized again in the A Minor Triple Concerto for flute, violin, clavier, and string orchestra. There the movement is in C major. Curiously, the top voice is assigned to the harpsichord and the middle voice to the flute, while the violin provides *pizzicato* figuration.

Performance:

Notice the original slurs in mm. 3, 5, and 7, which give a particularly expressive emphasis to the anacrustic quarter.

The

Fourth Sonata in E Minor (BWV 528)

borrows its first movement from the introductory Sinfonia of Part II of Cantata 76 (see p. 130). In the cantata movement the *oboe d'amore* and the *viola da gamba* carry the melodies. From the verbal context ("Hasse mich nur recht, feindliches Geschlecht"—"Hate ye me well,

231. See, for example, the awkwardness created by two successive entries of the theme in the same voice at the top of p. 32 and p. 32, 2, 5.

foul fiends of Hell!")[232] it follows that the expression of the *Adagio* introduction is to be interpreted as meek, that of the *Vivace* as defiant. Perhaps the head of the theme of the *Andante:*

was also generated from the first four eighths of the introduction:

The last movement (*Un poco Allegro*—with emphasis on "*poco*") was once supposed to have stood as middle movement between the Prelude and the Fugue in G Major (see p. 142). The glory of the sonata is the *Andante,* with its array of ever new counterpoints set against the theme involving leaps of a fourth, and with its surprising stretto at the end.

A variant of the second movement in D minor (Peters edition, I, p. 94) is shorter by two measures than the later version. This variant shows especially well how the first draft was enriched and made more emotional by the "diminution" and by the more active progression of the bass.

Performance:

1st movement: *Adagio,* ♪ = 70; *Vivace,* ♩ = 96.

2nd movement

3rd movement

The

Fifth Sonata in C Major (BWV 529)

is in form the largest, in technique the most difficult, and in its style the one best suited to the organ of all the sonatas. All three move-

232. *Tr.* Henry S. Drinker.

233. Consult the Table of Ornaments in the *Klavierbüchlein für Friedemann Bach* (the last example).

ments are in developed concerto form, the first with a complete *reprise*. Bach had once intended the *Largo* to stand between the Prelude and the Fugue in C Major (II, 1). (See p. 145.)

The structure of the *first* movement is:

Principal Section: mm. 1-51
Subordinate Section: mm. 51-72
(in which the principal theme is announced in the form of fragments tossed in!)
Principal Section: mm. 72-84
Subordinate Section: mm. 84-105
Principal Section: m. 105 to the end.

The principal sections should be played with the *Plenum* of both manuals, the subordinate sections with bright principals and mutations. Tempo: ♩ = 92-96 (no faster!)

The structure of the second movement is:

Principal Section: mm. 1-12
Subordinate Section: m. 13-
Return of the Principal Section: in the alto in m. 21; in the soprano in m. 25
Subordinate Section: m. 33-
Return of the Principal Section: in the soprano in m. 41; in the alto in m. 45. (Notice that the parts are exchanged.)

Performance: the principal section with light reeds, the subordinate section with the Quintaton and flutes (or some other combination of flue stops). Tempo: ♪ = 66.

The form of the *third* movement is more difficult to grasp, since the principal theme also appears in the subordinate sections (also in stretto):

Principal Section: mm. 1-29
Subordinate Section: mm. 29-43
Principal Section (quoted) in the minor: mm. 43-59
Principal Section in stretto: mm. 59-73
Principal Section (quoted) in the minor: mm. 73-119
Subordinate Section: mm. 119-133
Principal Section (quoted) in the minor: mm. 133-149
Principal Section (stretto): mm. 149-163

The 1st, 4th, and 8th sections are in the major (T—D—T); the three sections that merely quote the principal theme (sections 3, 5, and 7) are in the three relative minor keys (A minor, E minor, and

D minor); the two sections based on the second theme (sections 2 and 6) are again in the major (T and S). Sections 2, 4, 6, and 8 are of exactly the same length: 14 measures each. Sections 3 and 7 are again equal in length: each 16 measures. Section 1 corresponds in length to sections 7 and 8 combined.

Registration: brighter and more brilliant than the 1st movement, ♩ = 96-104.

Articulation of the individual movements:

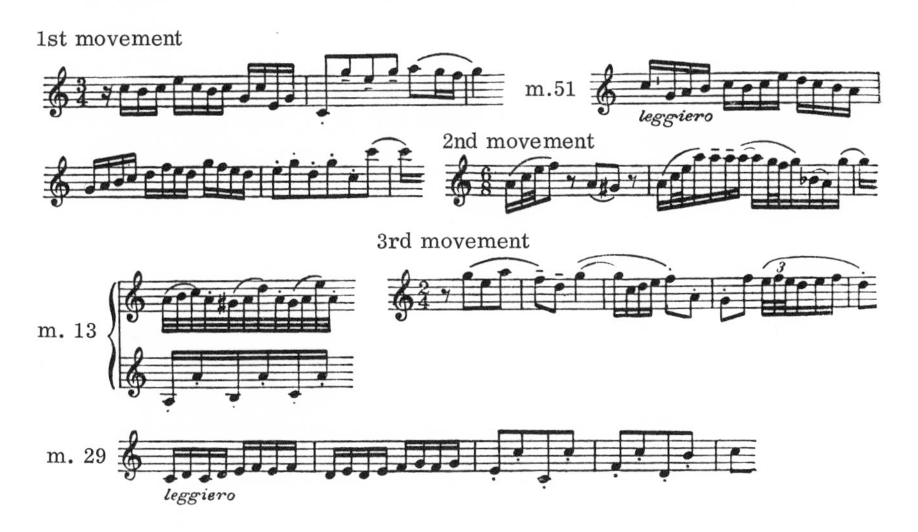

The

Sixth Sonata in G Major (BWV 530)

shines with a truly spring-like lustre. In the first movement, which begins like the *unisono* of a concerto for stringed instruments, the three small homophonic interpolations (mm. 37, 85, and 137) are set off distinctly from the four principal sections; similarly, in the third movement, the two subordinate sections beginning in mm. 19 and 42 are also set off.

In our effort to understand the musical expression of the sonata the glorious *Lento* in E minor causes us the most trouble. Its declamation is a lofty rhetoric, which may strike us today as slightly cold and pedantic. Underneath, however, is concealed a lyrical ardor typically baroque, of which we receive no hint until mm. 5-8 of the second part.

Performance:

1st movement

3rd movement, ♩ = 88.

SEPARATE TRIO MOVEMENTS

Possibly the

Trio in D Minor (IV, 14; BWV 583)

was written before the sonatas. It shows a certain relationship to the Great G Minor Fugue; with slight modifications the beginning would read:

The motive:

is also familiar from the same fugue. As Griepenkerl himself remarks in the Preface, the greater part of the ornaments may be dispensed with. ♩ = 69.

For knowledge of the

Trio in G Major (IX, 3; BWV 1027a)

we are indebted to Max Seiffert. This work is an arrangement of an arrangement. Bach transcribed his G Major Sonata for *viola da gamba* and obbligato harpsichord as a trio sonata for two flutes and *basso continuo*. Then, from this version he again transcribed the last movement as a trio for organ. The necessary simplification of the bass was cleverly done. Toward the end, eleven measures of the original were omitted, probably because the bass line was too difficult. 𝅗𝅥 = 80.

An additional

Trio in G Major (IX, 8; BWV 586)

also discovered by Seiffert and published for the first time in 1904, is actually a composition by Telemann which Bach transcribed for organ. Professor Karl Anton passed on this information in a review of my new edition of Vol. IX in *Musik und Kirche* (1942, Nos. 3-4). 𝅗𝅥 = 76.

Even the

Aria in F Major (IX, 5; BWV 587)

is not by Bach but by Couperin, as the Belgian organist Hennie Schouten determined. In fact, it is from the collection that appeared in 1726, entitled *Les Nations: Sonades et Suites de Simphonies en*

Trio. There it was Courante II from *"La Françoise"* and was for two violins, 'cello, and *basso continuo.*[234] Therefore, my argument in the Preface to Vol. IX, for the authenticity of this piece is untenable. The argument was that "no one else at that time wrote trio movements with so demanding a pedal part." It should be qualified to read: "No one else at that time transcribed for the organ trio movements with so demanding a pedal part."

Bach took over Couperin's composition without making any great changes, except that he omitted a number of ornaments. The parallel fifths, p. 17, 2, 10, remain, therefore, as also a pedal part ranging to e¹, although no organ in Leipzig had this note in its compass. If this piece was transcribed along with the sonatas, as we may assume, Bach must have become acquainted with Couperin's collection very soon after its appearance. ♪ = 112.

Two more works may be dated in Bach's first Leipzig period, at least according to the latest extant copy. These are the Preludes and Fugues in G Major and C Major. These two form a pair, at least to the extent that in both works Bach had considered inserting a trio movement between Prelude and Fugue.

Prelude and Fugue in G Major (II, 2; BWV 541)

Spitta ascribed the autograph to the year 1724 or 1725 by comparing its paper with that of cantata parts.[235] An earlier manuscript, of J. P. Kellner, gives the first thirteen measures of the third movement of the E Minor Sonata as "trio which is to follow the first movement"; they were crossed out, however, because (the movement was) "composed only thus far in the composer's autograph." It is interesting that here (and in the Prelude and Fugue in C Major) Bach had considered converting the duality of prelude and fugue into a sonata of three movements. By inserting this slow trio movement he would have had a "sonata" comprising three movements of different structural types. In the final revision, however, he gave up this idea. Significantly, none of the organ sonatas of the nineteenth century seized upon this happy idea again.

Klotz[236] accepts as possible, or probable, that in two further instances Bach had expanded the two-part form of prelude and fugue to

234. ". . . pour violons et une basse d'archet. . . avec clavecin." See *Oeuvres complètes de François Couperin* (Paris: Editions de l'Oiseau Lyre, 1932-33), Vol. IV, pp. 153-161.

235. *Op. cit.*, III, 208.

236. "Über Bachs Orgeln," pp. 202f.

the three-part form by insertion of a middle movement; i.e., that the Aria in F Major (see above) was placed between the Toccata and the Fugue in F Major, and that the isolated Trio in D Minor (see p. 140) stood between the Fantasy and the Fugue in G Minor. This conjecture, however, rests on a less sound foundation.

In no other organ work of Bach do we find, as we do here, a basic mood so expressive of an abundance of youthful happiness. One might therefore assume that it was composed during Bach's happiest period: in Cöthen. The Prelude and Fugue are related closely in spirit and also in their themes; yet the distinguished authorities Heuss and Straube have declared themselves in favor of another interpretation of the Fugue.

According to Heuss it develops, after a "joyfully vigorous" beginning, into "inner discontent." According to Straube the entire Fugue signifies a resigned turning-back from the "cheerfulness of the Prelude" to the "realities of existence." The strong dissonances in the last third of the Fugue and the connection of its subject with the Weimar cantata *Ich hatte viel Bekümmernis (I had great heaviness of heart)*[237] seem to support this interpretation.

Nevertheless, I cannot agree with it. In spite of being in the minor mode, the cantata theme has something playful about it, and assumes an even happier, more triumphant mood in the major. By the displacement of the center of gravity at the end, it is even turned back into something almost roguish. Without its ornamentation it reads:

Similarly, the minor dissonances toward the end of the Fugue are not to be interpreted as pessimistic; rather, the introduction of dissonance here signifies a deepening of the feeling of happiness.

All similar moods that Bach had embodied in earlier pieces—in the Preludes VIII, 11, and IV, 2, in the first movement of the G Major Toccata for clavier, and in the G Major Prelude and Fugue of the *Well-Tempered Clavier*—seem to be epitomized here and heightened to a final masterly expression.

The main theme enters after eleven measures of a spirited toccata-like running passage[238] ("a general upbeat"). In its harmonic answering of tonic by dominant and dominant by tonic, it anticipates formations like the subject of the E♭ Major Prelude. Equally "modern" is the three-part form that shows through. The writing is strict even when it is in six parts; when necessary, parallels were

237. This is Cantata No. 21. The theme is used in the minor in the first chorus.
238. This should be divided between the hands exactly according to Bach's instructions.

removed by crossing of parts. It is a pity that Bach had no d^3 available for the end of the Prelude. The writer plays the passage like this:

The following features of the Fugue are noteworthy: the homophonic interpolation at the top of p. 12 (cf. the C Minor Fugue, II, 6) and the congestion just before the end, which we have already encountered in the Passacaglia, and which we shall meet again in the C Major Fugue (II, 7). Especially beautiful are the two strettos, reserved till now, which follow the release of the streams of tone from this congestion. (The first stretto is at the ninth above, the second at the fourth below; both are at the distance of half a measure.) The final feature is the *quinta vox* beneath the triumphant pedal point on g^2 in the soprano. (Bruhns would have given this entry to the pedal, thus creating a double pedal.)

Performance: The Prelude (♩ = 112) requires a brilliant, clear, but not too shrill *Plenum* on the HW; it should be played without altering the tone quality. The Fugue (♩ = 96) demands the warm sound of principals, which should be increased to a *Plenum* with reeds for the last section (from the top of p. 13 on). If the manuals are coupled, a transition to an adjacent manual may be made like this on p. 11, 4, 1:

239. This is the ornament in the BG; the Peters edition shows only *tr*.

With manuals uncoupled, one should go to the adjacent manual at p. 11, 3, 3. The return to the HW: r.h., p. 12, 3, 1, last quarter; l.h., p. 12, 3, 4, 2nd quarter.

The *Fugue*

at a less lively tempo:

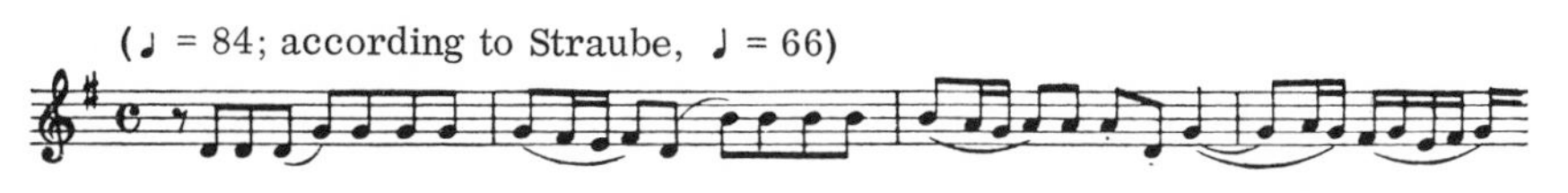

The

Prelude and Fugue in C Major (II, 1; BWV 545)

has come down to us in two autograph manuscripts: a fair copy of 1730 and an earlier one, in which the *Largo* of the fifth trio sonata is interpolated as middle movement. A first version of the Prelude is preserved in the form of a copy (BWV 545a); this begins:

and ends:

240. See the Peters edition, Vol. II, p. 88, where at "x" it reads f² instead of d², probably through an oversight.

It shows that Bach did not add until later the first three measures and the four corresponding measures at the end. These are like two towers which flank the broad middle structure. This, in turn, is laid out in three sections, with the emphasis on the outer sections, so that the following terraces result:

mm. 1-3 — 4-11 — 12-16 1/2 — 16 1/2-27 — 28-31.

At the beginning, measure 1 is for 6 parts (the e^2 is correctly a half note in the Peters edition, but in the BG incorrectly changed to a quarter); mm. 2 and 3 are for 5 parts; the following measures for 4 parts; and the middle section for only 3 parts; whereupon the number of parts is again increased to the end. For this reason the architectural design will be recognized clearly, even without any change in registration.

Bach wrote *Pro Organo Pleno* above the work, thus demanding a majestic *Plenum*-registration on the HW. Straube writes fittingly, "Let the organist seek to reproduce in his registration the magnificence and splendor of the *Meistersinger* orchestra." The tempo should be broad, ♩ = 66 (not *allegro*); the *Praller* in the pedal

(omitted in the Peters edition) provide external support for this conclusion.

In its basic outline the subject of the Fugue resembles the subject of the first fugue in the *Well-Tempered Clavier,* but it is even simpler: the two descending thirds, f—d and e—c, answer the ascending tetrachord (see below).

The three-part form of the Fugue, its modulation scheme—everything lies plain and open as rarely in Bach. The almost too "bourgeois" chordal ending is not so strict in its voice-leading as are the corresponding passages in the G Major Prelude. A change of manual seems not to have been intended, yet the three sections should be distinguished from each other by changes in registration; and the intensification at the end, plainly demanded by the sequences, must be impressive. Tempo, 𝅗𝅥 = 72. Articulation:

CHAPTER 14

THE LAST GREAT WORKS OF THE LEIPZIG PERIOD

(*ca.* 1730-1740)

For Bach the period between the *St. Matthew Passion* and the *B-Minor Mass* (1729-1737) meant the attainment of an eminence for which he had struggled every step of the way. Maturity and depth were the marks of this second master period. Yet from here, during his last creative period, he was to climb still higher to the abstractions of his last contrapuntal works.

The harvest had been brought in. At the same time—possibly for some time—Bach had seen with perfect clarity how very much of a stranger to his period he had become. He saw his sons go the way of the new art, but did not follow them. He took not a single step outside the world he himself had built. Instead, he summoned all his powers for the creation of works which, without concession to the taste of the day, raised to unprecedented heights the expressive means of this period now drawing to a close.

Even in purely technical matters this was true. It is improbable that, around 1740, anyone other than possibly Kittel or Krebs would have had the technique to play the E Minor Fugue or the *Third Part of the Clavierübung*. And what musician of this transition period—in part *galant*, in part *empfindsam*—would have had the capacity to comprehend the intrinsic greatness of these gigantic works?

In these last works, also, Bach availed himself of the concerto form for his preludes; once he even used it for a fugue (the E Minor). But the difference between these works and earlier ones lay in the style of their themes. In the Dorian and F Major Toccatas this form had been combined with toccata themes in sixteenth-note motion; in the trio sonatas the themes were like those of chamber music. Now they became monumental, but within this general quality there was still great variety, as may be imagined. It was as if Bach had wanted to prove that this aristocratic art form could be used for every manner of expression in the hands of a composer of genius.

The modulatory scheme of the five Preludes in question—the C Minor, the C Major, the B Minor, the E Minor, and the E♭ Major—is almost exactly the same: T—D—S—T. In the E Minor only, there is an additional entry in the RM (G major). In the Preludes in C Major and E♭ Major the thematic material of the subordinate sections is derived directly from the principal section. In the Preludes in C Minor, B Minor, and E Minor the subordinate sections are free transformations of the principal section.

We notice a very great variety, however, in the way Bach connects these parts with each other. In the E♭ Major Prelude, for reasons linked with its "program," they are separated clearly from each other; in other works—the C Minor Prelude, for example—they are so welded together that no analysis can specify the point at which one section passes over into the next. The organist who would like to register according to the structure often does not know where to find the correct points for transition from one manual to another (see pp. 149ff.).

The fugues show even greater variety. They are as different in form as their subjects are in style. All are alike only in placing form at the service of expression with greater freedom and excellence than formerly. Only in respect to the C Minor Fugue does this judgment need to be qualified somewhat.

In the fugues, complexes oppose each other as do the sections of a concerto movement. The unbelievably daring and unique form of the E Minor Fugue even attempts to unite the two completely dissimilar elements of fugue form and concerto form!

Thus, these last five great preludes and fugues constitute the lofty conclusion of Bach's free organ works. They are, in fact, the final supreme culmination of German composition for the organ immediately before the profound decline which lasted for more than a hundred years.

Prelude and Fugue in C Minor (II, 6; BWV 546)

According to Spitta's hypothesis, the C Minor Fugue, like the Fugue in F Major, originally had another, shorter, Prelude for which Bach later substituted the present one. Spitta reasoned that "their grander structure offers too great a contrast to the fugues, and betrays the period of Bach's highest mastery."[241] Like an immense double chorus, the beginning of the Prelude is constructed above a

241. *Op. cit.*, I, 590.

pedal point on C. The "motive of grief" (cf. the C Minor Fantasy, III, 6, and the chorus "O man, bewail thy grievous fall" from the *St. Matthew Passion*) is heightened here to exaltation.

Abruptly and precipitously the rise of the Neapolitan sixth chord breaks forth from the waves of the triplets and the sequence, fighting its way upward step by step:

In this passage all movement seems to come to a standstill before it flows into the broad, sweeping cadence. What a wealth of great effects!

The double theme with which the subordinate section is introduced in m. 25 is prepared in the soprano and bass in mm. 21 and 23:

In this theme the halves and quarters stand firmly against the triplet rhythm; but, with its deeply emotional expression, this theme holds even the subordinate sections up to the tension and majesty of the principal section. Some organists fail to realize this fact and consequently play the subordinate sections with expression and tone that are too trivial. Once—in mm. 109-111 (p. 40, 3, 2)—this music assumes an expression almost Beethovenian.

The performance of this gigantic work (♩ = 88) requires two equal, uncoupled manuals, each with a powerful *Plenum*. The structure of the Prelude is as follows:

Principal Section: mm. 1-24/25
Subordinate Section: mm. 25-48/49
Principal Section: mm. 49-52/53
Subordinate Section: mm. 53-70
Principal Section: mm. 70-96/97
Subordinate Section: mm. 97-119/120
Principal Section: mm. 120-144.

It is surely no accident that these 12 x 12 = 144 measures arrange themselves freely into groups of 24 + 24 + 48 + 24 + 24 measures (disregarding small discrepancies). The manual transitions are as follows.

The principal section (HW), mm. 1-24/25; the transition to the subordinate section (OW) is made by playing c^1 simultaneously on both manuals with the l.h.:

The transitions in mm. 49 and 53 are made as follows:

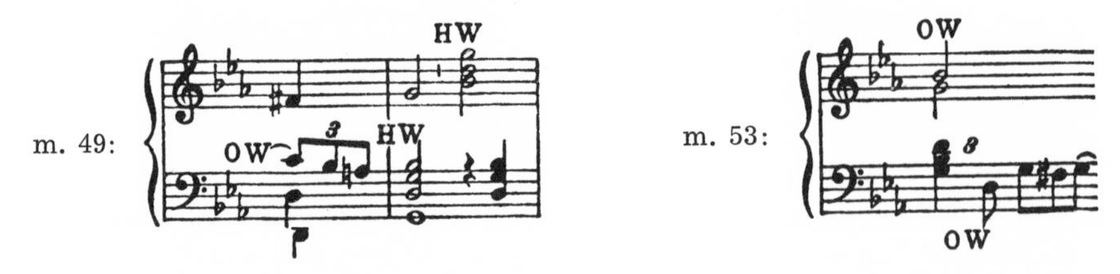

In m. 77 the r.h. goes back to the HW on the 4th quarter; in m. 78, the l.h. on the 2nd quarter; in m. 105, after the 1st note, again to the OW; return to the HW in m. 120, as in m. 49.

Readings: Whether it was intentional or an oversight on Bach's part that there is an $e^{\flat 1}$ instead of b♭ in the *reprise*, p. 41, 2, 1, must be left undecided. The meter signature for the Prelude and Fugue is given variously in the manuscripts as 𝄵 and C.

The *Fugue* is not quite the equal of the Prelude. It is for five parts, but fails to maintain the five consistently. It makes the start of a double fugue, yet only the head of the second subject (m. 59) is introduced and developed separately. The complete form of the second subject, used when combined with the first subject, reads:[242]

Finally, there is the intensification of the dominant, reminds one of Beethoven, just before the last entry of the subject in the pedal. Spitta objected to this passage as being "in its purpose. . . quite foreign."[243] The Fugue is nevertheless a magnificent piece of music, above all in the beauty of its principal subject, with its a b b a' structure and extension of a' which reminds one of the A Major Fugue.

242. Curiously, Straube seems to have overlooked the importance of this passage in his edition.

243. *Op. cit.*, I, 592.

Primarily the performance must make clear the construction. Measures 1-58 should be played on the HW with a full chorus of principals. Straube lengthens m. 59 to a measure of 3/2:

but one should find a *ritardando* in m. 58 and a shortening of the cadential chord sufficient, without giving up the duple meter. Measures 59-86 on the OW, then again on the HW to m. 115; here, on the second note, to the OW, without the usual echo-effects; return to the reinforced HW in m. 140: soprano on the 2nd quarter, alto on the 4th quarter, with the tenor following in m. 142. Tempo: 𝅗𝅥 = 116.

There are many possible ways of articulating the subject. The following is recommended:

(in no case may the g and e♭ in m. 4 be separated!).

Prelude and Fugue in C Major (II, 7; BWV 547)

The Prelude is fitted together in an unsurpassable unity from a quadruple chain of connecting motives, without any further additions:

The ostinato motive in the bass:

(related to the "carillon" motive in the organ chorale "In dir ist Freude") is derived from m. 2 of the beginning. In its idiom the Prelude is closely related to the opening chorus of Cantata 65, *Sie werden aus Saba alle kommen (All they from Sheba shall come)*, composed for Epiphany, 1725:

244. This reading from the BG is better than that of the Peters edition, in which "*tr*." appears above the 3rd note.

conclusion:

No doubt can exist, then, that this is joyous, festive music. But why does one hear it so seldom? Probably only because, as in the Dorian Fugue, the material is so concentrated that the player does not know how to organize it formally. The continual crossing of tenor and bass also adds to the difficulties of making it sound well in performance. The Prelude should be played only with a very full pedal (not coupled). I have never heard the work sound as I imagine it in my mind. The exultant dissonances at the end and their triumphant resolution make the heart leap. But what organ gives the ultimate in tone and expression? The only organization by manual transitions that Bach himself could have made is: m. 31 to the OW (l.h. on the 1st quarter, r.h. on the 2nd) and, in mm. 52-53, back to the HW again (first the alto and then the tenor and soprano). A steady, distinct rhythm, linked with rich articulation:

will have to compensate for whatever the organ may owe the music in tone quality. Tempo: ♩. = 60 (no faster!).

The customary evaluation of the Fugue falls even farther short of its importance. The reason is that Bach delays the pedal-entry of the subject a long time, thereby also delaying the magnificent combination of the subjects reminding one of the Overture to the *Meistersinger*. Consequently, the listener, who does not know what is to come, becomes impatient, especially when the player considers it suitable to begin the Fugue *piano*, as many do. In no other fugue by Bach does the subject appear so many times (more than fifty!). It is therefore quite superfluous to bring it into prominence here and there; instead, the organist should try to play off the four large exposition groups against each other:

mm. 1-15 HW (almost every note here is thematic!);
m. 15 (2nd half) to the OW;
m. 27 to a 3rd manual;
m. 34 the alto goes to the reinforced (possibly coupled) OW on the 3rd quarter; the other parts in m. 35;
m. 48, 3rd quarter (l.h.), return to the HW, coupled meanwhile.

The first two expositions present the subject in direct motion; the 3rd (m. 27) in contrary motion (inversion); the 4th in a stretto of statements in contrary and direct motion; and the 5th (from the entrance of the pedal on) in numerous strettos, with the subject in augmentation in the bass. This unprecedented combination of subjects is also jammed with dissonances; as in the Prelude, these are resolved gradually above a tonic pedal point. In this passage the fugue still surpasses the subject.

It has already been mentioned that Bach's most artificial fugues are not always his most important ones. This may be true, but here artificiality is placed at the service of an idea. As an example of the greatest mastery of an artisan it embodies a transcendental idealism reminiscent of Schiller.

The curve of the subject is related to that of the B Major Fugue in Part II of the *Well-Tempered Clavier*, the late entrance of the bass to that of the C Minor Fugue.[245] The leap from a dissonance in measure 30 is curious:

From the very first note on, the *performance* should make clear to the listener both in sound and in tempo (♩ = 54) the grandeur of this music. Consequently, a *Plenum* should be used on all three keyboards, the pedal with strong reeds, uncoupled, and the assignment to manuals as outlined above.

245. It is not acceptable, however, to conclude from these facts, as does the *Volks-Spitta*, that the time of origin of the work was between the years 1742 and 1744.

The

Prelude and Fugue in E Minor (II, 9; BWV 548)

is a composition so great both externally and internally that Spitta was justified in saying that its conventional title no longer suffices to suggest to our period a true idea of its grandeur and power; "it should be called an organ symphony in two movements."[246] The internal relationship of the Prelude and the Fugue is that of contrast: the heavy restraint of the Prelude is relaxed in the Fugue, which is the boldest and freest Bach ever wrote.

Once more we are obliged to admire the homogeneity of the thematic material in a prelude. The first principal section (mm. 1-18/19) is merely a single long-drawn-out melodic curve. In it one figure grows out of another. From it, also, is fashioned the thematic material of the first subordinate section (mm. 19-32/33). The second subordinate section, beginning in m. 51, seems at first glance to be presenting a new motive. Later (m. 90), however, the inversion of the dotted motive:

shows clearly its derivation from:

(m. 15). It, too, then, is derived from the principal theme, which is based on this same descending melodic progression. All these figures that have grown from each other are combined in so many different ways that the resulting impression is that of one single immense organism. The sequences give the movement a special significance; rising and falling in the ponderous rhythm of entire meas-

246. *Op. cit.*, III, 210.

ures, they raise and lower the musical structure like the hull of an enormous ship that is pounding through the waves of the sea.

In *performance* the music may be allotted to three manuals according to the division of the movement into one principal and two subordinate sections. The structure of the movement is as follows:

Principal Section:	mm. 1-18/19
1st Subordinate Section:	mm. 19-32/33
Principal Section:	mm. 33-50/51
2nd Subordinate Section:	mm. 51-68/69
1st Subordinate Section:	mm. 69-80/81
Principal Section:	mm. 81-89/90
2nd Subordinate Section:	mm. 90-93/94
1st Subordinate Section:	mm. 94-114/115
2nd Subordinate Section:	mm. 115-120/121
1st Subordinate Section:	mm. 121-124/125
Principal Section:	mm. 125 to the end.

Here, also, examples of symmetry are worthy of note: mm. 51-80 and 90-114 correspond exactly to each other; in the first major division, mm. 1-51, the lowest point of the harmonic progression lies exactly in the middle, in mm. 24-26. There are other examples of symmetry as well.

The movements should be played broadly and sound massive; not, as we hear most frequently, *allegro*. Widor and Schweitzer seem to me to approach the proper tempo more nearly with ♩ = 50 than Griepenkerl with ♩ = 60 or Straube with ♩ = 66.

The Fugue is not only the most daring, but also the most difficult technically of all of Bach's fugues—if one sets 𝅗𝅥 = 69 as minimum tempo. It is in three-part form with a complete *reprise* of the principal section, in this feature resembling the C Minor Fugue (III, 6). In the middle section, the subject of the fugue emerges only here and there from the midst of a sparkling toccata. Fugue, concerto, and toccata, therefore, are combined here in a manner comparable only to that employed in the Finale of the *Ninth Symphony* a hundred years later.

The subject drives out from the tonic toward both sides, widens to an octave, and then returns to the tonic. It is far more than "harmony broken apart," as both Pirro and Frotscher[247] describe it. It is carried along by an irresistible rhythmic impulse which is communicated to the counterpoints as well. Both demand the most vital articulation:

(see: next page)

---

247. *Op. cit.*, p. 895: "zerlöste Harmonik."

Straube interprets the subject in the following way:

Interpretations are indisputable, yet to me only the articulation seems possible for the eighths in m. 3 (see the tenor in m. 8 and the bass in m. 21). Concerning the trill in the 4th measure, see p. 51.

The toccata-like middle section begins with a rocking figure which could have had its prototype in Bruhns (Prelude and Fugue in G Major,[248] the interlude before the second fugue). This figure seems to roll the subject back up:

Even the basses underneath the following sixteenth-note scales[249] are based on the subject

(see m. 21). Later, the intervals are contracted and developed into a new motive,

Anything other than caprice, therefore, prevails in this middle section, which creates an impression of being wholly improvisatory.

The *performance* of the Fugue is shown clearly in that the principal section and the *reprise* are to be played on the HW with *Organum Plenum;* in the middle section two subordinate manuals may alternate, each having the clear, luminous sound of mixtures.

---

248. *Orgelwerke, op. cit.,* No. 1, p. 7.

249. The scales in quarters and in sixteenths moving in the same direction at the same time have their model in the organ chorale "Vom Himmel kam der Engel Schar."

Tempo, 𝅗𝅥 = 72. The first note in the soprano, p. 74, 3, 2, should read b^2, not a^2.

Prelude and Fugue in B Minor (II, 10; BWV 544)

The careful, elegantly-written fair copy of this work which Bach prepared—one of the most beautiful music manuscripts in existence[250]—gives evidence in a purely external way of the high rank held by this work. But even its tonality and its themes are linked with the most consecrated areas of Bach's music. The chromatic sequences of the Prelude are similar to those in the first Kyrie of the *B-Minor Mass,* and its melismas closely resemble those in the aria "Erbarme dich" of the *St. Matthew Passion.* Couldn't passages from the aria like this:

or the end:

also appear in the organ prelude? This Prelude, therefore, differs completely from the E Minor Prelude in basic mood, in spite of their close formal relationship. In its lyricism and in its sorrowful mood the Prelude is like an aria from a Passion.

Many an interpreter has failed in the difficult task of trying to do justice simultaneously to the architectonic structure of this work and to its expression of feeling. One course would be to follow the expression, as Spitta[251] suggested in his sensitive interpretation and Straube realized in his edition. Yet it might be felt that the inscription *Pro Organo Pleno* would oblige us to sweep aside all romanticism with a masterful *forte* tone and *tempo ordinario*. Ideally, the player ought to try to combine the two by finding a *Plenum* combination in keeping with the special quality of this work. The tempo and performance should be *affettuoso*—as Bach significantly directed for the B minor movement of the Fifth Brandenburg Concerto; i.e., about

250. This MS has appeared in facsimile print (Universal Edition).
251. *Op. cit.*, III, 209-210.

♪ = 80 (Widor and Schweitzer's ♪ = 63 is too slow). A lighter, more transparent registration on the OW will contrast with the *Plenum* of the HW (notice the original *staccato* marks); and the construction will be brought out by changes of manual:

Principal Section:	mm. 1-16/17
Subordinate Section:	mm. 17-26/27 (one would do well, however, to play the r.h. in m. 26 as a general upbeat on the HW, the l.h. following in m. 28)[252]
Principal Section:	mm. 27-42/43
Subordinate Section:	mm. 43-49
Principal Section:	mm. 50-68/69
Subordinate Section:	mm. 69-78 (according to Klotz[253] from m. 73 only)
Principal Section:	mm. 78, r.h. (l.h. from m. 79) to the end.

The *Fugue* we would hardly count among Bach's more important ones—to judge by its unpretentious subject. If it is, nevertheless, equal to the Prelude and inwardly forms a unit with it, this is due to its huge development. The section for manuals alone, interpolated in mm. 28-58, frees the subject from its monotony and—to use a term from modern psychology—introversion. At the end of this development section, a new theme[254] breaks through like a ray of sunlight from a cloud:

It comes as power from above that "helpeth our infirmities,"[255] and carries the subjects together to the end in a grand intensification.[256]

Thus the construction is also shown clearly:

Principal Section:	mm. 1-27/28 (registered with a tranquil principal-combination)
Middle Section:	mm. 28-58 (within this section mm. 35-40 may be further shaded off)

252. See p. 43.
253. *Op. cit.*, p. 275.
254. As second countersubject; the first appears at the very beginning of the Fugue.
255. Romans 8:26, "Likewise the Spirit also helpeth our infirmities. . ."
256. Frotscher sees the Fugue differently (p. 899): flowing along quietly, peacefully, without any sustained animation, and without contrapuntal subtleties.

Principal Section: m. 59 to the end (on the coupled, reinforced HW, and with a gradual increase to the end)
Tempo: ♩ = 60-69.

Prelude and Fugue in E-Flat Major (III, 1; BWV 552)

Bach's last free organ work is also one of the most brilliant jewels in the reliquary of his art. As is well known, its two parts were separated originally, for they constituted the beginning and the end of the *Third Part of the Clavierübung* (see p. 268). Prelude and Fugue may be understood fully only in connection with this collection and were probably written expressly for it. Nevertheless, Griepenkerl, who was the first to place the Prelude and Fugue together, could refer to Forkel as his authority for doing so.

While in other preludes and fugues of Bach we cannot know what the composer "had in mind," here we stand on firmer ground. It is only natural to assume that the two pieces are closely allied with the "Organ Mass" that they enclose—not only externally, but also internally. Traditionally, the three-part Fugue has been interpreted as a symbol of the Trinity. Then, recently, Steglich advanced the theory, quite convincingly, that the Prelude also should be so interpreted. It contributes to "the representation of the all-embracing triune power of God. The splendid, majestic Prelude, resembling an overture, affords an insight, as it were, into the influence of this power in the world. It sets forth the three themes, sharply delineated and structurally clear: the essence of a Sovereign in the authentic first theme; the dual character of Christ as the Son of God descending to man, and the Savior born of man, in the second theme; and the descent and diffusion of the Holy Spirit in the third."[257]

Ranging from e♭¹ to e♭², the first theme is "authentic." Its proud, majestic, downward motion becomes meek in the second ("plagal") theme, with e♭¹ as its central point:

257. Rudolf Steglich, *Johann Sebastian Bach* (Potsdam, 1935), p. 146.

Even its continuation, in whose fervent expression Steglich professes to recognize the "Savior," is derived from the principal theme:

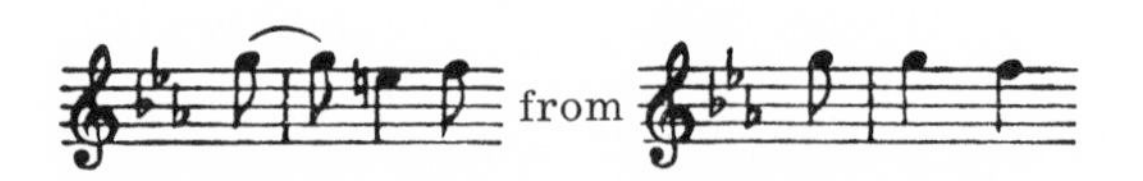

as is also the third theme, shooting down with great spirit:

The scale is converted into a "flight of stairs" in the pedal:

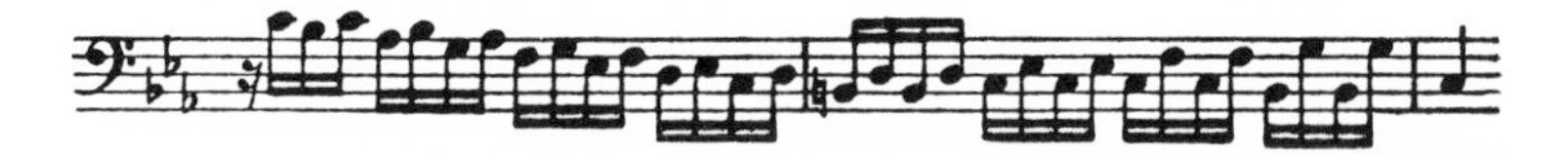

The structure of this magnificent work is therefore perfectly clear:

Principal Section:	mm. 1-32 (twice 16 mm., each 4 + 12)
1st Subordinate Section:	mm. 32/33-50/51 (here also 16 mm., which becomes 18 by repetition of mm. 45-46)
Principal Section:	mm. 51-70/71
2nd Subordinate Section:	mm. 71-97/98 (*manualiter*)
Principal Section:	mm. 98-111
1st Subordinate Section:	mm. 111/112-129/130
2nd Subordinate Section:	mm. 130-173/174 (*pedaliter*)
Principal Section:	mm. 174 to the end.

In no other organ work of Bach are there found so many four-measure groupings. The articulation is also meaningful. The characteristic rhythm of the French overture loses its frigidity when the slurs given by Bach himself are observed. These "bind back" the sixteenth to the dotted eighth: . As a result, the rhythm becomes warm and vital. The staccato marks in the second theme are also original. The echo passages indicated by *forte* and *piano* do not invalidate the direction *Pro Organo Pleno;* a *Rückpositiv* registered *forte* and a *Brustwerk* registered *piano* may support the *Plenum* of the *Hauptwerk*.

The manual transition in mm. 50/51 may be made as follows:

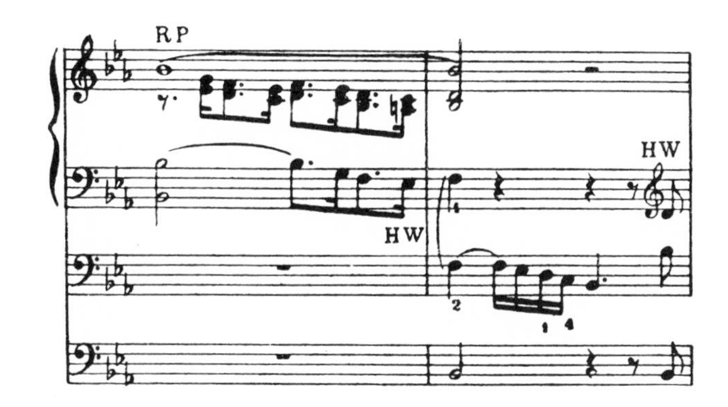

in mm. 97/98 (and correspondingly in mm. 173/174) thus:

In mm. 32 and 111 the chord should be shortened by the last three sixteenths.

Certain errors are not infrequently heard when the Prelude is performed, even by good players. These are too gross and massive a registration, and a tempo that is not kept uniform throughout—too broad at first and then almost doubled for the first subordinate section. Mainly, however, the dotted rhythm is not carried out strictly enough: it should be performed between ♩. ♬ and ♩.. ♬. Registration: HW, *Plenum*, with all the mixtures and with reeds; RP, brilliant; BW, like an echo of the RP. Tempo: ♩ = 96.

The *Fugue*, "with a glance now no longer turned toward earth, but upward as if toward heaven, sees the Trinity glorified" (Steglich). The remarkable form of the Fugue is not, as some scholars think, a reversion to the multisectional form of Buxtehude. It may be understood only in terms of its symbolism: there are three fugues with three subjects, and yet they are one, like the three persons of the Godhead. Here, in its expression of the ineffable, music has achieved something for which the plastic arts and poetry of all periods have striven in vain: a real representation of the Trinity through the medium of art.

The subject of the first fugue—and thus the principal subject of the whole work—has the pure and noble quality of the old *a cappella* music; we seem to hear a choir of human voices in a service of worship. The subject no longer touches the root of the tonic chord, but rises solemnly from the fifth to the octave. (Busoni felt that two fugue subjects in the *Well-Tempered Clavier* were preliminary stages in the development of our subject: those of the fugal section in the E♭ Major Prelude in Book I and of the E♭ Major Prelude in Book II.)

The second subject flows along serenely and meekly; it is joined by the first subject, which lifts it up and draws it to itself. The third subject, as if floating with outspread wings, is united presently with the first subject, each permeating the other most deeply. The second subject even seems to be implicated in the sixteenth notes:

Stretto has been kept in reserve to this point; now, in two strettos, the Fugue proceeds to the overwhelming height of the close, a height never at any time to be understood on the basis of its form but only from its spiritual content. The gradation of the meter from ¢ to 6/4 and then to 12/8 has a counterpart in the three Kyrie fughettas (see pp. 273f.).

Performance:

1st Section: HW, with a more mellow, more "vocal" *Plenum* than that used for the Prelude.
2nd Section: BW; from the combination of the two subjects on, the RP.
3rd Section: on the HW, coupled; with the same volume used for the Prelude.

Tempo: 1st Section, 𝅗𝅥 = 72 (with dignity, not fast); 2nd Section, ♩= 144; 3rd Section, ♩. = 72; i.e., the whole work as if in *one* tempo.[258]

258. See also Arthur Mendel, "A Note on Proportional Relationships in Bach Tempi," *The Musical Times* (Dec., 1959), pp. 683-685.

CHAPTER 15

COMPOSITIONS FOR ORGAN WITH ORCHESTRA

Many organists will be taken aback by this title, since Bach, of course, wrote no concertos for organ with orchestra. His cantatas, however, contain no less than 25 movements with obbligato organ. Sixteen of these are vocal movements; 9 are opening sinfonias. A chronological survey results in the following picture:

1. Cantata 71, *Gott ist mein König,* for the Inauguration of the Council in Mühlhausen on Feb. 4, 1708, contains a duet for soprano ("Soll ich auf dieser Welt mein Leben höher bringen") and tenor ("Ich bin nun achtzig Jahr") in which there is a free soprano part for the organ in addition to the b.c.
2. Cantata 47, *Wer sich selbst erhöhet, der soll erniedriget werden,* composed for Sept. 22, 1720, according to Spitta's conjecture,[259] contains a soprano aria, "Wer ein wahrer Christ will heissen," with b.c. and solo violin or obbligato organ.
3. Cantata 172, *Erschallet ihr Lieder,* composed for Pentecost (May 28), 1724, contains a duet for soprano and alto, "Komm, lass mich nicht länger warten," in which two independent instrumental parts are added to the two vocal parts: either for violin and 'cello or for *Organo obligato.* The organ ornaments the chorale "Komm heiliger Geist, Herre Gott," which is shortened somewhat.
4. Cantata 188, *Ich habe meine Zuversicht,* composed for the 21st Sunday after Trinity, October 29, 1730, or October 14, 1731, was to begin with the complete Concerto in D Minor for clavier (three movements), transcribed for organ. This transcription has not been preserved, however. During the course of the cantata the organ appears obbligato once more: with the alto aria "Unerforschlich ist die Weise."
5. Cantata 35, *Geist und Seele wird verwirret,* composed for the 12th Sunday after Trinity, August 12, 1731, contains in Part I both an introductory sinfonia and two alto arias with obbligato organ; in Part II, again an introductory sinfonia and an alto aria. Spitta[260] conjectures, probably correctly, that the two "symphonies" represent the outside movements of a lost concerto; and the first aria (A minor,

259. *Op. cit.,* II, 12f.
260. *Op. cit.,* II, 447.

6/8), as a *Siciliano*, its middle movement. (The first 9 measures of this concerto are reproduced in the BG, Vol. XVII, p. XX.)

6. Cantata 49, *Ich geh' und suche mit Verlangen,* composed for the 20th Sunday after Trinity, probably August 26, 1731, contains as introductory symphony the organistic, simplified third movement of the Concerto in E Major for clavier;[261] a bass aria, "Ich geh' und suche mit Verlangen," with b.c. and obbligato organ; and a closing duet for soprano (c.f., "Wie bin ich doch so herzlich froh") and bass ("Dich hab' ich je und je geliebet") with strings, *oboe d'amore,* and obbligato organ.

7. Cantata 29, *Wir danken dir, Gott,* composed for August 27, 1731, for the Inauguration of the Council in Leipzig, contains as opening symphony a transcription of the E Major Prelude for unaccompanied violin—transposed to D major—for string orchestra, 2 oboes, 3 trumpets, *timpàni,* and b.c. with obbligato organ; in addition, it has an aria, "Halleluja, Stärk' und Macht," for alto, b.c., and *Organo obligato,* which is identical with the major part of a previous tenor aria, except that it is set a fifth lower; in the alto aria the organ takes over the part of the solo violin in the tenor aria—a fourth higher, however.

8. Cantata 27, *Wer weiss, wie nahe mir mein Ende,* composed for the 16th Sunday after Trinity, September 9, 1731, contains an aria for alto, "Willkommen! will ich sagen, wenn der Tod an's Bette tritt," with *Oboe da caccia* and *Organo obligato* (reading thus following the part itself; in the original score it reads "*Cembalo obligato*").

9. Cantata 169 for alto, *Gott soll allein mein Herze haben,* composed for the 18th Sunday after Trinity, either September 23, 1731, or October 12, 1732, contains as introductory symphony with obbligato organ the first movement of the Concerto in E Major for clavier, transposed to D major. Two of the following alto arias have obbligato organ: the first, "Gott soll allein mein Herze haben," adds to the alto a florid part, apparently of free invention; the second, "Stirb in mir, Welt," is a remodelling of the *Siciliano* of the concerto mentioned above, transposed to B minor and expanded from 37 to 46 measures.

10. Cantata 170 for alto, *Vergnügte Ruh', beliebte Seelenlust,* composed for the 6th Sunday after Trinity, July 20, 1732, contains two arias with obbligato organ. The first, "Wie jammern mich doch die verkehrten Herzen," is without b.c.; in its place the violins and violas in unison form the lowest part; added to this are two florid parts for obbligato organ, to be performed *a 2 Clav.* The second

261. The Concerto in E Major for clavier was apparently not written till after the version for organ and orchestra, as its more elaborate writing shows; both versions, however, appear to go back to a vanished violin concerto (see the older variants of the second movement in the BG, Vol. XVII, p. 314).

aria, "Mir ekelt, mehr zu leben, drum nimm mich Jesu hin," calls for obbligato organ besides strings, b.c., and *oboe d'amore*.

11. Cantata 146, *Wir müssen durch viel Trübsal in das Reich Gottes eingehen,* written for Jubilate Sunday, probably of the year 1734, uses as introductory symphony the older version of the first movement of the D Minor Concerto for clavier, transposed for the most part an octave lower; whether this is the same version that had been used for Cantata 188 is not known. As opening chorus the second movement of the cantata ingeniously builds a four-part choral setting above the complete instrumental part of the second movement of the concerto (*Adagio,* G minor). Here also the solo part is set an octave lower.

And what is the upshot of all this?

It is clear that most of the questions arising concern the conductor of cantata performances and his organist rather than the independent organist. I have given as detailed and complete a list as possible, however, to arouse interest in performance of these pieces. The arias and particularly the instrumental movements are far too little known, and they are in part glorious pieces.

To begin with, we understand the disappointment of most Bach scholars with regard to the narrow limits set here for display of the organ. In none of the arias or duets does the organ have any more importance than any obbligato melody instrument. In Cantatas 47 and 172 it is indicated expressly as a substitute for a violin (wanting, for some reason). Only in Cantata 27 does the organ part exceed the compass of any of the melody instruments of the time; but it is important here that the movement was intended originally for the harpsichord. Is the organ then obliged to come forward with a tone that is rich and loud?[262]

Some of these trios for one vocal part and two organ parts sound equally as enchanting as the six trio sonatas for organ. But is the organ really to play only two parts? Isn't it also required to take over the b.c. simultaneously? The alto aria of Cantata 29 shows clearly that it is not obliged to do so: the figured *continuo* part appears in addition underneath the unfigured two-part setting for the obbligato organ. But even without this proof we could state with certainty that a performance of these movements on two manuals and pedal (as, for example, the Breitkopf & Härtel edition of Cantata 169 requires) would be in thoroughly poor taste—since the bass doesn't take the pedal of the organ into consideration at all. No, the organist has nothing to play other than his obbligato part; another player and another instrument (a harpsichord, perhaps) must be at hand for

262. Notice how Mozart, in the slow movements of his piano concertos, sometimes gives the piano a simple one-part melody, which the orchestra has to accompany.

realization of the b.c. If no other instrument can be procured, the realization of the "figuring" is omitted, just as it is omitted in the three-part movements of the six sonatas for violin and obbligato harpsichord, while it *is* performed whenever a movement of this kind is composed for three melody instruments; then the keyboard player has only to accompany, i.e., play the b.c. and realize its figures. In all matters of this sort the Baroque was governed far more by external circumstances than we are today.

A search has been made for the external reason that may have induced Bach to assign a large number of movements to the organ, particularly during the years 1730-1732. Bernhard Friedrich Richter occupied himself with this problem in the *Bach-Jahrbuch* for 1908.[263] He rejected the hypothesis set up by Rust and Spitta, that during these years the Thomas Church had acquired a new *Rückpositiv* playable independently; he believed, rather, that, because of the rebuilding of the Thomas School, the *Positiv* there could have been installed in the church for a few years.

But even earlier, Bach had required the organ obbligato, or permitted its alternate use, in Cantatas 71, 47, and 172. This fact escaped Richter, however, so that his interesting explanations are therefore not of basic importance for this problem.

It is indicative of the uniformity of Bach's style that he could venture to place movements from chamber music works or concertos at the head of his church cantatas as introductory symphonies. Since almost all of the clavier concertos are transcriptions of violin concertos, even in them the music for the clavier is frequently for only two parts: melody and bass. It is just the same, of course, in the additional arrangement for organ. The effect of some of these movements is nevertheless quite extraordinary. Nothing more brilliant was ever written for organ and orchestra than the famous overture to the Cantata for the Inauguration of the Council (No. 29). No movement from Handel's organ concertos can compare with it. The *perpetuum mobile* of the Prelude for unaccompanied violin is like a torrent of fire, entrusted to the organ. And how Bach transformed the seeming polyphony of the violin prelude into a real polyphony for large orchestra; how everything here blossoms and lives! We cannot concur with Spitta's restrictive judgment of this transcription.[264]

No less ingenious is the introductory movement of Cantata 146. How daring to bring the irresistible spirit of this concerto movement into an inner connection with the subject "Wir müssen durch viel Trübsal das Reich Gottes eingehen" through their programs! Perhaps even more to be admired, in the following introductory chorus, is the way a four-part choral setting is constructed around the em-

263. Pages 49-63, "Ueber Seb. Bachs Kantaten mit obligater Orgel."
264. *Op. cit.*, II, 449f.

bellished melody and the ostinato string accompaniment. A performance of this movement that will sound well is of course difficult to achieve, yet is most nearly achieved with a numerically small chorus. It is a great pity that the transcription of the third movement (see Cantata 188) no longer exists. If it did, we should have a D Minor Organ Concerto by Bach which would soon be resounding in many concert halls and churches.[265]

The introductory movement of Cantata 169 is quite different from these two large overtures. It is a piece of music of springlike grace. In it the organ is to be handled basically as in chamber music, since we are dealing with a solo cantata. The first two movements of the E Major Concerto for clavier are used here; the third movement is used in Cantata 49. If the three movements were brought into one uniform tonality (either E major or D major) we should have a second organ concerto with orchestra by Bach!

In contrast to the movements just mentioned, the introductory symphonies of Part I and Part II of Cantata 35 lag far behind in musical value. Viewed as a whole, however, in the 25 movements in which the organ appears obbligato either with voices or orchestra, a wide and as yet little-cultivated field is open to the organist.[266]

B. ARRANGEMENTS OF CHORALES

CHAPTER 16

MUSICAL LANGUAGE OF THE CHORALE PRELUDES

When we take the step from the free works of Bach to his arrangements of chorales we enter a world in which other laws besides the musical are valid. The arrangements of chorales are not absolute music, but are obligated primarily to the "word." This fact is basic to an understanding of both their style of expression and their types of form.

---

265. I am aware that the authenticity of the D Minor Concerto for clavier is in doubt. The philological considerations which have been advanced, however, do not, in my opinion, stand up against the convincing internal authenticity of this very work. If any one of Bach's clavier concertos was composed by him, it must have been this one!

266. Wolfgang Auler published several of these movements recently. (Mainz: Schott's Söhne).

Their place in the church service resulted automatically from the triple task assigned the organ in the Lutheran service of the baroque era: to "prelude," to "alternate," and to accompany.

Least interesting to both composer and organist was the four-part accompaniment of the congregational singing, a custom which was first adopted during the course of the seventeenth century. The prelude could be either a free organ work or one based on a chorale. With respect to the liturgy the latter naturally took precedence. It was not merely a servant of the liturgy, however, but left ample opportunity for free play of the imagination. When congregation (or choir) and organ were to perform the stanzas of a chorale alternately, only the organ chorale was considered, of course; this could also substitute for a free introduction to a hymn.

For the fulfillment of these various tasks German composers for the organ created three species of form: the "open" form of the *prelude fughetta* (usually on the first line of the melody); the "closed" forms of the *organ chorale* (i.e., one complete statement of the chorale melody—in any technique) and the *chorale fantasy* (which may be regarded as an extended organ chorale); and, as the third form, the "serial form" of the *chorale partita* (variations on the chorale patterned after secular folksong variations).

Of these forms, that of the organ chorale was by far the most important. One reason was that it could adapt itself to so many uses in the church service: it could introduce a hymn, play a stanza of a chorale *alternatim*, or serve "*sub communione*," i.e., as Communion chorale. In addition, its artistic possibilities were almost inexhaustible. It could be written for two parts (*bicinium*), for three, for four, or for more parts. The c.f. could remain in *one* voice throughout, or it could change from one to another. The melody could appear unornamented or embellished, etc. It is well known that Scheidt demonstrated all these formal possibilities in classical fashion in his cyclical variations on Evangelical hymns in the *Tabulatura Nova* (1624).[267] Now the aim was to bring greater life and spirit into the form.

The c.f. usually retains its "vocal" quality even in the organ chorale. The surrounding "instrumental" parts contrast with it in an artistically very happy and versatile manner. If the c.f. is unornamented and in large note values, as is usual in Scheidt and particularly in Pachelbel, it may be considered a symbol of the singing congregation: it stands forth, "objective," sacrosanct. When the remaining parts introduce a c.f. of this kind by imitating it in advance, line by line, they, too, symbolize the congregation. Individual voices lead in singing the chorale and establishing its prayerful mood until

267. And Sweelinck before him, as we have known since 1943.

the principal voice, as representative of the entire congregation, begins solemnly to intone it.

This style, found particularly in Pachelbel, has the advantage of close liturgical affiliation, but the disadvantage—sometimes clearly perceived—of artistic limitation. When the parts providing the counterpoint draw their thematic material from the c.f., but alter or paraphrase it, they are thus interpreting the chorale in a personal, subjective way until the leading part lifts us up dogmatically and objectively, so to speak, into the realm of inviolable truth. We are indebted to this fertile antithesis for a number of the most important works of Bach.

When the accompanying parts start out with motives quite independent of the c.f., progressing freely, the situation might be likened to that in which a clergyman begins his sermon by relating a personal experience and only later unexpectedly establishes its connection with his text.

If the c.f. itself is altered, that is to say, ornamented, then it, too, is drawn into the realm of the subjective. It loses its simplicity and clarity at the price of an expression which is personal and unique. In the music of the North Germans this form often had something superficial or trivial about it (Buxtehude's thirty small organ chorales, for example).[268] It was Bach who first raised it to its highest intellectual and spiritual level.

All the possibilities pointed out here were recognized in the seventeenth century, though at first only from the side of form. The composer was not yet obliged to reflect on the text or pretend to "express" it at all. It is therefore a mistake to try to set specific stanzas of text to the organ chorales of the pre-Bach period.

But mustn't the intellectual and emotional content of a hymn-tune necessarily have had an influence on the composition also? We are inclined to answer this question quite simply, "Yes." But we forget too easily that in so doing we are committing the error of conferring directly upon a melody the emotional content possessed by the text belonging to it. But that the melody alone, divorced from its text, can convey no definite character whatsoever, we shall understand easily if we bear in mind that texts of completely contrasting content were frequently set to one and the same melody. In the sixteenth century, for example, the Passion hymn "O Mensch, bewein dein' Sünde gross" ("O man, bewail thy grievous fall") and the Pentecostal hymn "Jauchz, Erd und Himmel, juble hell" ("Rejoice, earth and heaven, rejoice greatly") were sung to the same melody. Examples of this kind could be multiplied at will.

Within a hymn, also, the melody is obliged to keep at a certain neutral distance in relation to the changing content of the various

---

268. Spitta-Seiffert edition, Vol. 4.

stanzas. Only art music can reduce this distance by its various means and so interpret the melody that no one could possibly confuse an organ chorale on "O man, bewail thy grievous fall" with one on "Rejoice, earth and heaven, rejoice greatly."

It would exceed the scope of this work to trace the gradual enrichment and refinement of musical expression in the organ chorales from Scheidt to Bach. Music discovered first a fairly definite way of expressing sorrow or sadness; for example, Scheidt's chromatic setting of "Da Jesus an dem Kreuze stund" ("When on the cross the Savior hung").[269] In the second half of the seventeenth century the rapidly-growing refinement of instrumental expression, especially in violin music, was also transmitted to the organ chorale. The melismatic paraphrasing of the c.f. became more animated, and the harmony warmer and more pliable. A sixteenth-note motion, sustained throughout a work, could mean, in an *allegro*, an expression of constancy or joy. A certain reserve in tone and tempo could express devotion or mysticism. For a long time, however, all of these techniques remained very general and in no way binding. Not until after 1700 did the new "Doctrine of the Affections," just coming into vogue, require the composer to "take one emotion as his main objective"[270] in every melody. Frotscher[271] emphasizes quite correctly that by "affection" was meant "not sentiment or sentimentality in the romantic sense, but the sum of all the intellectual and spiritual powers . . . sensations such as elements of volition, such as ethical and religious feelings." When music wanted to translate into its own idiom such an "affection," which could be made known with perfect clarity only in the text, it had to set the stage deeper within and become "more an expression of feeling."[272]

In the cantata and the oratorio the relationship between text and music was expressed directly; important abstraction and absorption were required, however, before one could proceed in like manner with the purely imagined word in the organ chorale. The fact that in this art Bach remained "unique" (in both senses of the word) is to be attributed not only to the strength and depth of his personality, but also to the decline of the organ chorale after 1700. This was brought about by the undermining influence of the Enlightenment, which caused the form to sink rapidly to the level of an artisan's product.

After a century of rich development the organ chorale was gradually approaching a crisis. Its decline was arrested solely by the workmanlike diligence of Johann Gottfried Walther and the genius of

---

269. Peters 4393b, No. 5, pp. 28-35.
270. Mattheson, *op. cit.*, p. 145, par. 74.
271. *Op. cit.*, 902.
272. See Beethoven's comment on the title-page of his *Pastoral Symphony*, that this work was "more an expression of feeling than painting."

Johann Sebastian Bach. Otherwise, production, which had once been so plentiful, rapidly subsided.[273] Music detached itself from the church much as Beethoven, a scant hundred years later, in his symphonies emancipated himself from the social music of his time. In the midst of this notorious decline of the ecclesiastico-musical community life, Bach rescued the treasures of the Evangelical chorale by removing them from the clutches of fashion and preserving them for the little circle of "connoisseurs of work of this kind"[274] in a most artistic style unintelligible to the uninitiated.

His collections of chorales for the organ, therefore, have only a slight connection with the church service, even externally. A few decades earlier the German organ chorale would not have been conceivable without this association. The *Little Organ Book* was intended to serve the "beginning organist" as methodical instruction. The *Third Part of the Clavierübung* contained arrangements of a difficulty that far surpassed the technical ability of organists of around 1700. We may also ask what churchgoer of that period would still have been able to distinguish the chorale melody when it appeared in a form not readily intelligible even to a professional musician. If one contrasts the rationalistic shallowness of chorale-preludes by Telemann and others—which were therefore popular with congregations—with the depth of thought, the wealth of symbolism, and the emotional strength of Bach, the gap between the two worlds seems too wide to bridge.

For decades one of the most important aesthetic tasks connected with Bach has been that of investigating the wealth of these works in images, intellectual concepts, and symbolism, and of making them usable in practical way. Spitta had always avoided these problems, but Schweitzer—and almost simultaneously, André Pirro—proceeded to examine more carefully the dependence of Bach's idiom on the ideas supplied by the words. Schweitzer set up entire tables of motives: pictorial motives (step-, fall-, wave-motives, and others), "speaking" and "expressive" motives, etc. Even though some of Schweitzer's interpretations may seem contestable in details today, this path that has been trod so resolutely by the Alsatian and French students of Bach's aesthetics has led to an immeasurably clearer and more definite picture of Bach's music. In this way of thinking, of course, there lay the danger of sinking to the level of the *leitmotif* (see Luedtke's interpretations in the *Bach-Jahrbuch* for 1918). Research could not stand still, therefore, at the point reached by Schweitzer.

---

273. See "Orgelchoräle um J. S. Bach" in *Das Erbe deutscher Musik*—what evidence of incapability for Bach's period!

274. See the title-page of the *Third Part of the Clavierübung*, p. 268.

The period after the First World War sought to approach Bach from the point of view of the symbolism of numbers (Wilhelm Werker and Wolfgang Gräser). Schering's two articles on "Bach und das Symbol,"[275] however, were the first studies to take a definitive step beyond Schweitzer. Schering said of Bach's symbolism that it "is seldom a simple one, but tends to derive its kinetic energy and persuasive power from various superimposed intellectual fields of force."

The first essay dealt with the question of the canon as an artistic device in Bach. Schweitzer had not assigned it any importance. Schering contended that, in the uninterrupted striving of Western music for spiritualization, even the technique of the vocal canon had been raised to symbolical significance by Bach. In contrast to the earlier, purely artificial canonic technique (Fux), Bach had tried to express ideas in the text symbolically through the medium of canon; for example, "succession," "being joined together," "fulfillment of the law," and other similar concepts.

In the second article dealing with the "figurative" and the "metaphorical" in Bach, Schering investigated certain of Bach's stereotyped figures in respect to their connection with the rhetoric of the seventeenth and eighteenth centuries.[276] First came the "metaphorical" idiomatic expressions, under which Schering included all those which aspire to, or achieve, the power of picturization or illustration. "The nature of music offers unlimited possibilities for this, yet not all ages have made equal use of them." The metaphor is in detail what the symbol is in general: "a manner of expression which comprehends, along with the obvious and traditional, something secret and not obvious as well." Here Bach is perceived especially as an important representative of Rationalism. His production "was not nourished by a romantic frenzy of feeling; instead, he received his impulses from rational data. This sort of conception, foreign as it may appear to us in its manifestations and consequences, may in no case be put in competition with the romantic."

All these artistic devices establish relationships which can be well understood by the listener and yet not enter fully into the music. In the program symphonies of Berlioz and Liszt the program has meaning as an important part of the work of art, yet often runs along beside the music. The enjoyment and understanding of many of the large chorale preludes of Bach are also enriched by extra-musical associations of this kind. This fact does not make them easier to understand, however, but more difficult. "There arises that un-

275. *Bach-Jahrbücher* for 1925 and 1928 and, collectively, *Das Symbol in der Musik* (Leipzig: Köhler & Amelang, 1942).

276. Spitta also had something basic to say on this matter, *op. cit.*, I, 602ff.

pleasant feeling of there being more to be known and felt than understanding and feeling are capable of receiving simultaneously."

Moreover, the question as to which textual idea Bach had in mind is not always to be answered with certainty in an individual instance. In the organ chorale on "Alle Menschen müssen sterben" ("All men must die"), for example, the music expresses nothing of death or transitoriness. Did Bach then wish to express the bliss of the world to come in the floating rhythm of the counterpoint? Bach's music propounds riddles of this kind more than once; actually, a perfect solution can hardly be reached.

With the majority of the organ chorales, however, we stand on firm ground, for, as a rule, Bach singles out one idea from the profusion of possibilities and carries it through consistently, without mingling other ideas with it. The small organ chorales, especially those of the *Little Organ Book*, thus maintain a pictorial quality which seems to contradict the nature of music as a temporal art. They are not developed; they merely exist. They need to be understood as a whole first, and only then considered in the course of their parts.

However, to approach some of the large chorale preludes in the same manner is scarcely possible because of their dimensions; and their homogeneity affects one, on first hearing, not as a merit but as a defect. Once "wound up," however, they run off like an ingenious clockwork. Usually very great mental application and concentration on the entire melody are required in order not to allow the mind to tire or the attention lapse in listening to the marvelous fantasy "Komm, heiliger Geist, Herre Gott," with its nine phrases of the c.f. in the bass. In certain of Bach's large chorale arrangements, therefore, organists like particularly the very passages in which Bach himself digresses; i.e., gives up homogeneity of thematic development for the sake of expression of one line of text, as at the close of "O Lamm Gottes unschuldig," for example.

In order to attain an understanding of Bach's chorale arrangements for the organ, therefore, both the player and the listener must first of all be acquainted with the texts. Some of these may still be found in current hymnals. The organist who plays from the Peters edition may jot these down in his copy; best, as I have done in my editions,[277] above or below the c.f. The texts not generally familiar today (or at least their first stanzas) are included here.

Then the melody: how shall one recognize it from among the often widely digressing modifications, if one does not have it continually present in its plain form? We of today need years to become as well acquainted with some of these melodies as people obviously were in

277. *80 Chorale Preludes: German Masters of the 17th and 18th Centuries* (Peters No. 4448).

Bach's day. It is even better to have them at hand in a composition by Bach or one of the old masters. The editions of the writer, the *Orgelbüchlein* and the *Orgelchoräle Manualiter* (Bärenreiter), and the English edition of Bach published by Novello (London) meet this requirement.

But even with this acquaintance one can be helpless in the face of many organ chorales of Bach, if one does not understand their particular idiom. The first requirement is a conception of the form in general. It is usually easy to recognize. In addition, a recognition of the c.f. throughout all its forms and paraphrases is essential. This, of course, is less easy. In the following pages, therefore, the c.f. will be given in a musical illustration wherever it may seem necessary. The final requirement is a penetration into the meaning of this idiom and an understanding of its symbolism.

Understanding is facilitated for the audience when a setting of the chorale is sung in a public performance along with the organ chorale. Schweitzer was the first to place the two together. He always conceived the organ setting as a prelude to the chorale by the choir. This procedure is clear, yet when the organ chorale is not a prelude but an intellectual interpretation of the chorale itself, as is nearly always true of Bach's organ chorales, the reverse order is also possible: a presentation of the chorale in its plain, objective setting first, and then as "seen through a temperament."

Smaller organ chorales, which are individually too short, may be grouped together with other arrangements of the same melody, with other chorales of appropriate type, or with others proper for the same time of the church year. Such groupings have been attested since Bach's time.[278] For practical use in the church service only those are suitable, of course, whose melodies are still in use, and whose structure at least the educated person can understand today. Unfortunately these requirements are fulfilled by scarcely a third of Bach's organ chorales.

The youthful works are more easily understood by a congregation than those of the Leipzig period. The latter should not be used in a church service since they are arranged too artfully, and in addition lack the quality of a "prelude." At the beginning of a service a short, free prelude by Bach in the same tonality might precede one of the fairly short organ chorales. At Christmas, for example, one might group together the first movement of the Toccata in E Major and the chorale "Lobt Gott, ihr Christen allzugleich" (see p. 188). We organists must continue trying to bring the chorale preludes close to the congregation during the church service and in recital. How can they learn to understand them if they never have an opportunity to hear them, if these "treasures are never displayed"?

---

278. *Peters Jahrbuch* for 1904, p. 23.

CHAPTER 17

AUTHENTICITY AND CHRONOLOGY OF THE CHORALE PRELUDES

Nearly 150 arrangements of chorales are contained in Vols. V, VI, VII, and IX of the Peters edition; of these almost two-thirds are preserved in collections assembled originally by Bach himself. Hence, the authenticity of only about a third of these works comes into question. Since my new edition of Vol. IX (1940) has eliminated several spurious works, only two pieces need to be rejected from the present balance of the Peters edition as definitely not genuine. These are in Vol. VI: No. 1, "Ach Gott und Herr," and No. 24, "Gott der Vater, wohn uns bein." Their composer is Johann Gottfried Walther.

Until some fresh, reasonably certain clues are discovered, the question of authorship of a number of other pieces must be considered unclarified, even though Bach's authorship is probable for most of them: i.e., in Vol. V, No. 5 of the Appendix (p. 105); in Vol. VI, Nos. 21 and 28; in Vol. IX, Nos. 13, 15-17, 19-22, and 26.

It is equally difficult to establish a reliable chronology since, in all probability, even earlier (Weimar) works were admitted into the Leipzig collections. On the other hand, a classification set up according to the various types of form could be quite convincing; this, however, would break up the collections assembled by Bach himself: the *Third Part of the Clavierübung*, the *Eighteen Chorales*, etc.

We shall try to take a middle course by establishing a chronological order for the early works and dealing with their forms simultaneously. From the *Little Organ Book* on, however, the treatment will leave the autograph collections intact. The following picture results:

Partitas (Lüneburg, *ca.* 1702)
Arnstadt Congregational Chorales (Arnstadt, *ca.* 1705)
Introductory Fughettas (Arnstadt and Weimar)
Small Chorale Preludes (*Little Organ Book*, 1717)
Large Chorale Preludes handed down individually (Weimar)

The Leipzig Collections

The *Eighteen Chorales* (*ca.* 1715—*ca.* 1750)
The *Six Chorales* (the so-called "Schübler," composed 1728—1736; arranged, 1746)
The *Third Part of the Clavierübung* (1739)
The *Canonic Variations* (1746)

A classification by type of the forms which Bach cultivated is instructive primarily because it shows which forms he particularly favored:

1. Partitas: 4
2. Congregational Chorales: 7
3. Fughettas: 20
4. Chorale Fantasy: 1
5. Small Chorale Preludes; i.e., organ chorales without separation of the lines:
   a) *manualiter:* 5
   b) with pedal: 52 (46 of these in the *Little Organ Book*)
6. Large Chorale Preludes; i.e., organ chorales with their lines separated by interludes: 51
   a) c.f. unornamented ("vocal"); the counterpoints (c.p.) also unornamented and taken from the c.f.: 10
   b) c.f. unornamented; c.p. taken from the c.f. by "instrumental" paraphrase: 23
   c) c.f. ornamented; c.p. taken from the c.f. by paraphrase: 10
   d) c.f. unornamented; c.p. thematically independent of the c.f.: 8

Of these works—counting each variation comprised within a partita individually—7 are 2-part; 40, 3-part; 97, 4-part; 22, 5-part; and 1, 6-part.

The chorale melody appears in the soprano 63 times; in the alto, 5 times; in the tenor, 15 times; and in the bass, 15 times. It changes register 8 times; and in 14 pieces the c.f. is treated canonically.

CHAPTER 18

CHORALE PARTITAS AND CHORALE FANTASIES

The chorale partitas of the seventeenth and eighteenth centuries transferred to the chorale the technique and style of the secular song variations and, accordingly, were intended more for music-making in the home than for the congregational church service, more for the clavichord or the *Positiv* than for the large church organ. Usually the pedal was not required at all, or at most only in the last variation, and Bach's partitas were the first to presuppose a performance on two manuals.

This delicate and subtle art form sprang ultimately from the English virginal music of the sixteenth century, but Sweelinck, with his famous variations on "Mein junges Leben hat ein End,"[279] may properly be regarded as its originator. Scheidt treated only secular melodies in this technique,[280] and separated these pieces strictly from his arrangements of sacred *cantus firmi*.

Pachelbel transferred the secular partita technique to the chorale for the first time in his *Musikalische Sterbensgedanken*,[281] published in 1683. In contrast to the highly developed techniques of Sweelinck and Scheidt, Pachelbel's moderate craftsmanship in his partitas signified a marked decline. Georg Böhm first brought new life to the *genre*, and J. S. Bach followed him directly.

It was, in part, borrowed forms which were to instill new life into the partita. The suite had its influence, as witness the variations in the style of *allemande*, *courante*, and *sarabande* in Buxtehude's "Auf meinen lieben Gott."[282] Even the influence of the Neapolitan operatic aria was noticeable.

In Böhm and Bach the first variation is usually for two parts, like a coloratura aria with thorough-bass. It resembles the Neapolitan aria *ca.* 1700 in that the beginning of the melody is intoned briefly, whereupon an interlude follows, and only then is the beginning repeated and the melody continued. Riemann called this type the "motto aria" ("Devisen-Arie") because the beginning of the theme was set up like a "motto." But this stylistic peculiarity probably had a secular basis. In the theater, the very beginning of a vocal piece was often missed by the audience during the general inattention, and it was desired to give the singer an opportunity to start again when the house was quieter! Applied in the field of church music, however,—and some of Bach's arias are so considered—and ultimately in an arrangement of a chorale for the organ, this custom had an utterly absurd effect.

The only composer besides Bach to give this form a greater impetus was Lübeck, with his magnificent, but unfortunately unfinished, partita with obbligato pedal on "Nun lasst uns Gott den Herren."[283] Bach cultivated this form only in his youth and under the immediate influence of Böhm; aside from Bach, J. G. Walther also wrote partitas. The chorale partita began to decline soon after 1700 just as, of course, the *Positiv* as an independent instrument also died out rapidly in the eighteenth century.

---

279. *Alte Meister*, ed. Straube, No. 27, p. 77.
280. Samuel Scheidt, *Ausgewählte Werke für Orgel und Klavier*, ed. Hermann Keller. (Peters No. 4393b) Section IV.
281. Modern edition: Bärenreiter No. 1016.
282. Spitta-Seiffert edition, Vol. IV, No. 31.
283. Vincent Lübeck, *Orgelwerke*, ed. Hermann Keller (Peters No. 4437), No. 8, p. 45.

It is interesting to compare Bach's Partitas with those of Böhm.[284] Despite very great similarities,[285] it will be noticed how much more careful Bach's writing is than the often slapdash, "sloppy" (to use Bach's expression) work of Böhm. Only in Bach's first two Partitas does the first simple statement of the chorale use "handfuls" of notes indiscriminately, as does Böhm's "Ach wie flüchtig, ach wie nichtig." In the rest of the Partitas one finds scarcely any parallel intervals; only one set of chromatic parallel fifths, in fact, in the penultimate measure of "Christ, der du bist der helle Tag." I suspect, therefore, that Bach later touched up all the Partitas. We know that he revised "Sei gegrüsset, Jesu gütig," but it is probable that he revised the first two, as well.

In the Partitas another question is of greater interest than the reminiscences of Böhm. It is whether Bach's style was not already influenced by the text. We notice this tendency in only a few places. It is a long way from the Partitas to the *Little Organ Book!*

The last two variations of "O Gott, du frommer Gott" seem quite clearly to be representing the text of the corresponding stanzas of the hymn; as do—although less clearly—the last two variations of "Christ, der du bist der helle Tag." An English Bach scholar[286] made an attempt to interpret the first Partita in its entirety in terms of musical symbolism. Thus, he sees expressed in the soprano of the first variation, for example, "the prayer for God's assistance"; in the winding figures of the bass, "the wily Satan"; at the end, "the soul ascends to its peace, and the serpent sinks into the abyss," etc. As ingenious as this interpretation may be, one is obliged to remark that "If one can't get anything out of a work, one can read something into it." I believe that only during the course of a long inner development did Bach arrive at a musical idiom of a kind that is more precisely explainable.

How ought one to perform the Partitas? They are ideally suited to a *Positiv*, and Busoni gave a striking demonstration of how closely they are related to piano music in his inclusion of three variations from the first Partita (nos. 1, 2, and 7) in his *Fantasy after J. S. Bach;* in this there is no noticeable breach between Bach's style and Busoni's piano style. They might even be played on a large organ by using the tone sparingly; i.e., with *Positiv* registration—in other words, with characteristic foundation-stops, delicately colored here and there with mutations; a *Plenum* (mild) would be used only for the final variation.

---

284. See *Sämtliche Werke*, ed. J. Wolgast; Vol. I, *Klavier und Orgelwerke* (Leipzig: Breitkopf & Härtel, 1927), pp. 74ff.

285. Ernst Isler in the *Schweitzerische Musikzeitung*, 1930, No. 22, p. 728.

286. Rutland Boughton, *Bach, the Master: A New Interpretation of His Genius* (New York and London: Harper & Brothers, 1930).

1. Partite diverse sopra "Christ, der du bist der helle Tag"
Various partitas on "O Christ, Thou art the light of day"
(V, pp. 60-67; BWV 766)

Here Bach calls each individual variation "partita." The seven partitas correspond to the seven stanzas of the hymn, a German translation of the mediaeval evening-hymn "Christe, qui es lux et dies."

Christ, der du bist der helle Tag,	O Christ, Thou art the light of day
Vor dir die Nacht nicht bleiben mag,	Before which night must needs give way;
Du leuchtest uns vom Vater her	Thou shinest down from Heaven's height
Und bist des Lichtes Prediger.	And art the Preacher of the Light.
Erasmus Alber, *ca.* 1556.	*Tr.* Henry S. Drinker.

The naive "full-fisted" clavier setting of the chorale at the beginning will sound well only when played without pedal. The 2nd partita—i.e., the 1st variation—should be played with deep, intimate expression. It requires two manuals, although no instructions to this effect appear in the sources. Even three manuals may be used, in fact, if one does not wish to bring about the change from *f* to *p* by opening and closing the expression pedal.

The 4th partita (variation 3) bears a striking resemblance to the 3rd partita of Böhm's "Ach wie nichtig."[287] The 5th partita (variation 4) brings the c.f. in the tenor. The BG suggests playing it in the pedal with 8'; in order to do so, however, one would have to omit the ornamentation. In one manuscript the c.f. is assigned to a manual of its own, and the bass given to the pedal.

The 6th partita (variation 5) depicts the ascending and descending angels with gently undulating triplets. In the last partita the descending "tied" motives represent the "closing eyes," while the second section rings out in praise of the "Holy Trinity." In this variation a reed may be used for the pedal bass, which is added to strengthen the manual bass.

287. *Sämtliche Werke*, ed. Wolgast, Vol. I, pp. 73ff.

2. Partite diverse sopra "O Gott, du frommer Gott"
Various partitas on "O God, Thou Faithful God"
(V, pp. 68-75; BWV 767)

Here Bach employs a less familiar melody[288] (Hanover, 1646) used with the hymn. The 8 stanzas may be placed under the 9 partitas if no words are applied to the first plain setting. It seems certain that the 8th partita (variation 7) in its yearning chromaticism—the most expressive found in the early works of Bach— is an interpretation of stanza 7:

Lass mich an meinem End Auf Christi Tod abscheiden	Let nothing that may chance, Me from my Savior sever;

The last, greatly extended variation is quite as clearly a musical setting of the last stanza:

	Wann du die Toten wirst	And when the Day is come,
	An jenem Tag aufwecken,	And all the dead are waking,
	Wollst du auch deine Hand	Oh reach me down Thy hand,
	Nach meinem Grab ausstrecken	Thyself my slumbers breaking;
	Lass hören deine Stimm,	Then let me hear Thy voice,
	Und meinen Leib weck auf	And chance this earthly frame,
(Andante)	Und führ ihn schön verklärt	And bid me aye rejoice
(Presto)	Zum auserwählten Hauf.	With those who love Thy name.
	Johann Heermann, 1630.	*Tr.* Catherine Winkworth.

Bach has here transformed the beginning of the first phrase into a fanfare, which calls the dead from their graves and resounds from the ends of the earth:

The change of time from *Andante* to *Presto* is found also at the end of Böhm's Partita "Wer nur den lieben Gott lässt walten."[289] In gen-

288. Brahms's chorale prelude, Op. 122, No. 7, is based on this chorale tune.
289. *Sämtliche Werke*, ed. Wolgast, Vol. I, pp. 143ff.

eral the influence of Böhm is greater in this Partita than in Bach's first Partita, especially in the intolerable stretching and picking-apart of the c.f. in the 1st variation. In the 6th variation the music depicts the "vigorous steps" of the earthly pilgrim; in the 5th variation, the bass:

expresses the gesture of the hands stretched out imploringly; in the remaining variations the relation to the text is weaker. Frotscher evaluates this Partita in detail.[290]

3. Partite diverse sopra il Chorale "Ach, was soll ich Sünder machen?"
Various partitas on the Chorale "What shall I, a sinner, do?"
(IX, 26; BWV 770)

Ach, was soll ich Sünder machen?	What shall I, a sinner, do?
Ach, was soll ich fangen an?	Whither shall I turn for aid?
Mein Gewissen klagt mich an	Conscience waking brings to view,
Und beginnet aufzuwachen.	Sins that make me sore afraid.
Dies ist meine Zuversicht:	This my confidence shall be,
Meinen Jesum lass ich nicht.	Jesus, I will cleave to Thee.
Johann Flittner, 1661.	*Tr.* Catherine Winkworth

This Partita came to light in Switzerland during the period when Spitta was writing his biography, and he was the first to describe it.[291] It was not included in the Peters edition till 1940, and for this reason had remained unknown to many organists until then. To judge by both external and internal evidence,[292] it may pass for a work of Bach quite as well as the first two Partitas.

In spite of its "full-fisted" part-writing, which is far from strict, partita 1 has nevertheless been cleansed most carefully of parallel

290. *Op. cit.*, pp. 907ff.
291. *Op. cit.*, I, 211, fn. 45.
292. Besides the Swiss MS it is authenticated by a copy made by Krebs.

octaves. Partita 2 has its immediate prototype in the 2nd partita of Böhm's "Ach wie nichtig." Examples of the florid writing of the following variations also can be found easily in Böhm as well as in Bach's first two Partitas. The last two variations are more especially "North German": a rapturous-mystical *sarabande* and a long chorale fantasy (cf. "Christ lag in Todesbanden," VI, No. 15).

4. *Partita on "Sei gegrüsset, Jesu gütig," Partita on "Thee I greet, Thy love I treasure"*

(V, pp. 76-91; BWV 768)

Sei gegrüsset, Jesu gütig,	Thee I greet, Thy love I treasure,
Über alles Mass sanftmütig!	Tender far beyond all measure.
Ach, wie bist du so zerschmissen	Ah, how Thou wert mutilated,
Und dein ganzer Leib zerrissen!	All Thy body lacerated!
Lass mich deine Lieb ererben	Grant that I Thy love inherit,
Und darinnen selig sterben.	When I die, Thy blessing merit.
Christian Keimann, 1663.	*Tr.* Henry S. Drinker.

This is the most important Partita of the entire literature for organ. It is so different in appearance from the first three that we see at first glance that it must have been greatly revised later—probably for the last time in Weimar. At the very beginning the four-part chorale setting differs noticeably from the "full-fisted" settings of the first Partitas. Settings like this one, however, which we are accustomed to call merely "Bach chorales," Bach did not use before 1713, even in his cantatas. The final completion of the Partita, therefore, ought probably to be assigned to Bach's last Weimar period. The stylistic breach between the first variations and the pedal variations, which were composed afterwards, is unmistakable and places the artistic unity of the work seriously in question. The source material confirms this judgment.

One of the numerous manuscripts, probably the oldest, contains only four variations; *viz.*, 1, 2, 4, and 10. Variation 10 has a pedal part, of course, but nevertheless was probably written before the Weimar period. Two reasons may be given for this judgment. As a *sarabande*, it is closely related to the penultimate variation of "Ach, was soll ich Sünder machen." In addition, it is written for five parts with two sopranos in the manner of Tunder.

A Königsberg manuscript shows the text of the Communion hymn "O Jesu, du edle Gabe" under the music; it also brings the variations in a somewhat different order, although the first four are grouped together again, as above: 1, 2, 4, 10, 3, 5, 7, 11, 9, 6, and 8. In fact, the long pedal point at the end of the 8th variation permits the conjecture that Bach intended the work to end here. This, however, could have been only at a time when variation 11 was not yet composed. In short, it appears impossible to distinguish any organic plan of construction in this work which was revised so many times. It is quite as impossible, of course, to place specific stanzas under the individual variations. Luedtke[293] tried it—with both hymns—but without coming to any very convincing conclusions. Nevertheless, it would not seem impossible that Bach was thinking of stanza 6 of "O Jesu, du edle Gabe" when he wrote the ponderously mounting thirty-second notes of the 6th variation (c.f. in the bass). This reads:

Wenn die Höll' mich will verschlingen	When hell's fire, encircling slowly,
Und mit ihrem Feur umringen,	Threatens to consume me wholly,
Dein Blut, Jesu, mich verbirget	Thy blood, Jesus, me concealing,
Und all diese Feind erwürget.	And to all hell's fiends death dealing,
Dein Blut mich von Sünden wäschet	Of my sins removes all traces
Und der Höllen Glut auslöschet.	And the glow of hell effaces.

Tr. H. H.

According to both the majority of the manuscripts and the internal organization, variations 6 and 7 of the Peters edition should be reversed. In its rich coloratura the first variation shows a significant development beyond the first three Partitas. "Echo" effects are given up, and the long-drawn-out lines have become more animated. The ecstatic rhythm in the 8th variation seems to express the joy in heaven ("Wenn ich werde hingerücket," stanza 8 of "O Jesu, du edle Gabe"). The five-part conclusion *in Organo pleno* is masterful. Here every association with the old partita for *Positiv* has been abandoned.

One curious work, whose documentation is unreliable, may be mentioned in connection with the Partitas:

293. *Bach-Jahrbuch* for 1918, pp. 47-53.

Aus der Tiefe rufe ich (IX, 16; BWV 745)
From the depths to Thee I call

"The chorale appears at first in a 'full-fisted' setting for manuals alone. This is followed, as in 'Christ, der du bist der helle Tag,' by a single complete statement of the c.f., the background for this being almost romantic. Nevertheless, the piece clearly shows features of Bach's early style (cf. 'Christ lag in Todesbanden,' Peters VI, No. 15). Even in spite of all its immaturity I should not know who else should receive credit for this impassioned musical style." (See my Preface to Vol. IX.)

The only independent chorale fantasy in North German style also shows an inner connection with the Partitas and is from the same period. This work is:

Christ lag in Todesbanden
In death's strong grasp the Savior lay
(VI, No. 15; BWV 718)

Organists do not play this curious but peculiarly beautiful piece very often. It is true that one would hardly think of Bach as its composer. To judge by its style one might suppose its composer to be Böhm; to judge by its form, a composer from the circle around Buxtehude.[294]

The first two lines of the chorale are presented at first in two parts (as in the corresponding variations of the Partitas), with the melody ornamented and with an introduction somewhat like a thorough-bass; then in three parts with advance imitation.

---

294. Fritz Dietrich gives a detailed analysis of this piece in the *Bach-Jahrbuch* for 1929, pp. 7-12.

The "fantasy" style begins only in the second section of the chorale: the fifth line of the hymn is spun out in mm. 27-33; the sixth is treated in triplet rhythm, mm. 33-42; the echo at the end of this line introduces a development of the seventh line, in echo style, which comprises some twenty measures, and which treats the first half of this line at first, and then the second:

By this division the line was torn apart in the middle of a word, but breaks of this kind were an everyday occurrence in the North German fantasy.

The last line, "Hallelujah," presents the chorale three times in large note-values without coloration, after the manner of Bruhns; for example, his "Nun komm der Heiden Heiland."[295] Here, however, the chorale notes are surrounded by sixteenth notes.[296] The final statement is in the pedal. Here, the manner in which the work struggles through from a rapturous mood to real grandeur creates a beautiful effect. The way the right hand is called upon, at the end, to restrike the tonic which is already being held in the pedal is a curious feature and suggests performance on the harpsichord.

CHAPTER 19

THE ARNSTADT CONGREGATIONAL CHORALES

To the young organist of the Church of St. Boniface in Arnstadt, the development of his skill and the free play of his ability in the toccata and the fugue may, in the beginning, have seemed more important than did the organ chorale. Moreover, he dumfounded his congregation by his youthfully ingenious harmonizations of the chorales. When in March, 1706, he had to account for having overstayed

295. *Orgelwerke;* No. 4.
296. Even these embellish the line:

The marking *"piano"* in this measure is wanting in the BG.

by nearly three months the leave of absence he had been granted for the journey to Lübeck, he was also reproved "for having hitherto made many odd variations in the chorale, and blended with it many strange tones, so that the congregation became confused by this. In the future he must, when he wishes to introduce a *tonus peregrinus*, maintain it and not interrupt it too quickly with something else, or, as has been his habit up till now, even play a *tonus contrarius*."[297] The student Rambach then stated further that "the organist Bach had hitherto played somewhat too long, but after he had received a note from the Superintendent about this, he had immediately gone to the other extreme and made it too short."

Probably none of us, his associates in the craft, will be able to refrain from a certain wry pleasure when we read this reprimand which our greatest colleague received and had to swallow! We have no choice but to show our high respect for the expert knowledge of music theory possessed by the Consistory of the Count of Schwarzburg, but we don't even know for certain what they meant by a *tonus "peregrinus"* or *tonus "contrarius."*

In contrast to other commentators I suspect that by *"tonus"* they meant tonality: if he wished to touch upon a foreign tonality, then he must remain in it and not leave it again immediately or even select harmonies that do not fit the tonality of the melody at all. That this censure was justified we see from some of Bach's chorale harmonizations that have been preserved by some lucky chance. These are so daring, in fact, that one would have to admire a congregation that could sing to them. Their harmonies are unique within all the works by Bach based on chorales; on the other hand, the interludes between the lines, with their runs in thirty-second notes, follow a use—or, we might better say, abuse—of the period. This treatment was repressed for the first time toward the end of the eighteenth century and finally disappeared completely during the nineteenth century.

The most interesting fact about these works is that Bach took them as a starting-point for works based on chorales, in which a singing congregation was no longer taken into consideration, yet which still clearly show their derivation from the congregational chorale. It is striking that, as in the fughettas, Christmas hymns predominate here also. There are six[298] settings of this kind in all; in performance they all require the *Plenum* of the *Hauptwerk*.

---

297. Cf. *The Bach Reader*, p. 52.

298. For four of these, sketches something like figured basses have come down to us, but were not included in the Peters edition. (See the BG, XL, pp. 158ff.)

Allein Gott in der Höh sei Ehr
All glory be to God on high
(IX, 14; BWV 715)

A setting which fairly "swarms" with "*tonis peregrinis et contrariis.*" Notice the sixth line, for example; this is harmonized almost completely with diminished-seventh chords! Similarly,

Gelobet seist du, Jesu Christ
All praise to Jesus' hallowed name
(V, Appendix, No. 1; BWV 722)

with the bold deceptive cadence at the end of the first line. Further (handed down in defective condition):

Herr Jesus Christ, dich zu uns wend
Lord Jesus Christ, be present now!
(IX, No. 18; BWV 726)

The following work goes an important step farther:

Lobt Gott, ihr Christen allzugleich
Let all together praise our God
(V, Appendix, No. 6; BWV 732)

Here, in the very first line the exultant attack is treated as a motive by all the voices. The interlude between the first and second lines is kept polyphonic beneath the sustained melody tone. In the third line an ecstatic soprano voice soars above the c.f. In short, a brilliant organ chorale of great originality has grown out of an accompaniment for the congregation.

In dulci jubilo
(V, Appendix, No. 3; BWV 729)

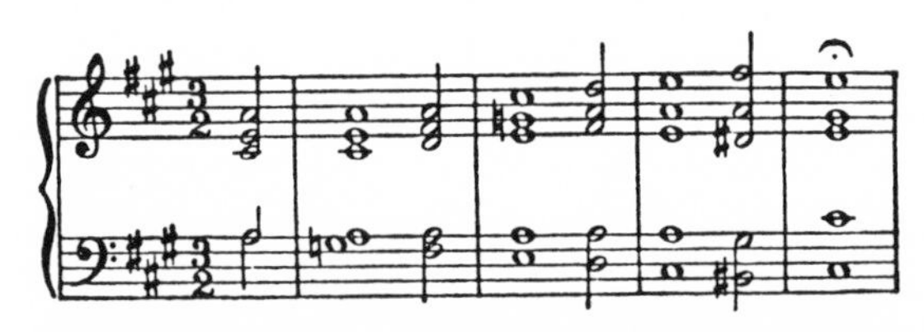

Here the eighth-note (and later the triplet) rhythm of the interludes streams through the massed chords of the chorale as if in exuberant jubilation, and resolves them. The pedal probably drops out from m. 23 to m. 38. Should the tenor in m. 3 actually read g♯? The BG cautiously puts f♯ instead, but the original g♯ seems more in keeping with the ingenuity of these settings.

Vom Himmel hoch, da komm ich her
From heaven above to earth I come
(V, Appendix, No. 7; BWV 738)

Here the rhythm of sextuplets, carried out uniformly, permeates the chorale setting from the very beginning. Only the monophonic interludes, in which the angels of Christmas Eve ascend and descend, still suggest derivation from a congregational chorale. Along with this formal restraint the harmony is also held within normal limits. The fact that the conception of the groups of sixteenths alternates repeatedly between and gives the rhythm of this piece a special drive.

We should mention in this connection the only sketch of an accompaniment for congregational singing that we have by Bach from a later period: the strictly five-part accompaniment—probably having originated in Weimar—for

Herr Gott, dich loben wir
Lord God! our praise we give
(VI, 26; BWV 725)

Luther's German translation of the Old Church *Te Deum laudamus*. We can see both from the presence of an accompaniment and from its type how foreign the monophonic Gregorian chant had become to Bach's generation. How slowly this exultant antiphony of two monophonic choirs must have been sung by the Weimar congregation; how heavily the five-part harmonies cling to the melody! At the same time, Bach does not accomplish the thing easily: everywhere he is trying to follow the text in his musical idiom, as when he has a vibrant eighth-note motion begin at "All Engel und Himmelsheer" ("To Thee all angels cry aloud; the Heavens, and all the Powers therein"), or introduces a fervent chromaticism at "Nun hilf uns, Herr, den Dienern dein" ("We therefore pray Thee, help Thy servants. . . ."). In spite of its many beauties, however, this setting may be used neither for accompanying a congregation nor as an organ chorale.

CHAPTER 20

CHORALE FUGHETTAS, CHORALE FUGUES, AND CHORALE TRIOS

a) CHORALE FUGHETTAS

The South German organists had solved the problem of "handling the chorale singing by having a thematic prelude precede it,"[299] by using as introduction a fughetta on the first line or sometimes even the first two lines of the hymn. Pachelbel brought this technique to Central Germany, where Johann Christoph Bach elevated it to his favorite form in his *44 Choräle zum Praeambulieren*. His fughettas, however, are still on a very modest level of professional ability, and certainly many an organist at that time improvised better and more imaginatively.

Then Commer published three small fughettas in his *Musica Sacra* under the name of J. S. Bach. These agree closely as to form with the fughettas of Johann Christoph, but are more flexible in their style. It is therefore not impossible that we have before us the earliest of Bach's youthful works. He could have composed them under the influence of his uncle, possibly soon after leaving Eisenach, hence probably in Ohrdruf, between his eleventh and fourteenth years. Because they were not sufficiently authenticated, they failed to find acceptance either in the Peters edition or in the BG. From what source Commer obtained them is not known to me.

I included two of these fughettas in my *Kunst des Orgelspiels*[300] as practice pieces for beginners. It is disconcerting that the first of these is entitled "Nun ruhen alle Wälder," since this text does not appear elsewhere among Bach's works. The beginnings are as follows:

299. Frotscher, *op. cit.*, p. 510, "die Choralgesänge vorhero thematice praeambulando zu tractiren."
300. Peters No. 4517, pp. 30 and 31.

Nun ruhen alle Wälder (BWV 756)
Now all the woods are sleeping

Herr Jesu Christ, dich zu uns wend (BWV 749)
Lord Jesus Christ, be present now!

Herr Jesu Christ, mein's Lebens Licht (BWV 750)
Lord Jesus Christ, Light of my life

The earliest fughettas of Bach identified positively may have originated in Weimar. The influence of Walther may not be considered here, however, since he almost never wrote in the form of the prelude fughetta. It is also curious that these pieces are almost exclusively preludes on Advent or Christmas hymns. The expressive counterpoints are noteworthy, and the fughettas acquire their characteristics from them rather than from the chorale melody. In

Gottes Sohn ist kommen (V, 20; BWV 703)
Once He came in blessing

(3-pt, *manualiter*)

a motive in sixteenths hovers about the pastoral c.f. In

Nun komm, der Heiden Heiland (V, 43; BWV 699)
Savior of the nations, come

the countersubject is derived from the c.f.:

and thus enhances the delicate charm of this piece. In

Lob sei dem allmächtigen Gott (V, 39; BWV 704)
To God we render thanks and praise

(3-pt, *manualiter*)
(for the text, see p. 202)

Bach transforms the c.f. into the dance rhythm of 3/2 meter and adds to it a counterpoint frankly enthusiastic. In

Herr Christ, der einig Gottes Sohn (V, 23; BWV 698)
O Thou, of God the Father

(3-pt, *manualiter*)

a countersubject appears together with the c.f.;[301] in mm. 11-13 the second line of the chorale is added to these two, all three voices being in stretto; in mm. 15 and 16 the first line is "diminished" and the second line similarly shortly afterwards:

301. Cf. Zachow, "Jesu, meines Lebens"; Alberti, "Herzlich lieb hab ich dich" (*80 Chorale-Preludes*, Nos. 40 and 46, Peters No. 4448).

In

Gelobet seist du, Jesu Christ (V, 18; BWV 697)
All praise to Jesus' hallowed name

(4-pt, *manualiter*)

the subject appears no less than 12 times within 14 measures, always accompanied by the same descending scale motive—symbol of the Son of God descending to earth—so that episodes are completely lacking.

In

Christum wir sollen loben schon (V, 7; BWV 696)
Now must we Jesus laud and sing
or
Was fürchtst du, Feind Herodes, sehr?
Herod, why dreadest thou a foe?

(4-pt, *manualiter*)

Bach appears to have composed with the alternative hymn in mind, to judge by the vigorous rhythmical treatment and the harmonization. The counterpoint is taken from the eighth-note ending of the c.f. Here, also, as in the preceding fughetta, the pedal might take over the final entry.

One may use foundation stops as registration for the first two of these little fughettas, the *Plenum* of a subordinate manual for the last four.

Two additional fughettas with obbligato pedal are probably not by Bach.

Das Jesulein soll doch mein Trost (IX, 17; BWV 702)
The Christ Child shall be still my Hope

although contained in Kirnberger's collection and authenticated by other copies, is a stiff, ungrateful setting, which develops the first two lines of the hymn in stretto from the very beginning. In addition:

Der Tag, der ist so freudenreich
This day, so rich in joy and love
(BG XL, 55; not in Peters; BWV 719)

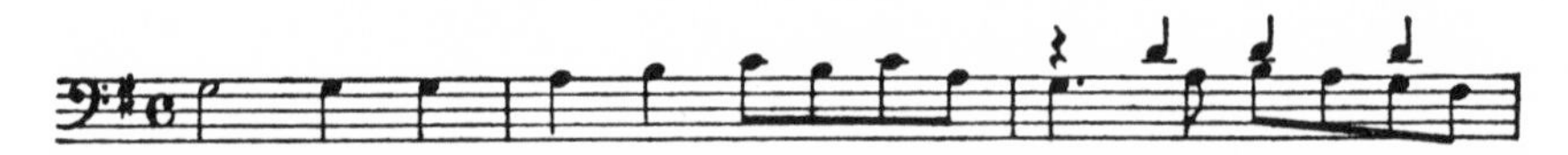

The only source for this fughetta is the collection *Chorales Which May Be Used as Preambles during the Divine Service, Composed and Published by Johann Christoph Bach, Organist in Eisenach.*[302] Two fughettas, on the first and the second lines, are here linked together by a three-measure transition.

We may consider the Weimar fughettas studies in a form that Bach seemed to drop all at once or at least discontinue for a long time apparently unused. Not till the period of his greatest maturity and mastery did he revert to this form to imbue it with its highest spiritual quality in the eight small settings in the *Third Part of the Clavierübung* (see p. 268).

One additional isolated fughetta shows so many traits of the late master-period that we should like to accept it as having been composed in Bach's last creative period (perhaps as a preliminary study for the *Canonic Variations?*). It is the fughetta on

Vom Himmel hoch, da komm ich her (VII, 54; BWV 701)
From heaven above to earth I come

302. *Choräle, welche bei währendem Gottesdienst zum Präambulieren gebraucht werden können, gesetzet und herausgegeben von Joh. Christoph Bachen, Organ. in Eisenach.*

A countersubject consisting of scale passages appears against the first line of the c.f. (in quarter notes), a treatment similar to that in the fughetta on "Gelobet seist du, Jesu Christ" and other Christmas chorales. Added to this, the second and third lines (in eighths) appear in artistic strettos that are mastered with astonishing ease. This treatment continues until the homophonic turn at the end almost craftily dissolves the magic.

Performance: bright, light foundation-stops, 8', 4', and 2'; ♩ = 96.

b) CHORALE FUGUES AND CHORALE TRIOS

In three of his Weimar works Bach expanded the chorale fughetta into the chorale fugue. (By "fugue" we do not mean an organ chorale with a fugal introduction of each line, but a fugue which is free in construction and whose subject is taken from a chorale.) All three show such a magnificent flow of invention that one would like to suppose they were improvisations that were written down.

The fugue on

Allein Gott in der Höh sei Ehr (VI, 11; BWV 716)
All glory be to God on High

(3-pt)

is so constructed that, after a short exposition of the first line, the second appears in a form that one does not immediately grasp:

and in the third section both lines appear together in an unforced stretto (the second line with slight changes), to which the first two lines are added as a c.f. in the pedal in large note values. Registration, a *Plenum;* at the end, strong pedal-reeds. The writer plays the last entry of the c.f. in the soprano an octave higher (from eight measures before the end through the first quarter of the penultimate measure). The tempo, a spirited allegro (𝅗𝅥 = 126-138).

The

Fuga sopra il Magnificat (VII, 41; BWV 733)

(5-pt)

is quite as fluent and as easily contrived as the preceding, but far surpasses it in technique and in the way it takes shape. Its subject is Mary's Hymn of Praise in St. Luke I, vv. 46 and 47:

Mei - ne Seel er-hebt den Her - ren, und mein Geist freut sich Gott's mei-nes Hei - lands.

Its stirring counterpoint resembles that of the fughetta on "Lob sei dem allmächtigen Gott." From the floods of fantasy the subject emerges only here and there, twice in stretto. (For these strettos a pedal with 8' pitch may assist.) Bach keeps the pedals in reserve for some time; finally they present the c.f. in whole notes. From this entry on, the fugue takes a fresh, powerful impetus and proceeds to its magnificent ending. The chorale theme disappears from the manual once the pedal has begun to speak.

A sparkling *Plenum* of the *Hauptwerk* without reeds, a pedal *Plenum* with reeds, a lively tempo (𝅗𝅥 = 84), and a firm, masculine rhythm are the indispensable requirements for a performance of this delightful piece.

The third fugue, on "Wir glauben all an einen Gott" (VII, 60), combines fugal and ostinato techniques; it is in the *Third Part of the Clavierübung* and will be discussed there (p. 278). A chorale-treatment of "Vom Himmel hoch, da komm ich her" (VII, 55), to which Bach gave the name *Fuga* is discussed on p. 229.

CHORALE TRIOS

By this heading we do not mean three-part treatments of a continuous c.f., but two *concertante* trios, whose subjects Bach derived by paraphrasing one line of the chorale: "Allein Gott in der Höh sei Ehr" (VI, 7) and "Herr Jesu Christ, dich zu uns wend" (VI, 27).

They represent perhaps the most daring and remote combination into which the chorale can enter with forms essentially alien to it. Both pieces are among the *Eighteen Chorales* and will be discussed there (p. 258 and p. 250).

CHAPTER 21

THE "ORGELBÜCHLEIN" AND OTHER SMALL ORGAN CHORALES

LITTLE ORGAN BOOK[303]

Containing Instruction for a Beginning Organist in Developing a Chorale in all Kinds of Ways; and along with this, in Acquiring Skill in his Study of the Pedals, since in Chorales of the Kind found here, the Pedal is Treated as Wholly Obbligato.

Solely in Praise of God Most High;
That all Mankind may Learn thereby.

Autore
Joanne. Sebast. Bach
p.t. Capellae Magistro
S(erentissimi) P(rincipis) R(egnantis)
Anhaltini Cothensiensis

Bach gave this title to a collection of small organ chorales planned to cover the entire liturgical year, from Advent to the Sunday nearest All Souls Day, in 164 chorales. Only 45 were completed, however.[304] After Bach's removal to Cöthen, the work was left unfinished. Since Bach referred to himself in the title as conductor *pro tempore* to the Prince of Anhalt-Cöthen, he must have started on the collection between his appointment and his departure from Weimar; that is, in the autumn of 1717. It is not unlikely that he beguiled the time while under arrest in Weimar (see p. 22) by composing these 45 chorales! Of the first 40 numbers, Advent to Easter, all but eight were composed; of the last hundred, only six.

Since Bach was on the point of accepting a position that had nothing to do with church music, we understand the purpose of the collection. It probably was begun "solely in praise of God Most High," but its

---

303. A somewhat different translation of the title page may be seen in *The Bach Reader, op. cit.,* p. 75.

304. Another, older, autograph contains only 26 chorales.

primary purpose is pedagogical. It claims to help "a beginning organist" both "in acquiring skill in his study of the pedals" and "in developing a chorale in all kinds of ways." That is, it claims—like the Inventions—to be simultaneously a method for acquiring technique in playing and in composing for one who is eager to learn. Long ago the *Little Organ Book* achieved classic recognition for its importance in instruction, as the best organ method of all time for developing imagination and technique equally, for those who have the rudiments behind them. (In Bach's day it was not necessary to teach these first.) Furthermore, it has long since become indispensable to us in the church service as a book of organ chorales for all seasons of the church year.

With two exceptions, Nos. 13 and 20, all the chorales present the c.f. in the soprano, either plain or slightly embellished (in line with the motivic structure of the accompanying parts), as the clearest way of presenting it without preludes or interludes. The c.f. is embellished and to be played on a separate manual only three times (in Nos. 16, 24, and 42). In an additional nine chorales Bach specifies two manuals, either to let a canon stand out clearly (Nos. 21, 31, and 35) or to give distinctness to running parts in inner voices (Nos. 2, 9, 10, 19, 26, and 40). The setting is almost always for four voices; only once is it for three (No. 40), twice for five (Nos. 21 and 35), and twice for a mixture of four and five parts (Nos. 1 and 17).

One can imagine how the settings of the *Little Organ Book* grew from plain four-part settings of the chorales. Much as a sculptor chisels his figures from a block by cutting material away, the composer works out motives by loosening up the compact setting. In so doing he obtains figures beginning with an up-beat. These result primarily from the insertion of rests. The ostinato basses demonstrate this technique with particular clarity, as for example in No. 32:

becomes:

At the beginning of the tenor part of No. 37,

from:

comes:

In the use of this technique Bach had many models, of course, especially in the area of the chorale partita.[305] In the deep and immediate relationship between text and music, however, Bach had no model, but himself became a model. Schweitzer attributed such importance to this fact that he placed the *Little Organ Book* in the very center of Bach's aesthetics as the "dictionary of Bach's musical language"[306] and characterized it as "one of the greatest achievements in music in general."[307]

Since then, perhaps the *Little Organ Book* has been overestimated from time to time. Within Bach's total output of organ chorales it still represents only one type, and it is surely surpassed in spiritual significance by a number of the large settings. Let us also guard against a "picture hunt" in the *Little Organ Book,* for not all of the settings submit to an interpretation in terms of pictures or ideas. The type of interpretation that is possible will be shown with the individual chorales.

The editors of the Peters edition had attached no importance to the intimate connection among the chorales or their order in the *Little Organ Book,* and (in Vol. V) arranged the chorales in alphabetical order along with others. In 1928 I edited the *Little Organ Book* after the original for the Bärenreiter-Verlag, and included texts, four-part choral settings of the chorales, and remarks on origin and performance. I should like to refer the reader to this edition for details that I shall pass over here. In the meantime an edition without commentary, but following the original, has been issued by Peters (No. 3946). In the following pages the first stanza will be given of those hymns whose texts may be presumed not to be generally familiar today.

Performance: As a rule, a combination of foundation stops will be suitable for performance of the one-manual pieces among the chorales of the *Little Organ Book;* c.f.-combinations or reeds (see No. 2) for those in which a melody is to be brought out prominently. The sound of a high-baroque mixture is no longer suitable for any of these chorales; a few, Nos. 3, 17, 22, and 27, for example, permit the use of the *Plenum* of a subordinate manual. The tempo in many chorales is slower than that a congregation would use in singing, even though we assume that congregations of Bach's day sang appreciably

305. Fritz Dietrich in the *Bach-Jahrbuch* for 1929, p. 28.
306. *Op. cit.*, II, 55; see also I, 284.
307. *Op. cit.*, I, 284.

slower than do those of today. The tempo selected, however, must be one that still permits the chorale note to be felt as the beat note.

THE ADVENT AND CHRISTMAS CYCLE

1. *Nun komm, der Heiden Heiland (V, 42; BWV 599)* *Savior of the nations, come*

Nun komm, der Heiden Heiland Der Jungfrauen Kind erkannt, Des sich wundert alle Welt, Gott solch Geburt ihm bestellt.	Savior of the nations, come, Offspring of a virgin's womb, In the fulness of the time! Praise and wonder, ev'ry clime!
Ger. Tr., Martin Luther, 1524, of "Veni redemptor gentium," by St. Ambrose, 374.	*Tr.* Anon., 1743.

This very first organ chorale makes a reasonably certain interpretation extremely difficult. Perhaps the "suspended" effect of the ties, and the slowly descending motive

symbolize the descent of God's Son to His human lowliness: "God such birth for Him ordained." The tempo must be slow and solemn (♩ = 40).[308] One can imagine light foundation-stops or a mild *Plenum* as registration.

2. *Gott, durch deine Güte* or *Gottes Sohn ist kommen (V, 19; BWV 600)* *God, in Thy great Goodness* or *Once He came in blessing*

In Canone all' Ottava, a 2 Clav. e Ped.

Gottes Sohn ist kommen Uns aller zu Frommen Hie auf dieser Erden In armen Gebärden, Dass er uns von Sünde Freie und entbinde.	Once He came in blessing, All our ills redressing, Came in likeness lowly, Son of God most holy, Bore the Cross to save us, Hope and freedom gave us.
Johann Roh, 1544.	*Tr.* Catherine Winkworth.

308. The metronome markings given here differ repeatedly from those I put in my Bärenreiter edition (in the Appendix) in 1928. All suggestions of this kind, of course, have only a relative validity.

Bach composed with the second text in mind, as he usually did when he assigned two chorale texts; the canon signifies that God's Son fulfilled the Law. The only original instruction for registration is found here: "*Prinzipal* 8'" for the right hand, "*Trompete* 8'" for the pedal; it is certainly sober enough. Klotz,[309] to be sure, advocates the hypothesis that, in common with Netherlands traditions of the sixteenth century, this registration meant: "manual *Prinzipal, Oktaven, Quinten, Mixturen,* and pedal *Trompete* with pedal coupler." I cannot agree with this opinion—primarily because Bach's instruction "for two manuals and pedal" would then not make sense. The left-hand part probably should be registered with 16', as in "Wo soll ich fliehen hin" (VII, 63). Bach's Weimar organ had a *Trompete* in the pedal and extended to f^1 (as I tried to make plausible on p. 34). The stop indications are therefore probably to be taken literally. 𝅗𝅥 = 72.

3. *Herr Christ, der einig Gottes Sohn,* or
Herr Gott, nun sei gepreiset
O Thou, of God the Father, or *Lord God, our praise we render*
(V, 22; BWV 601)

Herr Gott, nun sei gepreiset, Wir sagen frohen Dank, Dass du uns Gnad erweiset, Gegeben Speis und Trank, Dein Mildigkeit zu merken, Den Glauben mehr zu stärken, Dass du seist unser Gott.	Lord God, our praise we render And happy thanks do give, That Thou us grace dost tender— Food, drink, that we may live, Thy tenderness perceiving, Our faith more strength re- ceiving, That Thou art our true God.

Tr. H. H.

Here again, not the Advent text, but the "table hymn," a grace sung at meals, seems to have supplied the inspiration for Bach's musical idiom: the "beatific-peace rhythm" [rhythm figure] here signifies splendor and strength in its spreading out of the chords. (Cf. Böhm's Prelude in C Major and "Gelobet seist du, Jesus Christ"; Walther's "Vom Himmel hoch, da komm ich her," and others.) ♩ = 56.

309. *Musik und Kirche,* 1941, p. 109.

4. *Lob sei dem allmächtigen Gott (V, 38; BWV 602)*
To God we render thanks and praise

Lob sei dem allmächtigen Gott,	To God we render thanks and praise,
Der unser sich erbarmet hat,	Who pitied mankind's fallen race,
Gesandt sein'n allerliebsten Sohn	And gave His dear and only Son,
Aus ihm geboren im höchsten Thron.	That us, as children, He might own.

Tr. Moravian Hymnal.

Here a new symbolism enters: the basses of Nos. 4-7, which are strikingly similar in their stepwise descending progressions, signify the descent of the Godly Majesty to men. This symbolism and that of the ascending and descending angel hosts give the Christmas chorales a feature in common, as does the use of canon the Passion chorales. The symbolism of the inner parts is independent. In these, redeemed humanity gives thanks to Almighty God. The kinship of the sixteenth-note motive with the motives in Nos. 5 and 7 should also not be overlooked. ♩ = 52.

5. *Puer natus in Bethlehem (V, 46; BWV 603)*
A Child is born in Bethlehem

Puer natus in Bethlehem	A Child is born in Bethlehem,
Unde gaudet Jerusalem.	Exult for joy, Jerusalem!
Halleluja! Halleluja!	Alleluia! Alleluia!
Latin, 14th c.; *Ger. tr.*, Anon., 1553.	*Tr.* H. M. MacGill, 1876.

The inner parts here seem to represent the rocking of the cradle, as in No. 7. Schering[310] explains them by the mental image of "wrapping," the passage being similar to one in the *Christmas Oratorio* of Schütz ("and wraps him in swaddling cloths"). According to Schweitzer, the bass must signify "a constant succession of deep obeisan-

310. *Das Symbol in der Musik*, p. 76.

ces"[311] of the kings before the Child Jesus; but it is even more probable that it symbolizes the divinity of Christ and His descent to mankind, thus corresponding to Nos. 4 and 6. 𝅗𝅥 = 76.

6. *Gelobet seist du, Jesu Christ (V, 17; BWV 604)*
All praise to Jesus' hallowed name

a 2 Clav. e Ped.

Gelobet seist du, Jesu Christ,	All praise to Jesus' hallowed name,
Dass du Mensch geboren bist	Who of virgin pure became
Von einer Jungfrau, das ist wahr;	True man for us! The angels sing,
Des freuet sich der Engel Schar	As the glad news to earth they bring.
Kyrieleis!	Kyrie eleison!
From the Latin sequence "Grates nunc omnes reddamus," 14th century; *tr.* Martin Luther, 1524.	*Tr.* Richard Massie, 1854.

How closely together the Christmas chorales of the *Little Organ Book* must have been composed, this chorale happens to show very clearly. It conforms to Nos. 4 and 5 in its bass line and anticipates No. 7 in the "hooked" progression of the inner parts (rocking of the cradle). ♩ = 54.

7. *Der Tag, der ist so freudenreich (V, 11; BWV 605)*
This day, so rich in joy and love,

a 2 Clav. e Ped.

Der Tag, der ist so freudenreich	This day, so rich in joy and love,
Aller Kreature,	Joy to all creation,
Denn Gottes Sohn vom Himmelreich	God's Son came down from Heav'n above
Über die Nature	Down from His high station,
Von einer Jungfrau ist geborn.	Of mortal maid to be the Son,
Maria, du bist auserkorn,	Thou, Mary, wast the Chosen One,

311. Schweitzer, *op. cit.*, II, 62.

Dass du Mutter wärest.	Thou the Blessed Mother.
Was geschah so wunderlich?	What the miracle thereby?
Gottes Sohn vom Himmelreich	Christ the Son of God on High
Der ist Mensch geboren.	Became of man the brother.
Ger. Tr. of "Dies est laetitiae," 1529	*Tr.* Henry S. Drinker.

Bach becomes a genre-painter in his little picture for this pre-Reformation German translation of the "Dies est laetitiae"; the slightly jolting movement of the middle parts represents the rocking of the Child's cradle, while another echo of the festive rhythm of Nos. 4-8 may be traced in the bass. ♩ = 58.

8. *Vom Himmel hoch, da komm ich her (V, 49; BWV 606)*
From heaven above to earth I come

In the four Christmas chorales next following, Bach is thinking above all of the appearance of the angels on Christmas Eve, and he depicts, in the eighth-note steps of the pedal, the ascent and descent of the heavenly hosts. Thus, this chorale may be interpreted as misty and delicate quite as well as lustrous and splendid. ♩ = 69.

9. *Vom Himmel kam der Engel Schar (V, 50; BWV 607)*
To Shepherds, as they watched by night

a 2 Clav. e Ped.

Vom Himmel kam der Engel Schar	To shepherds, as they watched by night,
Erschien den Hirten offenbar,	Appeared a troop of angels bright;
Sie sagten ihn'n: ein Kindlein zart,	Behold the tender Babe, they said,
Das liegt dort in der Krippen hart.	In yonder lowly manger laid.
	Tr. Richard Massie.

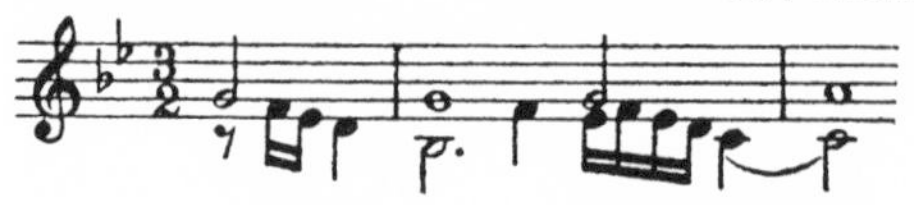

Here the scale passages of the tenor and bass depict with a clarity almost too realistic Jacob's ladder on which the angels ascend and descend. The two manuals, which Bach demands only in the interest of clarity, should not contrast. ♩ = 108.

10. *In dulci jubilo (V, 35; BWV 608)*

Canone doppio all'Ottava a 2 Clav. e Ped.

Since the melody scarcely leaves the tonic chord, it has been treated canonically in all periods: from Sicher's book of tablatures in the sixteenth century to Praetorius and Walther, and right up to our own time. Bach even treats the four voices in double canon up to m. 24. In genuine baroque gaiety little *putti* whirl about in triplets, and blow on silver trumpets (in the jostling quarter notes). Since it is probable that none of Bach's organs had an f♯ in the pedal, he himself doubtless played the c.f. an octave lower with the *Kornettbass* 4' on his Weimar organ. The fifth part, entering at the end, belongs in the manual. In this chorale Bach clearly differentiates duplets (♩♩) from triplets (♩♪ with 3). 𝅗𝅥 = 88.

11. *Lobt Gott, ihr Christen, allzugleich (V, 40; BWV 609)*
Let all together praise our God

In this piece, also, we find musical "Jacob's ladders" in the pedal and Christmas joy in the inner parts, which move without interruption and as if on wings! ♩ = 80.

12. *Jesu, meine Freude (V, 31; BWV 610)*
Jesu, priceless treasure

Bach admitted this chorale into the Christmas cycle as expressive of "the mystic adoration"[312] in spite of the fact that textually it makes no reference to Christmas. The unusually low register of the c.f. and the autograph instruction "*Largo*" give the work a peculiarly deep solemnity. Once again we have an example of the uniformity of Bach's musical idiom: while the ties found in the middle voices have a meaning similar to that of the ties in "Nun komm, der Heiden Heiland," the treatment of the ostinato bass is analogous to that of "In dir ist Freude,"—and yet in what contrasting moods in the two chorales! ♪ = 63.

13. *Christum wir sollen loben schon (V, 6; BWV 611)*
Now must we Jesus laud and sing

Canto fermo in Alto

Christum wir sollen loben schon,	Now must we Jesus laud and sing,
Der reinen Magd Marien Sohn,	The maiden Mary's Son and King,
So weit die liebe Sonne leucht't	Far as the blessed sun doth shine,
Und an aller Welt End reicht.	And reaches earth's most distant line.
Ger. tr., Martin Luther, 1524, of "A solis ortus cardine" by Coelius Sedulius	*Tr.* George MacDonald, 1876.

Among the four-part organ chorales of Bach this is the only one (exclusive of canons) to place the c.f. in the alto. This chorale also has the most ethereal quality of any of the compositions in the entire *Little Organ Book*. The c.f. is already somewhat concealed, as an alto, yet the accompanying voices envelop it even more with soft veils that are woven out of it, note for note—a veiling in awe before the Mystery.

312. Schweitzer, *op. cit.*, II, 64.

Only a good performer should make an attempt to bring the c.f. into prominence on a separate manual. ♪ = 58.

14. *Wir Christenleut' (V, 55; BWV 612)*
We Christians may

Wir Christenleut, Han jetzund Freud, Weil uns zum Trost ist Christus Mensch geboren, Hat uns erlöst, Wer sich des tröst Und glaubet fest, soll nicht werden verloren.	We Christians may Rejoice today, When Christ was born to com- fort and to save us; Who thus believes No longer grieves, For none are lost who grasp the hope He gave us.
Caspar Füger, 1592.	*Tr.* Catherine Winkworth.

We also encounter the triumphal rhythm ♬♩♩♩ ♪, among other places, in the Great C-Major Prelude (II, 7). In its simplified version in the pedal it is related to the eighth-note motive of "Komm, Gott, Schöpfer, heiliger Geist." ♩. = 48.

END OF THE YEAR AND THE NEW YEAR

15. *Helft mir Gott's Güte preisen (V, 21; BWV 613)*
Ye Christians in this nation!

Helft mir Gott's Güte preisen, Ihr lieben Kinderlein, Mit G'sang und andern Weisen Ihm allzeit dankbar sein, Vornehmlich zu der Zeit, Da sich das Jahr tut enden, Die Sonn sich zu uns wenden, Das neu Jahr ist nicht weit.	Ye Christians in this nation! Come all, and praise with me Our Maker's preservation, In joyful harmony, Even at this present time, When we new date our season, And have the greatest reason To love our Lord Divine.
Paul Eber, *ca.* 1580.	*Tr.* John Christian Jacobi, 1722.

As in No. 13, the counterpoint here does not contrast with the c.f., but is constructed from it

and thus "helps," unceasingly, "to praise God's goodness."[313] ♩ = 60.

16. *Das alte Jahr vergangen ist (V, 10; BWV 614)*
The old year now hath passed away

a 2 Clav. a Ped.

Das alte Jahr vergengen ist,	The old year now hath passed away,
Wir danken dir, Herr Jesu Christ,	We thank Thee, O our God, today,
Dass du uns in so grosser G'fahr	That Thou hast kept us through the year,
So gnädiglich behüt't hast dies Jahr.	When danger and distress were near.
Jakob Tapp, 1588.	*Tr.* Catherine Winkworth.

In this unprecedented piece the music expresses a degree of grief and melancholy that seems justified neither by the text nor by the melody. It is a lament for the transitory nature of the worldly, which the coloration of the c.f. elaborates in an expression of profound sorrow, intensified by the chromaticism of the accompanying parts. The ending in major was dictated by the unusual cadence of the chorale melody. Bach's ornamentation exaggerates this cadence (a a g♯), however, with a series of yearning appoggiaturas climbing to the sixth above, and then lets it subside into the major, as if in blissful exhaustion. ♪ = 66.

313. Here (and occasionally below) a brief quotation from the German chorale has been given a more literal translation than was possible for the translator of the chorale as a whole. (*Tr.*)

17. *In Dir ist Freude (V, 34; BWV 615)*
In Thee is gladness

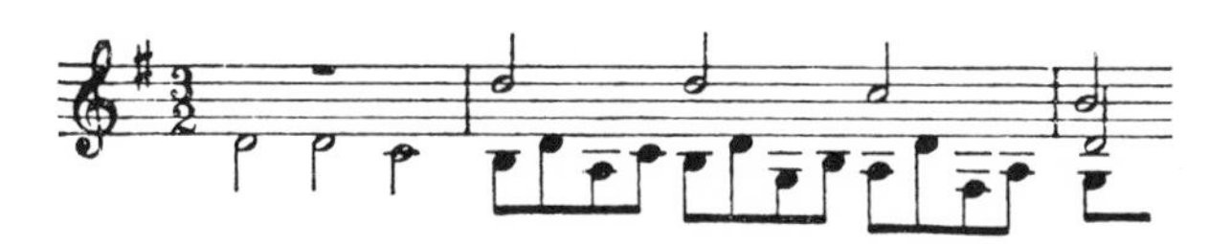

As grief was intensified in the preceding chorale, here gladness is heightened into exuberance. The melody was originally a Venetian dance-tune. The bass, for which Pirro[314] conjectured that Bach used the *Glockenspiel* of his Weimar organ, revolves about itself, as if in an eddy:

This is the only chorale in the *Little Organ Book* that fails to present the c.f. without a pause. Overflowing with joy, the advance imitations repeat the beginning of the tune until, in mm. 9 and 10, and then again in mm. 26 and 27, the c.f. itself enters. In mm. 34-37 it appears in the bass. Not until the second half of the tune is it carried through continuously, partly embellished and not entirely easy to recognize:

(The articulation marked here is designed to point up the tones of the melody.) 𝅗𝅥 = 84.

18. *Simeon's Song of Praise: Mit Fried und Freud ich fahr dahin*
In peace and joy I now depart
(V, 41; BWV 616)

The "joy rhythm" (simplified in the pedal to) expresses the happy trust of the chorale; cf., moreover, the "Lauda-

314. *Op. cit.*, p. 75.

mus" of the *B Minor Mass*, the organ chorales "Wer nur den lieben Gott lässt walten" (No. 43) and "Von Gott will ich nicht lassen," and, in addition, the first and second movements of the C Major Toccata as examples of the range of this formula. ♩ = 42.

19. *Herr Gott, nun schleuss den Himmel auf (V, 24; BWV 617)*
Lord God, now open wide Thy Heav'n

a 2 Clav. a Ped.

Herr Gott, nun schleuss den Himmel auf, Mein Zeit zu End' sich neiget, Ich hab vollendet meinen Lauf, Des sich mein Seel erfreuet; Hab gnug gelitten, Mich müd gestritten, Schick mich fein zu, der ewgen Ruh, Lass fahren, was auf Erden, Will lieber selig werden.	Lord God, now open wide Thy Heav'n, My parting hour is near; My course is run, enough I've striv'n, Enough I've suffer'd here; Weary and sad, My soul is glad That she may lay her down to rest; Now all on earth I can resign, But only let Thy Heav'n be mine.
Tobias Kiel, 1620.	*Tr.* Catherine Winkworth.

The text, which also refers to Simeon's death, inspired Bach to paint a picture of wonderful vividness. With the c.f. and the voice accompanying it, which travel the road to eternity hand in hand, as it were, are associated the restlessly ascending and descending sixteenth notes, as a picture of the unrest in earthly life and the vigorous (according to Schweitzer, "uncertain"[315]) steps of the pilgrim in the pedal. One needs to have all these associations clear in one's mind beforehand, not to become bewildered by the profusion of images. ♩. = 60.

THE PASSION

20. *O Lamm Gottes, unschuldig (V, 44; BWV 618)*
O Lamb of God, most stainless!

Canone alla Quinta

315. *Op. cit.*, II, 62.

Among the seven Passion-chorales of the *Little Organ Book* (Nos. 20-26) there are no less than four in which the c.f. is set in canon. Bach uses it here as symbol of the fulfillment of the divine law by the Son. In "O Lamm Gottes" the lamentation of Christ in the "motive of grief"

is added in wonderful contrast (cf. the final chorus of Part I of the *St. Matthew Passion*). If performed on one manual, the canon will hardly be heard. Matthäi[316] proposes three manuals (the c.f. on the middle manual), but the imitating part (alto) may then become insignificant in comparison with the leading part (tenor). The direction *"Adagio"* is also to have a bearing on the registration. ♪ = 69. The antepenultimate note in the soprano in measure 3 probably should read a^2, not g^2.

21. *Christe, du Lamm Gottes (V, 3; BWV 619)*
Lamb of God, our Savior

In Canone alla Duodecima a 2 Clav. e Ped.

Bach calls for a distribution of this five-part setting on two manuals, so that each hand takes one c.f. part and one accompanying part.[317] The canon will come into greater prominence, however, if one uses three manuals here, also, and plays the c.f. in the tenor on the lowest manual, its imitation in the soprano on the highest, and the two alto parts (divided between the hands) on the middle manual. The scale, descending slowly and heavily, symbolizes the descent of Christ from His Divinity into human sorrow. 𝅗𝅥 = 40.

22. *Christus, der uns selig macht (V, 8; BWV 620)*
See the Lord of Life and Light

In Canone all' Ottava

Christus, der uns selig macht,	See the Lord of Life and Light,
Kein Bös's hat begangen,	Savior meek and lowly,

316. *Vom Orgelspiel*, p. 219.

317. Cf. the large arrangement of "Vater unser im Himmelreich" (VII, 52, p. 279).

Der ward für uns in der Nacht
Als ein Dieb gefangen,
Geführt vor gottlose Leut
Und fälschlich verklaget,
Verlacht, verhöhnt, und verspeit,
Wie denn die Schrift saget.

Ger. tr. of "Patris sapientia, veritas divina" by Michael Weisse, 1531.

Taken like a thief at night,
Bound by hands unholy,
See the sinless Son of God
Shameful mockings bearing,
Bitter taunts, a crucial rod,
Doom of sinners sharing.

Tr. J. Troutbeck.

Here the canon, which is carried out with relentless power between the "highest" and the "lowest" parts, signifies the surrender of God's Son to the Powers of Darkness. The expression of defiance in the rhythm 𝄾♪ ♬♪ ♪ (cf. "Christ ist erstanden") and the sadness in the chromaticism of the inner parts give this piece almost an excess of expressiveness. It should be played with powerful tone and inflexible rhythm. ♩ = 66.

23. *Da Jesus an dem Kreuze stund (V, 9; BWV 621)*
When on the Cross the Savior hung

Da Jesus an dem Kreuze stund
Und ihm sein Leichnam ward verwund't,
So gar mit bittern Schmerzen,
Die sieben Wort, die Jesus sprach,
Betracht in deinem Herzen.

Johann Böschenstein, ca. 1515.

When on the Cross the Savior hung,
And that sore load that on Him weigh'd
With bitter pangs His nature wrung,
Seven words amid His pain He said;
Oh let them well to heart be laid!

Tr. Catherine Winkworth.

Here Bach sketches the scene on Golgotha: the outstretched cross

with the drooping, lifeless body of the Crucified:

in addition, Mary and the disciple, who raise their hands imploringly:

—a "Lamentation of Christ" worthy of the Passions of Dürer. ♪ = 72.

24. *O Mensch, bewein dein' Sünde gross (V, 45; BWV 622)*
O man, bewail thy grievous fall

a 2 Clav. e Ped.

O Mensch, bewein dein' Sünde gross,	O man, bewail thy grievous fall,
Darum Christus seins Vaters Schoss	For which Christ left His Father's hall
Äussert' und kam auf Erden.	And came to earth from heavèn.
Von einer Jungfrau rein und zart	He of a virgin maiden pure
Er für uns hier geboren ward,	Was born, of man the Savior sure,
Er wollt der Mittler werden.	And came earth's ills to leaven.
Den Toten er das Leben gab,	The dead He raised again to life,
Und legt dabei all Krankheit ab,	The sick he loosed from pain and strife,
Bis sich die Zeit herdrange,	Until the time appointed
Dass er für uns geopfert würd,	That He for us should shed His blood
Trug unsrer Sünden schwere Bürd	And take on Him our sins' dark load,
Wohl an dem Kreuze lange.	Stretched on the Cross ac-cursèd.
Sebaldus Heyden, 1542.	*Tr.* Charles Sanford Terry. [318]

318. *The Four-Part Chorals of J. S. Bach: With the German Text of the Hymns and English Translations*, ed. Charles Sanford Terry (Oxford University Press, 1929).

This most famous coloration in the *Little Organ Book* shows how far Bach had surpassed his North German models and his own early attempts in this form—particularly in the Partitas. He gives a spiritual meaning to this technique for a profound meditation upon the hymn; ideas take the place of pictures, and the idiom does not become more graphic until the last lines of the stanza: "that He should be sacrificed for us" is expressed by the chromaticism of the bass, and by the laborious dragging of the inner parts; "long on the cross" by the dreamlike *Adagissimo* at the end, with its other-worldly modulation to C♭ major.[319] The player must give the piece a sensitive (*adagio assai*), but not weak, registration, and give it a poetic reading, for every note here is inspired! ♪ = 54.

25. *Wir danken dir, Herr Jesu Christ (V, 56; BWV 623)*
To Thee, Lord Jesus, thanks we give

Wir danken dir, Herr Jesu Christ,	To Thee, Lord Jesus, thanks we give,
Dass du für uns gestorben bist,	Who diedst for us, that we might live,
Und hast uns durch dein teures Blut	And thro' Thy holy precious blood
Gemacht vor Gott gerecht und gut.	Hast made us righteous before God.

Tr. August Crull.

The "steps" in the bass express faith; the work as a whole, however, like its text, seems somewhat flat and conventional after the previous splendors. ♩ = 66.

26. *Hilf Gott, dass mir's gelinge (V, 29; BWV 624)*
O help me, Lord, to praise Thee

a 2 Clav. e Ped.

Hilf Gott, dass mir's gelinge,	O help me, Lord, to praise Thee,
Du edler Schöpfer mein,	Great Shepherd of Thy sheep,
Die Silb in Reimen zwinge	In grateful phrases worthy
Zu Lob dem Namen dein,	Of Thee, who watch dost keep!
Dass ich mag fröhlich heben an	Help me in song my voice upraise

319. A similar turn is found at the end of Pachelbel's Fantasy in E♭ Major.

Von deinem Wort zu singen;
Herr, du wollst mir beistahn.

Heinrich Müller, 1531
(or earlier)

For Thy blest Word so holy,
And guide my feeble praise!

Tr. Charles Sanford Terry.[320]

The musical setting is quite as forced as is the text. The unremitting triplet-rhythm signifies constant endeavor, while the chorale is forced into canon as the syllables are into rhymes.[321] ♩ = 48.

EASTER

27. *Christ lag in Todesbanden (V, 5; BWV 625)*
In death's strong grasp the Savior lay

After the last two fairly weak chorales the splendid Dorian Easter hymns again give Bach's inspiration a powerful stimulus; the motive

symbolizes the rolling-away of the heavy stone from the tomb. The chorale should be played *maestoso* with *Organo pleno*. ♩ = 56.

28. *Jesus Christus, unser Heiland (V, 32; BWV 626)*
Jesus Christ, our Lord and Savior

Jesus Christus, unser Heiland,
Der den Tod überwand,
Ist auferstanden,
Die Sünd hat er gefangen.
Halleluja!

Martin Luther, 1524.

Jesus Christ, our Lord and Savior,
Is victor over death.
He is arisen,
Our sins has He imprisoned.
Halleluja!

Tr. Henry S. Drinker.

320. *The Four-Part Chorals,* ed. Terry, No. 176.
321. A reference to line 3 of the German stanza, of which a literal translation might read: "force the syllables into rhymes."

Possibly the ties in the eighth-note motive stand for the bonds of death; the quarters, which mount grandly in the bass, the triumph over death. ♩. = 58.

29. *Christ ist erstanden (V, 4; BWV 627)*
Christ is arisen

"Here the whole church rejoices with full, resonant voice and with inexpressible joy." Thus spoke the sixteenth century about this oldest and most magnificent of all Easter hymns. Bach conceived its three stanzas as a unit and composed each individually as he did the stanzas of "O Lamm Gottes unschuldig." The delightful Gregorian melody here loses all its energy—as in "Herr Gott, dich loben wir" (p. 189)—since it is forced into a counterpoint of halves against sixteenths. Bach also knew the melody only in its corrupt state and altered it still further by changing the second note, g, to g♯. The three sections of this chorale, nevertheless, constitute a magnificent piece of music. The first stanza, with its strict, syncopated rhythm ("syncope" means "a cutting up"—here the bonds of death?) is followed by a second stanza with almost the same harmonic basis but with an entirely different motivic structure. This motive symbolizes not only the "binding," but also, in its ascending motion,—for example, the tenor in measure 3—the Resurrection. The third stanza, "Alleluia," seems, in its irresistible rhythm, no longer to have any tendencies toward tone-painting.

It is perhaps best to play the first stanza on two manuals, even though Bach did not expressly prescribe it. The last stanza may bring an increase in both tempo and volume. 𝅗𝅥 = 46-52.

30. *Erstanden ist der heilig Christ (V, 14; BWV 628)*
The blessed Christ is ris'n today

Erstanden ist der heilig Christ,	The blessed Christ is ris'n today;
Halleluja!	Alleluia. Alleluia.
Der aller Welt ein Tröster ist.	Of all mankind to be the stay.
Halleluja!	Alleluia. Alleluia.
Anon. *Tr.* of "Surrexit Christus hodie," 1544.	*Tr.* Anon.

Here an exultant upward-movement lays hold of all the parts; even the leaps in the pedal symbolize the Resurrection. 𝅗𝅥 = 96.

31. *Erschienen ist der herrliche Tag (V, 15; BWV 629)*
The day hath dawned—the day of days

In Canone all' Ottava a 2 Clav. e Ped.

Erschienen ist der herrliche Tag,
Dran niemand g'nug sich freuen mag,
Christ, unser Herr, heut triumphiert,
All sein Feind er gefangen führt.
Hallelujah!

Nicolaus Heermann, 1560.

The day hath dawned—the day of days,
Transcending all our joy and praise:
This day our Lord triumphant rose;
This day He captive led our foes.
Hallelujah!

Tr. Arthur T. Russell, 1851.

The canon between the outer parts illustrates the triumphal progress of Christ, who "captive led our foes," while the inner parts exult in the rhythm ♩ ♫ ♩. 𝅗𝅥 = 84.

32. *Heut triumphieret Gottes Sohn (V, 28; BWV 630)*
Today God's only-gotten Son

Heut triumphieret Gottes Sohn,
Der vom Tod ist erstanden schon,
Halleluja!
Mit grosser Pracht und Herrlichkeit,
Des danken wir ihm in Ewigkeit,
Halleluja!

Today God's only-gotten Son
Arose from death and triumph won,
Alleluia, Alleluia!
In mighty pomp and rich array;
His therefore be the praise alway.
Alleluia, Alleluia!

Tr. G. R. Woodward.

As with "In dir ist Freude," Bach enhances the dance rhythm of the melody with the "leaps for joy" in the *basso ostinato*[322] and the sparkling rhythm of the inner parts. The hymn will pass equally for an Easter hymn or for an Ascension hymn. 𝅗𝅥 = 92.

PENTECOST

33. *Komm, Gott, Schöpfer, heiliger Geist (VII, p. 86; BWV 631)*
Come, Holy Ghost, Creator, come

Komm, Gott, Schöpfer, heiliger Geist, Besuch das Herz der Menschen dein; Mit Gnaden sie füll, wie du weisst, Dass dein Geschöpf vorhin sein.	Come, Holy Ghost, Creator, come, And visit all the souls of Thine: Thou has inspired our hearts with life; Inspire them now with life divine.
Tr. Martin Luther, 1524, of "Veni Creator Spiritus."	*Tr.* Catherine Winkworth.

The Peters edition did not include this piece in Vol. V, since it occurs in expanded form (VII, 35) among the large chorale preludes (see p. 260). In its brevity it does, in fact, give a fragmentary effect. According to Steglich's interpretation[323] the bass, which begins each time on the 3rd eighth, is an "expression of the occurrence of the descent of the Holy Ghost at Pentecost," represented by "the melody's floating down from above to the ground-bass." He also interprets the sixteenths of the inner parts in terms of musical symbolism as "the cloven tongues of fire of Pentecost manifested musically."[324] When he goes still farther, however, and professes

322. Schweitzer sees in them the Old Testament (Isa. 63:3) picture of the "treading of the winepress." *Op. cit.*, II, 63.
323. *J. S. Bach*, p. 122.
324. Acts 2:3.

to see an "obvious picture of the heart" in the three eighths ("visit the heart of man") not all will be able to follow him. ♩. = 50.

34. *Herr Jesu Christ, dich zu uns wend (V, 25; BWV 632)*
Lord Jesus Christ, be present now!

This hymn, attributed to Duke Wilhelm II of Weimar, is "a model of liturgical prayer" according to Wilhelm Thomas. In Weimar it was sung every Sunday before the sermon. Bach's musical setting is also a fervent prayer. The melody of the bass meekly follows the c.f. in the soprano in shorter steps and permits itself "to be led to the truth" by it. Even the inner parts pray continually: "Lord Jesus Christ." ♩ = 48.

35. *Liebster Jesu, wir sind hier (V, 37; BWV 633)*
Blessed Jesu, at Thy word

In Canone alla Quinta a 2 Clav. e Ped.

Curiously, this was written down in two versions. It is ornamented in one version, which either no longer pleased Bach, or appeared to him pedagogically unsuitable, so that he revised it slightly and left the c.f. "*distinctius*," i.e., unembellished in the first line, for greater clarity. The canon becomes really audible only in a performance on three manuals—technically not easy. Possibly the canon is a symbol of "be wholly drawn to Thee."[325] ♩ = 52.

---

325. Fritz Jöde made an arrangement of this piece for two vocal parts and strings.

OF THE TEN COMMANDMENTS

36. *Dies sind die heilgen zehn Gebot (V, 12; BWV 635)*
These are the holy ten commands

Dies sind die heilgen zehn Gebot,
Die uns gab unser Herre Gott
Durch Mose, seinen Diener treu
Hoch auf dem Berg Sinai.
Kyrie eleis.

Martin Luther, 1524.

These are the holy ten commands,
Which came to us from God's own hands
By Moses, who obeyed His will,
Standing upon Sin'i's hill.
Have mercy, Lord!

Tr. George MacDonald.

In this rather dry arrangement the inner parts attempt to impress the Commandments firmly upon us by means of constant repetition of the first phrase in double diminution—25 times in all. 𝅗𝅥 = 40.

THE LORD'S PRAYER

37. *Vater unser im Himmelreich (V, 48; BWV 636)*
Our Father, Thou in heav'n above

It was shown at the start (p. 198) how we may imagine this unpretentious organ chorale to have developed from the four-part setting of the chorale melody. The three anacrustic sixteenths are derived from the beginning of the melody by inversion. Everything here is humble, intimate prayer. In mm. 2 and 10 the last note of the c.f. should be played as an eighth note. ♪ = 60.

CONFESSION

38. *Durch Adams Fall ist ganz verderbt (V, 13; BWV 637)*
When Adam fell, the human race

Durch Adams Fall ist ganz verderbt	When Adam fell, the human race
Menschlich Natur und Wesen,	Was doomed to condemnation;
Dasselb Gift ist auf uns vererbt,	Bereft were we of innocence,
Dass wir nicht konnten g'nesen	Sin's poison wrought destruction.
Ohn Gottes Trost,	But thanks to God,
Der uns erlöst	Who spares the rod,
Hat von dem grossen Schaden,	From death have we been taken.
Darin die Schlang	The Serpent Eve
Evan bezwang,	Didst once deceive
Gott's Zorn auf sich zu laden.	Beholds his power shaken.

Tr. Charles Sanford Terry.[326]

In its concreteness this chorale is one of the most famous examples in the *Little Organ Book:* the descending diminished sevenths of the ostinato pedal depict the "Fall"; the third, altered from major to minor, the "Corruption"; together, the two produce a harmony of unparalleled boldness. ♪ = 69.

JUSTIFICATION

39. *Es ist das Heil uns kommen her (V, 16; BWV 638)*
Salvation now is come to earth

Nos. 38 and 39 are a pair of contrasts, as are Nos. 16 and 17. The joyous rhythm of sixteenths in the manual and eighths in the pedal suffuses the setting with health and strength. ♩ = 66.

326. *The Four-Part Chorals*, ed. Terry, No. 76.

CHRISTIAN CONDUCT

40. *Ich ruf zu dir, Herr Jesu Christ (V, 30; BWV 639)* *Lord, hear the voice of my complaint*

a 2 Clav. e Ped.

Ich ruf zu dir, Herr Jesu Christ,
Ich bitt, erhör mein Klagen;
Verleih mir Gnad zu dieser Frist,
Lass mich doch nicht verzagen!
Den rechten Glauben, Herr, ich mein,
Den wollest du mir geben,
Dir zu leben,
Dem Nächsten nütz zu sein,
Dein Wort zu halten eben.

Johannes Agricola, 1529.

Lord, hear the voice of my complaint,
To Thee I now commend me,
Let not my heart and hope grow faint,
But deign Thy grace to send me.
True faith from Thee, my God, I seek,
The faith that loves Thee solely,
Keeps me lowly,
And prompt to aid the weak,
And mark each word that Thou dost speak.

Tr. Catherine Winkworth.

This chorale is the only one for three voices in the *Little Organ Book*. (Alto and tenor have been drawn together into one voice.) The middle voice is meekly imploring (cf. No. 23), protected symbolically by the (autograph) slurs indicating *legato*, while the eighths of the bass depict the restless throbbing of the heart (cf. "O Schmerz, hier zittert ein gequältes Herz" in the *St. Matthew Passion*). ♩ = 40.

HYMNS OF CONSOLATION

41. *In dich hab ich gehoffet, Herr (V, 33; BWV 640)* *In Thee, Lord, have I put my trust*

In dich hab ich gehoffet, Herr,
Hilf, dass ich nicht zu Schanden werd
Noch ewiglich zu Spotte,
Das bitt ich dich, erhalte mich,
In deiner Treu, Herr Gotte!

Adam Reissner, 1533
(*Tr.* of Psalm 131)

In Thee, Lord, have I put my trust,
Leave me not helpless in the dust,
Let me not be confounded;
Let in Thy word, my faith, O Lord,
Be always firmly grounded.

Tr. Catherine Winkworth.

This is marked *"Alio modo"* because it is a setting of the alternative (minor) melody. For a setting of the major melody, see p. 240. The motive signifies constancy. ♩ = 50.

42. *Wenn wir in höchsten Nöten sein (V, 51; BWV 641)*
When in the hour of utmost need

Coloration is also employed here with great depth of meaning: for the anxiety and longing in the heart of man "that is restless until it repose in Thee."[327] Even the accompanying voices join in prayer with the beginning of the melody: . Spitta showed that this chorale was the model for the large setting. ("Vor deinen Thron tret' ich hiermit," VII, 58). (See p. 260.) ♪ = 58.

43. *Wer nur den lieben Gott lässt walten (V, 54; BWV 642)*
If thou but suffer God to guide thee

The rhythm we encountered in No. 18, and for which further examples were given there, also governs this piece. A *Plenum* would carry it off very well. ♩ = 46.

44. *Alle Menschen müssen sterben (V, 2; BWV 643)*
Hark! a voice saith, all are mortal

327. See *The Confessions of St. Augustine*, Bk. I, p. 1 (Tr. Edward B. Pusey, D. D., *Modern Library*, New York, Random House, 1949).

The melody ("Jesu, meines Lebens Leben") cannot be found in Bach's hymnals as a funeral hymn. The interwoven accompanying parts, with their suspensions, which speak of "the great glory that is prepared for the godly,"[328] harmonize with its peaceful serenity. ♩ = 48.

45. *Ach wie nichtig, ach wie flüchtig (V, 1; BWV 644)*
O how cheating, O how fleeting

Ach wie nichtig, ach wie flüchtig	O how cheating, O how fleeting,
Ist der Menschen Leben!	Is our earthly being!
Wie ein Nebel bald entstehet	'Tis a mist in wintry weather,
Und auch wieder bald vergehet,	Gathered in an hour together,
So ist unser Leben, sehet!	And as soon dispersed in ether.
Michael Franck, 1652.	*Tr.* Sir John Bowring, 1825.

In this last chorale of the *Little Organ Book* Bach again portrays a double image: the *quasi-pizzicato* bass symbolizes the "futility" of human existence; the inner parts, passing by shadowlike, its transitoriness—a *chiaroscuro* like an etching by Rembrandt. The sixteenth-note motion is found with the same meaning both in Bach's cantata of the same title and in the secular music of the period; for example, in Adam Krieger's song, "Der Unbestand ist ihr verwandt," etc. ♩ = 63.

In addition to the *Little Organ Book*, several more chorales may be mentioned that are not included in it. First of all,

Herzlich tut mich verlangen (V, 27; BWV 727)
My heart is filled with longing

328. See I. Corinthians, 2:9, ". . . the things which God hath prepared for them that love Him."

One would like to see in this imperishable arrangement of the glorious melody the ideal type of the *Little Organ Book*, and it is not clear to us why it did not find acceptance there, or indeed, why Bach did not once write down this melody in advance among the 164 chorales of which he had planned to make settings. With an almost unnoticeable movement and animation of the simple four-part setting the voices start to speak and the rests to breathe; the expression does not become more insistent or more specific until the last line, "O Jesu, komm nur bald" ("O Savior, quickly come"). A very slow tempo is traditional for this chorale (♪ = 66); similarly, a light registration which keeps the c.f. from being brought into sharp prominence.

Liebster Jesu, wir sind hier (V, 36; BWV 706)
Blessed Jesu, at Thy word

This is perhaps the simplest and the least pretentious organ chorale by Bach. From this version of the melody—a variant of that found in No. 35 of the *Little Organ Book*—and from the very vocal treatment of the parts, I favor a late origin rather than an early one. ♩ = 52.

Two other arrangements of the same melody (V, Appendix, Nos. 4 and 5; BWV 730 and 731)

and

make a rather disagreeable impression and—if genuine Bach—probably originated as early as the Arnstadt period.

Even an ornamented arrangement of

Herr Jesu Christ, dich zu uns wend (V, 26; BWV 709)
Lord Jesus Christ, be present now!

fails as yet—particularly in the coloration—to show the clarification and spiritual quality of the ornamented chorales in the *Little Organ Book*. ♩ = 48.

Ach Gott und Herr (IX, 12; BWV 714)
Alas, my God

Per Canonem

The minor melody does not occur elsewhere in Bach, but only the master himself could have written this compact setting in which almost every note is thematic.

Performance: on two manuals, with rather harsh tone. 𝅗𝅥 = 63.

Auf meinen lieben Gott (IX, 15; BWV 744)
In God, my faithful God

Per Canonem

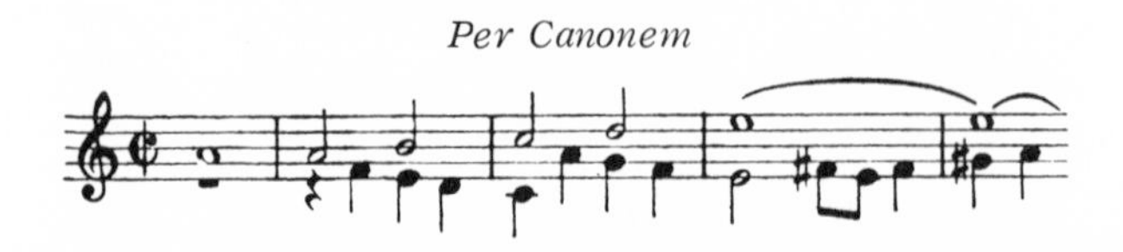

In technique this piece is patterned so strikingly after the preceding chorale that here perhaps Krebs was copying his teacher Bach. (See the Preface to Vol. IX.) The unpleasant parallel fifths in the final measure were removed in the editions of Hertzog and Körner, the passage being emended to read:

Two additional organ chorales refrain from using the pedals, since the scalewise progression of the counterpoint would make a performance *pedaliter* too difficult: the three- to four-part setting of

Wer nur den lieben Gott lässt walten (V, 53; BWV 690)
If thou but suffer God to guide thee

(♩ = 76) and the small arrangement of "Vater unser im Himmelreich" in the *Third Part of the Clavierübung* (see p. 281).

Three further organ chorales *manualiter* in three-part writing and with sensitively ornamented c.f.—suggested by the tone of the clavichord, which is delicate but flexible—appear in the *Little Clavier Book for Friedemann Bach*. The first of these also occurs in the larger of Anna Magdalena's music books. Since Bach separated the c.f. clearly from the accompanying parts, however, these pieces may be played on two manuals. They require a particularly subtle registration (the c.f. under control of the swell shades, if necessary).

They are the following:

Wer nur den lieben Gott lässt walten (V, 52; BWV 691)
If thou but suffer God to guide thee

There is an interesting variant of this work with extended prelude and interludes in Vol. V, p. 111.

Jesus, meine Zuversicht (V, Appendix, No. 2; BWV 728)
Jesus Christ, my sure Defence

to be played *adagio assai* in tempo and tone (♩ = 42); and the unfinished arrangement of

Jesu, meine Freude (V, 112; BWV 753)
Jesu, priceless treasure

which I completed for my editions of the *Klavierbüchlein für Friedemann Bach* and the *Orgelchoräle Manualiter* (both published by Bärenreiter). ♩ = 50.

Finally, there is one more piece to be mentioned in this connection. It presents the c.f. twice in succession, the second time beginning on the dominant:

In dulci jubilo (IX, 19; BWV 751)

Discovered by Seiffert, it was included in Straube's anthology *Alte Meister* (Peters edition, No. 3065) in 1904, and was immediately played a great deal. It is a pastorale which one may compare without hesitation to Pachelbel's "Vom Himmel hoch, da komm ich her" in 12/8 meter.[329] Nevertheless, both form and style make Bach's authorship seem very doubtful. 𝅗𝅥 = 138.

329. See *Orgelwerke*, ed. Matthäi, Vol. II, Nos. 5a and 5b.

CHAPTER 22

THE MISCELLANEOUS LARGE CHORALE PRELUDES

By this, the usual terminology introduced by Griepenkerl, we mean those organ chorales which present the various lines of the c.f. separately, and introduce each line by a prelude. We shall classify them in four groups:

The First Group: 10 chorales. The "Scheidt-Pachelbel organ motet" presents the c.f. unornamented, in large note values, and introduces each line—or at least the first one—by an advance imitation (usually at half-value) of the unembellished c.f. The style of both the c.f. and the contrapuntal parts is vocal.

The Second Group: 23 chorales. These also present the c.f. unembellished, but derive the contrapuntal parts from it by an often very free paraphrase; in contrast to the vocal style of the c.f., the style of the other parts is instrumental.

The Third Group: 10 chorales. In these chorales the c.f. is embellished; the counterpoint is derived from the c.f. as in the Second Group. Thus the chorale melody is never really heard, though it is always present in disguise.

The Fourth Group: 8 chorales. These chorales contrast a thematically independent counterpoint with the unembellished c.f.

Within each group the chorales have been arranged chronologically as far as possible.

FIRST GROUP

Vom Himmel hoch, da komm ich her (VII, 55; BWV 700)
From heav'n above to earth I come

(4-pt, c.f. in the bass)

This work is probably one of Bach's earliest, as is shown by the doubling of the manual bass by the pedal (in imitation of Pachelbel). Another evidence of immaturity is that the seven advance imitations of the first line follow each other regularly at the same distance of two-and-a-half measures. Nevertheless, the piece is not without charm for the very reason of its naiveté, and it can still be used in the church service today. ♩ = 116; c.f. in the pedal with reed tone; *Plenum* of the HW.

Durch Adams Fall ist ganz verderbt (VI, 21; BWV 705)
When Adam fell, the human race

(4-pt, c.f. in the soprano)

(text, see p. 221)

In the first publication of Bach chorale preludes by Schicht at the beginning of the nineteenth century, this chorale bore the remark *"a cappella."* This marking was suppressed by the editors of the BG. B. F. Richter published the work as a motet in Vol. XXVI of the publications of the Neue Bach-Gesellschaft. He suspected that originally it had been the opening movement of a chorale cantata (like "Ach Gott, vom Himmel sieh darein," perhaps), but that the arrangement for organ had been made by Bach himself. The performance will have to be governed accordingly. 𝅗𝅥 = 76.

Ich hab mein Sach Gott heimgestellt (VI, 28; BWV 707)
My cause is God's, and I am still

(4-pt, c.f. in the soprano)

Ich hab mein Sach Gott heimgestellt,
Er machs mit mir, wie's ihm gefällt.
Soll ich allhier noch länger leben,
Ohn Widerstreben
Will ich sein'm Willen mich ergeben.

Johannes Leon, 1589.

My cause is God's and I am still,
Let Him do with me as He will;
Whether for me the race is run,
Or scarce begun,
I ask no more—His will be done!

Tr. Catherine Winkworth.

Here we probably have before us a very early, clumsy work of Bach. Spitta[330] judged that, "with its irregular canonic treatment the chorale . . . might have derived from Walther." Walther, however, always wrote more "according to rule" than did the youthful Bach. Even the reckless harmonic treatment scarcely gives rise to any doubts of Bach's authorship.

Wir glauben all an einen Gott (IX, 24; BWV 765)
We all believe in One true God

(4-pt, c.f. in the soprano)

In addition to a manuscript of the complete work (a treatment of four lines) which Roitzsch had published, there is another, consisting of the first two lines only, which Seiffert discovered in 1904. Probably Bach abandoned the idea of treating all nine lines in this style because that would have proved too long and monotonous.[331] He also rejected the idea of calling special attention to the c.f., as did Scheidt in similar settings, as for example the first movement of his arrangement of this same chorale. A performance requires the *Plenum* of the HW. 𝅗𝅥 = 88.

Gelobet seist du, Jesu Christ (VI, 23; BWV 723)
All praise to Jesus' hallowed name

(4-pt, c.f. in the soprano)

330. *Op. cit.*, I, 656.
331. Cf. the shortening of "Komm heiliger Geist, Herre Gott," p. 248.

In this work Bach "virtually plagiarized Pachelbel," as Dietrich proved in the *Bach-Jahrbuch* for 1929[332] by comparing it with Pachelbel's "Komm, Gott, Schöpfer, heiliger Geist."[333] ♩ = 108.

Gottes Sohn ist kommen (VI, 25; BWV 724)
Once He came in blessing

(4-5 pts, c.f. in the soprano)

For this fine, smooth work the edition of the BG, which goes back to a copy in the *Andreas Bach Buch,* is preferable to the Peters edition. There the lowest voice is for the manual in mm. 32 and 33 and reads:

(the pedal enters for the first time with the c.f.); the last notes of the pedal may be played an octave lower:

♩ = 112.

Vater unser im Himmelreich (VII, 53; BWV 737)
Our Father, Thou in heav'n above

This setting is still more compact and more inspired than the preceding. In the vocal treatment of all its parts it reminds one of the Canzona. Formally and in the displacement of the bar lines of

332. Pages 60-61.
333. See *Orgelwerke,* ed. Matthäi, Vol. 2, No. 15.

the last two phrases, it is modelled on the introductory pieces of Scheidt's cycles of chorales. 𝅗𝅥 = 69.

Further examples of this style are found in the *Eighteen Chorales:* "Wenn wir in hőchsten Nőten sein" (see pp. 260f.) and in the *Third Part of the Clavierübung:* the three large arrangements of "Kyrie, Gott Vater in Ewigkeit," "Christ aller Welt Trost," and "Kyrie, Gott heiliger Geist" (see pp. 271ff); also the two arrangements of "Aus tiefer Not schrei' ich zu dir" (see pp. 283f).

SECOND GROUP

(c.f., plain; the c.p. paraphrases the c.f.)

In this group, which is numerically the largest (23 chorales), the chorales have been arranged according to the number of their parts. It is noteworthy that almost all of Bach's three-part works based on chorales belong in this group.

Two-part:

Allein Gott in der Hőh sei Ehr (VI, 3; BWV 711)
All glory be to God on High

(*manualiter*, c.f. in the soprano)

Excepting the two-part variations of the Partitas we have before us here Bach's only *bicinium*. To the c.f. is added an extremely stirring counterpoint, rocking to and fro in light dance rhythms. Its extremities lightly allude to the melody of the first line. Spitta doubted its authenticity: "Bernhard Bach wrote somewhat in this style; still, a few important features warn us to be careful."[334] Apart from the fact that the authenticity of the piece is adequately verified, only Sebastian could have written a virtuoso piece of this kind, so pretentious technically. The *bicinia* of Telemann are even more closely related to this work than are those of Bernhard Bach.[335]

Performance: on two manuals. ♩ = 120.

334. *Op. cit.*, I, 656.
335. See my edition, Peters No. 4239.

Three-part:

Nun freut euch, liebe Christen g'mein (IX, 20; BWV 755)
Dear Christians, one and all, rejoice

(3-pt, *manualiter*)

is preserved in a single late manuscript only, and therefore not reliably authenticated. It is "a neatly worked-out piece that would do credit to any of Bach's contemporaries, but without reasonably clear traces of Bach's style." (See my Preface to Vol. IX.) ♩ = 132.

Christ lag in Todesbanden (VI, 16; BWV 695)
In death's strong grasp the Savior lay

(c.f. in the alto, *manualiter*)

This piece is somewhat tiring because of its length. With its long-drawn-out advance imitations it is more of a "chorale invention," particularly in the ending, which is not at all suited to the organ. The c.f. can be brought out if it is played in the pedal with 4' pitch. A variant of this chorale (VI, p. 104; BWV 695a) and, similarly, one of "Jesu, meine Freude" (p. 244)—both from the same manuscript source—put the c.f. in the pedal as bass.[336] They probably derive from a pupil of Bach and from a time when the tradition of entrusting an alto- or tenor-part to the pedal had already been lost. In the manuscripts the simple chorale follows; of this only the figured bass is jotted down, not the melody. ♪ = 116.

Allein Gott in der Höh sei Ehr (VI, 4; BWV 717)
All glory be to God on High

(*manualiter*, c.f. in the soprano)

336. Frotscher's conjecture (*op. cit.*, p. 933) that it should also be interpreted here as a middle voice (thus to be played with 2'?) seems untenable to me.

Although this chorale occurs in only one manuscript, it is signed "J. S. B." It is a cleanly and carefully written piece in the rhythm of a *gigue*. It produces the best effect when the alto and tenor are played on two separate manuals, and the c.f. in the pedal with 4'. ♩. = 108.

Nun freut euch, liebe Christen g'mein (VII, 44; BWV 734)
Dear Christians, one and all, rejoice

a 2 Clav. e Ped., canto fermo in Tenore

This *perpetuum mobile*, in style and in form a masterpiece, intensifies the "Christian joy" to exuberance. A dance motive is developed from the first three notes of the melody:[337]

as an illustration of the phrase "with exultation springing."[338] With a bright registration for the manuals (l.h. without 16'), 4' may be recommended for the c.f. in the pedal, rather than 8'. The final sixteenth-note run belongs in the manual (as with "In dulci jubilo" of the *Little Organ Book*). A variant (VII, p. 91; BWV 734a) includes the c.f. in the manual; Busoni made his much-played piano transcription from this variant. On p. 37, 1, 4, the last notes of the soprano should read e d e f♯, not e d c♯ f♯. ♩ = 120.

Wir Christenleut (IX, 23; BWV 710)
We Christians may

(text, see p. 207)

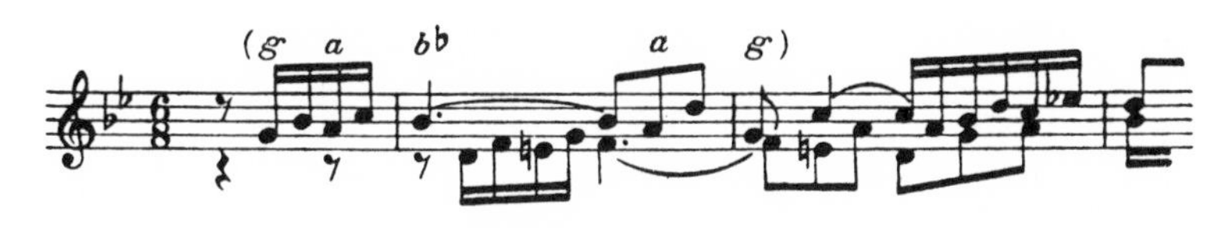

337. It is the original melody; the one that is current today (f/f c f b♭/a g f) was substituted for it as early as the sixteenth century, yet the first was retained for a long time—even up to the present—along with the second.
338. Dietrich in the *Bach-Jahrbuch* for 1929, p. 82.

This trio is also attributed to Krebs. In my Preface to Vol. IX I stated that "I am inclined to claim this piece for Bach. It is in a way 'correct,' as the rather sentimental period of Krebs was already past. I know of no example from the chorale works of Krebs (and these are for the most part rather weak, besides) in which he constructed an advance imitation as confidently as is done here, and put it in stretto immediately. Its continued use throughout the entire piece also has a counterpart in Bach in the three large settings of the Kyrie (Peters VII, No. 39 a-c). The piece may be placed on a level with the best chorale trios by Bach."

Performance: on 2 manuals and pedal with a mild 8'-reed. ♩. = 42.

Additional three-part settings within this group are found among the *Eighteen Chorales:* "Herr Jesu Christ, dich zu uns wend" and "Allein Gott in der Höh sei Ehr" (see pp. 250 and 258);[339] further, in the *Third Part of the Clavierübung:* two arrangements of "Allein Gott in der Höh sei Ehr" (see pp. 274f.); and in the *Six Chorales:* "Ach bleib bei uns, Herr Jesu Christ" and "Kommst du nun, Jesu, vom Himmel herunter" (see pp. 266 and 267); the first of the *Canonic Variations* on "Vom Himmel hoch, da komm ich her" (pp. 286ff.) also belongs here.

Four-part:

Wie schön leuchtet der Morgenstern (IX, 22; BWV 739)
O Morning Star! how fair and bright

(with migrant c.f.)

The authenticity of this chorale, which was first made known by Ritter in his *Geschichte des Orgelspiels und der Orgelkomposition,* is not fully established. If this work is by Bach, it must be from his Arnstadt period, since its style is altogether that of a North German chorale fantasy around 1700.

An additional, apparently somewhat later setting of the same chorale was left unfinished (23 mm., BG XL, p. 164). This fact is all the more regrettable since other than this we possess no organ chorale by Bach on this regal melody. Neither do we have one on "Wachet auf, ruft uns die Stimme," if we disregard the chorale trio

339. On pp. 196f. these two works were called "chorale trios"; both interpretations are possible.

found among the *Six Chorales*, which, of course, is a transcription from a cantata. Unfortunately we even have none on "O Welt, ich muss dich lassen."

Ach Gott vom Himmel sieh darein (IX, 13; BWV 741)
Ah God, from heav'n look down and see

(c.f. in the bass)

It is "preserved in several contemporary copies, among them Kirnberger's, but is apparently garbled. I agree with Naumann's conjecture in the Preface to BG XL that it is actually a work by Bach—to whom else could we attribute a stretto of the c.f. in double pedal? It is, however, an early, immature work corrupted by copyists." (See my Preface to Vol. IX.)

Ein feste Burg ist unser Gott (VI, 22; BWV 720)
A Mighty Fortress is our God

(2-4 pts, migrant c.f.)

Bach wrote this youthfully ingenious fantasy in 1709 for the rebuilt organ in Mühlhausen (see p. 20), as Spitta proved convincingly.[340] One manuscript contains the instruction: "*a 3 Clav.*" (not reproduced in the Peters edition); over the beginning of the left hand appears "*Fagotto,*" above that of the right, "*Sesquialtera.*" This does not mean, of course, that these two stops are to be used as solo stops, but that each should be prominent in a combination.

Mm. 1-20 are to be played on the OW and BW; the four measures following (c.f. colored, in the soprano) on the RP; mm. 24-33, in which the parts cross, are again played on the OW and BW; mm. 33-39 (the 5th line of the chorale, with coloration) presumably were again played on the RP. From m. 39 on, according to Spitta, the BW was coupled to the OW and "the full organ drawn" (?) in measure 50.

For the basses to the lines with coloration, on the RP, Bach used the new *Subbass 32'*; for the two lines with the c.f. in the bass, the

340. *Op. cit.*, I, 394ff.

new *Posaune 16'*. The loose form, reminiscent of the North German fantasies, together with the technique of frequently changing the register of the c.f., enabled Bach to produce this brilliant piece of music. ♩ = 96.

Fantasia[341] *super: Valet will ich dir geben*
Fantasy on "Farewell I gladly bid Thee"
(VII, 50; BWV 735)

(c.f. in the tenor)

This piece was probably composed in Arnstadt, as the variant printed in the Appendix to Vol. VII (p. 100; BWV 735a) shows. Later Bach revised it thoroughly, improved it, and gave it the gently rising ending, in which the soul is carried on high to its repose (as at the end of the large setting of "O Lamm Gottes unschuldig"). From the older version the breaking-up into motives still remains in the seventh line:

This was a treatment inoffensive to the North Germans, but one which Bach later could not endure. This chorale occurs in the *Andreas Bach Buch,* which is dated in Bach's Weimar period. This arrangement displays a pietistic tenderness, and the contrast between it and the following setting is extraordinarily great. The pedal should be played with 8' tone. ♩ = 84.

Valet will ich dir geben (VII, 51; BWV 736)
Farewell I gladly bid Thee

(c.f. in the bass)

---

341. Bach frequently called large chorale settings with the c.f. in the bass "*Fantasia.*"

The first setting expresses longing for death; this second setting, triumph over death. And it seems to us as though the latter interpretation were better suited to the stately melody, which reaches up so proudly. (This is said also in the thought of other texts sung to this melody, as for example, "Ist Gott für mich, so trete gleich alles hinter mich.") We are also acquainted with the spirited anacrustic figuration from the Arnstadt chorale, "Lobt Gott ihr Christen allzugleich" (see p. 188). From it was acquired the vigorous rhythm which paraphrases the c.f.—in the third line, for example—as follows:

(Reger derived inspiration from this piece for his chorale prelude "Jauchz, Erd' und Himmel, juble hell," Op. 67, No. 15.)

Performance: as for "Komm, heiliger Geist, Herre Gott" (pp. 247f.) ♩. = 76.

Additional four-part examples in this style appear among the *Eighteen Chorales* (pp. 245ff.): "Komm, heiliger Geist, Herre Gott" (VII, 36), "O Lamm Gottes, unschuldig" (VII, 48), "Nun danket alle Gott" (VII, 43), "Nun komm, der Heiden Heiland" (VII, 47), and "Jesus Christus, unser Heiland" (VI, 31 and 32); further, in the *Six Chorales* (pp. 262ff.): "Wer nur den lieben Gott lässt walten" (VII, 59); to which may also be added one five-part organ chorale: the large arrangement of "Vater unser im Himmelreich" in the *Third Part of the Clavierübung* (VII, 52; see below, pp. 268ff.).

THIRD GROUP

(c.f. colored; c.p. paraphrases the c.f.)

There are ten chorale preludes with embellished c.f. and a c.p. obtained by paraphrasing the c.f. Two early works will be mentioned first:

Vater unser im Himmelreich (IX, 21; BWV 762)
Our Father, Thou in heav'n above

Along with other evidence one notices the constraint felt by the composer (Bach?) in his uneasy effort, in paraphrasing the c.f., to bring the chorale notes on the accented parts of the measure, as for example, in the third line:

In dich hab ich gehoffet, Herr (VI, 34; BWV 712)
In Thee, Lord, have I put my trust

The great, austere text, with its rather tender major-melody ("Mit meinem Gott geh ich zur Ruh"), is also conceived in a tender, pastoral[342] manner: "The Lord is my Shepherd." In charming fashion the triplet rhythm is communicated to the c.f. in such a way that its entrance is hardly noticed. In the musical setting of the last line, however, the music makes a surprising rise toward fervor, even grandeur, particularly in the emphatic corroboration by the c.f. in the bass—for which one may use the pedal.[343] Bach calls the piece "Fughetta," since each line is introduced fugally. Mm. 5/6 of the tenor must read:

There are several additional four-part examples of this group in the *Eighteen Chorales* (pp. 245-261): "Komm, heiliger Geist, Herre Gott" (G major; VII, 37), "An Wasserflüssen Babylon" (VI, 12 b), "Schmücke dich, o liebe Seele" (VII, 49), "Nun komm, der Heiden Heiland" (VII, 45), and "Allein Gott in der Höh sei Ehr" (VI, 8 and 9).

Two settings in the manner of Tunder ("Jesus Christus, unser Heiland")[344] and Lübeck ("Nun lasst Gott dem Herren")[345] are for five parts with double pedal. Even though Scheidt had advised against

342. Tempo and rhythm are those of a pastorale in 12/8 meter, not those of a *gigue* (Frotscher, *op. cit.*, p. 933).
343. Here also Frotscher is in error when he speaks of a "sublimation"; the situation is the reverse.
344. See *Choralvorspiele alter Meister*, ed. Straube, (Peters No. 9124), p. 130.
345. See Lübeck, *Orgelwerke*, ed. Keller (Peters No. 4437), p. 45.

writing two pedal parts more than a fifth or an octave apart, "since one cannot reach other such [intervals] with the feet," the better-sounding wide compass was preferred around 1700.

Wir glauben all an einen Gott (VII, 62; BWV 740)
We all believe in One true God

Wir glauben all an einen Gott	We all believe in One true God,
Vater, Sohn und heil'gen Geist,	Father, Son, and Holy Ghost,
Der uns hilft aus aller Not,	Strong Deliv'rer in our need,
Den die Schar der Engel preist,	Praised by all the heav'nly host,
Der durch seine grosse Kraft	By whose mighty power alone
Alles wirket, tut und schafft.	All is made, and wrought, and done.
Tobias Clausnitzer, 1668.	*Tr.* Catherine Winkworth.

Actually, the only feature of this piece that is North German is the running passage at the end, which has no proper connection with the full, intimately warm composition. The upper pedal-part introduces the melody ahead of each line of the c.f.; before the second line it appears slightly disguised:

In *performance* one should differentiate the three sonorities of the two manuals and the pedal, omit 16' in the pedal, and try to bring out the vocal beauty of this setting by means of an expressive *legato* in all the voices. ♩ = 48.

This style achieves a quality even more spiritual in the chorale

An Wasserflüssen Babylon (VI, 12a; BWV 653b)
Beside the streams of Babylon

An Wasserflüssen Babylon	Beside the streams of Babylon
Da sassen wir mit Schmerzen;	Our weary vigil keeping,
Als wir gedachten an Zion,	When we remember Zion yon
Da weinten wir von Herzen.	We never cease from weeping.
Wir hingen auf mit schwerem Mut	We hang our harps, in our despair,
Die Harfen und die Orgeln gut	Upon the weeping willows there
An ihre Bäum der Weiden,	And mourn our degradation;
Die drinnen sind in ihrem Land;	All we hold dear our foes defame
Da mussten wir viel Schmach und Schand	And we must suffer slur and shame
Täglich von ihnen leiden.	In daily tribulation.
Versification of Ps. 137, Wolfgang Dachstein, 1525.	*Tr.* Henry S. Drinker.

Ever since Spitta it has been generally agreed that this composition was connected with Bach's trip to Hamburg in the year 1720 and with his playing in the presence of Reinken at St. Catherine's Church (see p. 23). This phenomenal achievement, however, is so far removed from an improvisation in the manner of the long-winded North German fantasies that the Hamburg journey can have been at best only the external motive for the working-out of a chorale prelude which strikingly reveals Bach's genius. The rhythm is that of a *sarabande*, and the c.f. is ornamented sparingly but expressively. Accompanying this c.f. we find not an ostinato bass, but a kind of ostinato soprano: the second soprano—at times adjusted to the tonality of the lines—laments unceasingly in eight-measure ritornellos in artistic stretto with the c.f.:

There is an insatiable melancholy in it, which almost blots out the pain. Here Bach shows us depths that at other times he does not reveal. Should we assume that, in later years, when double pedalling was no longer customary, he revised this miracle into a four-part setting and simplified it? (See the *Eighteen Chorales*, No. 3, pp. 248f.) ♩ = 60.

In the NBA[346] the editor, Hans Klotz, published another organ-chorale on "O Lamm Gottes unschuldig," which is not included in the Peters edition, in the BG, or in the BWV. The only source in which it is found is a manuscript of Johann Günther Bach, in which "G. [= Giovanni] S. Bach" is given as composer. It is an organ chorale for manuals alone, with anticipatory imitation of each line, and with its melody ornamented. It is followed by a simple version of the chorale, yet this also shows an ornamented melody. Its authentication is weak. Its style indeed shows influences of Bach, yet Bach himself would hardly have written for a Passion chorale such trivial passages in sixths as are found in the florid breaking-up of the last line of the chorale.

FOURTH GROUP

(c.f. plain, c.p. independent of the c.f.)

Only rarely, and for special reasons, did Bach introduce counterpoints that were thematically independent of the c.f.; this group, consequently, contains only eight chorales. Significantly, three of these are among the *Six Chorales* which are, for the most part, transcriptions from cantatas. These are: "Wachet auf, ruft uns die Stimme" (VII, 57), "Meine Seele erhebt den Herren" (VII, 42), and "Wo soll ich fliehen hin" (VII, 63). One chorale from the *Eighteen Chorales* is taken over from the *Little Organ Book:* "Komm, Gott Schöpfer, heiliger Geist" (VII, 35); and two appear in the *Third Part of the Clavierübung:* "Christ unser Herr zum Jordan kam" (VI, 17) and "Dies sind die heil'gen zehn Gebot" (VI, 19).

Only two isolated works, then, remain:

Wo soll ich fliehn hin? (IX, 25; BWV 694)
O whither shall I flee?

Wo soll ich fliehn hin, Weil ich beschweret bin Mit viel und grossen Sünden? Wo soll ich Rettung finden? Wenn alle Welt herkäme, Mein Angst sie nicht wegnähme.	O whither shall I flee? Depressed with misery? Who is it that can ease me, And from my sins release me? Man's help I vain have proved, Sin's load remains unmoved.
Johann Heermann, 1630.	Moravian Hymnal, 1754.

346. *Neue Bach Ausgabe*, Series IV, Vol. 3, p. 76.

This is apparently an early work, giving an effect of stiffness and monotony, but its authenticity has been adequately verified. Possibly the young Bach was intending to symbolize human helplessness by the constant repetition of the theme with its halting syncopations. (Cf. the cantata of the same name in the same key, No. 5.) In the trio of the same name from the *Six Chorales* Bach reached back into the store of motives of this youthful work (see p. 264).

Fantasia sopra: Jesu, meine Freude (VI, 29; BWV 713)
Fantasy on "Jesu, priceless Treasure"

In the first section of this piece, a theme that is expressive, and yet cannot be explained more precisely, is combined with the c.f. which wanders through all the registers. In the second section, which shows a change of meter and the marking "*dolce*"—the only *dolce* appearing in Bach's organ works—the c.f. is spun out in a very free way: mm. 1-11 of the 3/8 meter paraphrase the 7th line of the hymn; mm. 11-21, the 8th; mm. 31-38 and m. 42 to the end, the 9th. There is a striking similarity between this section ("Gottes Macht hält mich in Acht"), and the passage beginning "Gottes Macht hält mich in Acht" ("Might so vast leaves me aghast") in the motet of the same name, which was composed in Leipzig in 1723; this fact permits the assumption that the organ chorale might have originated at about the same time.[347] Although the fantasy was conceived for manuals alone, it will be advisable to give the c.f. to the pedal in the first section: lines 1-3 an octave lower with 4', lines 4 and 5 with 8'. A variant in D minor (VI, p. 110) presents all six lines in the pedal without discrimination as to pitch (cf. also p. 234). ♩ = 69; 2nd section, ♪ = 92.

347. Schweitzer, on the other hand, includes the Fantasy together with VI, 15, and VII, 54, 55, and 62, among the "admittedly youthful works, in which we can follow Bach's earliest development." *Op. cit.*, I, 293-294.

CHAPTER 23

THE "EIGHTEEN CHORALES"

Only a small number of Bach's settings of chorales may have been composed in Leipzig. In the master's last creative period, however,—from about 1738 on—we see him, like the aging Goethe, engaged in gathering together earlier, scattered works, looking them over once again, and arranging them in "collections." The result was that the *Well-Tempered Clavier* acquired a second part (1744) and no less than four collections of chorale preludes were assembled:

the *Third Part of the Clavierübung* (1739),
the *Six Chorales* (the so-called "Schübler," 1746),
the *Canonic Variations on a Christmas Hymn* (1746), and
the *Eighteen Chorales* (1750).

The first three of these anthologies Bach brought out in print, but while he was editing the fourth, death overtook him.

If this last collection is placed at the beginning of our discussion, the reason is that it contains wholly—or predominantly—works from the Weimar period. Probably it was destined for publication, like the other three, but failed to achieve it. We do not know what may have induced Bach to publish exclusively chorale works and yet none of the large preludes and fugues. Possibly it was a purely secular concern for sales, for he could have had greater hope of selling literature based on the chorale than of selling free works,[348] for which the church of Rationalism had less and less room and understanding. It is enough to know that in these collections he placed together those of his large works based on chorales that he himself considered the most valuable. Perhaps the large setting of "Valet will ich dir geben" and the Fugue on the *Magnificat* would have been worthy of inclusion as well.

The copying of the *Eighteen Chorales* fell within the last weeks of Bach's life. It reveals to us in a touching way the failure—at first gradual, and then swift—of the master's vital energy. The written characters, which had earlier shown such vigor, become uncertain and shaky. At the end of the fifteenth chorale Bach was obliged to hand over the pen to his son-in-law Altnikol, who wrote down the last three chorales at Bach's dictation; yet the last chorale again

---

348. Just as he also published neither the *Inventions* nor the *Well-Tempered Clavier* but *Six Partitas*, as *Opus 1*.

shows Bach's handwriting. Aware of the nearness of his own death, he changes the title to "Vor deinen Thron tret' ich hiemit." In the twenty-sixth measure his writing breaks off. His physical sight is blinded, but his spiritual vision sees heaven open. What other man has died as musician and Christian as did Bach?

For twelve of the eighteen chorales older versions exist which probably were revised and improved in Leipzig. For those who may wish to take a glimpse into Bach's workshop, therefore, no collection is as instructive as this one. It is only unfortunate that it is almost never the practical musician, but only the professional musicologist, who takes the trouble to compare the final versions with the earlier ones. For studying Bach's stylistic development these are quite as important as the sketch books, published by Nottebohm, for Beethoven.

Internally the *Eighteen Chorales* do not form a unit from any liturgical point of view.[349] Instead, Bach was intending to show, by large, significant examples, all the conceivable ways of arranging a chorale. We find in this anthology examples of ornamented *cantus firmus* in the soprano and in the tenor, all of which were composed in Weimar. Six settings in this style—Nos. 3, 4, 9, 10, 12, and 13—make up one-third of the collection. Later, in the *Third Part of the Clavierübung*, Bach no longer cultivated this type. There are also two magnificent fantasies with the c.f. in the bass (Nos. 1 and 11), two sparkling virtuoso trios (Nos. 5 and 14), three chorales with advance imitation of each line (Nos. 2, 7, and 18), and other forms. Taken all together, the differences in style (and in value) of the individual arrangements are so great that we cannot even say that the collection has any purely musical unity.

The title that Rust gave the collection in the BG, XXV, is neither autographic nor correct: *"Eighteen Chorales of Various Kinds, to be Performed on an Organ with Two Manuals and Pedal, Composed by. . . ."* He had merely patterned this title on the original title of the *Six Chorales*. Not all of the chorales require two manuals; No. 16 is for manuals alone.

In the NBA[350] the Canonic Variations are inserted before the last chorale because they appear in this position in Bach's autograph. The editor Hans Klotz, accordingly, counts 17 chorales, the Canonic Variations, and the chorale "Vor deinen Thron." This order may be correct philologically, but the musician will prefer the more meaningful compilation of the *Eighteen Chorales*, and furthermore, their separation from the *Canonic Variations*. This volume informs us of six additional readings besides the twelve old versions given in the Peters edition and the BG.

349. Luedtke made an attempt to draw up a unified sequence (*Bach-Jahrbuch* for 1918).

350. *Neue Bach Ausgabe*, Series IV, Vol. 2.

J. J.

1. *Fantasia*[351] *super "Komm, heiliger Geist, Herre Gott"* *Fantasy on "Come, Holy Spirit, come apace"* *(VII, 36; BWV 651)*

In Organo Pleno, Canto fermo in Pedale

Here, too, as in manuscripts of other works, Bach calls for the aid of Divine Grace with the initials *"J. J."* (*"Jesu juva"* = "Jesus, help!"), and he places Luther's German translation of "Veni, sancte spiritus" ("Come, Holy Spirit") meaningfully at the beginning of the collection. The animated theme that rapturously transforms the first line of the c.f. provides the building material for a magnificent F major toccata with c.f. added in the pedal. The organization results from the c.f., which is divided into its individual lines, the first of these proceeding directly out of the pedal point at the beginning in measure eight. Since the c.f. hardly modulates, the interludes make use of the opportunity for modulating to A minor, G minor, and D minor, as in the F Major Toccata. The thematic material consists of the main theme, the little rhythmic motive , and a few invocations: Her - re Gott. We have to compare Bach with his precedessors in order to perceive his enormous superiority: with Pachelbel's monotonously rolling sixteenths in "Nun freut euch, liebe Christen g'mein,"[352] for example; with Buxtehude's "Nun lob mein' Seel' den Herren";[353] or with Böhm's "Christe, der du bist Tag und Licht."[354] Walther alone comes reasonably close to Bach in his "Lobe den Herren, den mächtigen König."[355]

It is primarily the task of the organist not only to "boom" in the pedals and "whirl" in the manuals, but to play in a singing and inspired way, and thus restrain both the volume and the tempo (♩ = 84). The piece requires a majestic, but not shrill or harsh, *Plenum* of the HW and a registration for the pedals which contrasts with that of the manuals, not by the greatest possible volume but by its color—pure

351. See the footnote on p. 238.
352. See *Orgelwerke*, ed. Matthäi, Vol. 2, No. 13.
353. Spitta-Seiffert edition, Vol. III, No. 7.
354. *Sämtliche Werke*, ed. Wolgast, Vol. I, pp. 91ff.
355. *80 Chorale Preludes*, ed. Keller, No. 51, p. 84.

reed tone, without couplers. It also demands a firm, steady rhythm and a careful articulation of the manuals. Yet, however often one hears the Fantasy, these requirements are almost never fulfilled satisfactorily.

A variant (VII, 86; BWV 651a), which skips from the fourth line directly to the eighth (from p. 6, 1, 1, to p. 8, 3, 2), may be recommended for service use, and probably was even composed with practical use in view.

2. *Komm, heiliger Geist, Herre Gott (VII, 37; BWV 652)*
Come, Holy Spirit, come apace

Alio modo

(c.f. in the soprano)

This version probably derives from an earlier period of Bach; the spirited "Hallelujah"-ending, in particular, suggests North German prototypes. In value this second version is far lower than the first one, which displays a masterly compactness. The 3/4 meter forced Bach to keep both the c.f. and the advance imitations in the same note values, so that, after the very long and boring advance imitations, the c.f. does not enter with the necessary dominance. If we can come to terms with its form, however, we shall discover here, also, lyric beauties which repay a study of the piece. A variant (VII, 88; BWV 652a) was prolonged, in the rewriting, at the ends of a few lines only, and the ornamentation was simplified. The tempo should not be too slow. ♩ = 108.

3. *An Wasserflüssen Babylon (VI, 12b; BWV 653)*
Beside the streams of Babylon

Alio modo

(*a 4 voci*, c.f. in the tenor)

The marking *alio modo* has reference to the earlier five-part arrangement of the same chorale with double pedal (VI, 12a; BWV 653b; see pp. 242f.). Since the technique of double pedalling was steadily disappearing throughout the eighteenth century, Bach decided upon a revision and simplification to four parts; in this version he moved the c.f. from the soprano into the tenor.[356] In a manuscript of Krebs the two settings occur side by side. The second setting (Variant, VI, p. 103; BWV 653a) was also revised for inclusion in the *Eighteen Chorales*. The rhythm ♩♫ was sharpened into ♩. ♬—as in the first fugue of the *Well-Tempered Clavier*. Yet the inexpressible charm of the first five-part setting has vanished. ♩ = 63.

4. *Schmücke dich, o liebe Seele (VII, 49; BWV 654)*
Deck thyself, my soul, with gladness

(c.f. in the soprano)

Of the three large arrangements of an ornamented c.f. among the *Eighteen Chorales*, "Schmücke dich" has achieved an almost legendary fame. This came about through Schumann who, apropos of an organ recital in the year 1840 at the Thomas Church in Leipzig (the proceeds to go for a monument to Bach) had written about it: "Around the c.f. were hung gilded garlands, and such happiness had been poured into it that you yourself [Felix Mendelssohn] confessed to me that, if life were to deprive you of all hope and faith, this one chorale would restore them to you."[357]

Later, Pirro surpassed even this eulogy in *L'Orgue de J.-S. Bach*.[358] But doesn't this mean giving to this chorale an exceptional position to which it is not entitled? Don't the two others far surpass it: "Nun komm, der Heiden Heiland," with its gleam of mysticism, and the luminous chorale of the angels, "Allein Gott in der Höh sei Ehr"? Shall we support the thoughtless preference of the public for "famous" works?

Of course its beauty is not to be depreciated, either. In the rhythm of a *sarabande*, the chorale develops an ardent theme by paraphrasing the first line, and then continues independently with further development. Toward the end it even approaches a kind of *reprise*, so that this example shows Bach on a road along which he traveled farther in

356. Curiously, Spitta sees the process reversed. *Op. cit.*, I, 616.
357. See also Spitta, *op. cit.*, I, 618, fn. 356.
358. See pp. 64f. of the Eng. tr. of Pirro's book. (Details on this translation are given above, p. 7.)

the Schübler chorales: expanding the parts in opposition to the c.f. into independent periods. The five-part arrangement of "An Wasserflüssen Babylon" also has a bearing on this matter. ♩ = 56.

5. *Trio super: Herr Jesu Christ, dich zu uns wend (VI, 27; BWV 655)*
Trio on "Lord Jesus Christ, be present now"

a 2 Clav. e Ped.

It is curious what contrasts stand side by side in the *Eighteen Chorales;* next to the ardor of the last chorale appears a lively *concertante* trio, that seems to have nothing more in common with the chorale than the derivation of its theme from the beginning notes of the melody. We are almost surprised when, toward the end, the c.f. appears in addition, in the pedal; it could be omitted without our missing it. Like No. 14, this Trio[359] also is written in the exact style of the *Six Sonatas*. As a technical study, this excellently developed, clear, unusually consonant composition, which sometimes sounds like a *Glockenspiel*, is to be placed at least on a level with the *Sonatas*.

No fewer than three variants of this Trio have been preserved. The first (BWV 655a) and the third (BWV 655c) may be seen in the Appendix of Vol. VI of the Peters edition; the second (BWV 655b), in the BG only. They show how the formal layout of the Trio was gradually enlarged and the style improved in details.

In the first version, after an advance imitation of eight measures, the chorale enters in the bass. Here we have merely a three-part organ chorale with c.f. in the pedal; it belongs in the Second Group. The second version (BG XXV, p. 160) is curious: it shows us a trio of 29 measures without chorale (in contrast to the 73 of the final version), of which mm. 1-21 agree in layout with the final form, just as do the last measures again. Here, however, Bach has altered the theme to read:

We can imagine the third form as having arisen from a synthesis of the first two. It introduces the chorale again, restores the first

359. I am unable to agree with Dietrich's designation "chorale fugue."

version of the theme, and enlarges the first part by interpolating an extended section in the dominant. It was revised again only in details, but these apparent details are characteristic enough: parallel fifths, for example, had been left standing in the second measure:

Elimination of these gave the line marked polish:

This improved version of the motive was then used throughout the entire Trio. The registration may be thought of as analogous to that of the *Six Sonatas*. At the end a reed stop should be added in the bass. ♩ = 96.

6. *O Lamm Gottes, unschuldig (VII, 48; BWV 656)*
O Lamb of God, most stainless!

(3 stanzas)

As with "Christ ist erstanden," Bach here conceived the three stanzas as a unit, and composed them in succession: the first, three-part *manualiter* with slightly ornamented c.f. in the soprano; the second, similarly, but with the c.f. in the alto; the third, for four parts, with the c.f. in the pedal. The range of interpretation is extraordinarily great, from the almost dreamlike quality of the first stanza to the heroic grandeur of the third; the second stands between the two like a mediator.

Here, also, an older variant is extant (VII, p. 97; BWV 656a). This was improved in a number of details in the first two stanzas; only one passage in the third stanza (notated in 9/8 meter) had a stronger reading (p. 49, 1, 4):

The beginning of the first stanza appears incorrectly as tenor instead of alto in all the editions; it is correct in the variant. The emotional, madrigalesque rest in the second measure is noteworthy; it teaches us to understand correctly the musical expression of the first stanza: in spite of the luminous key of A major, it embodies an inexpressibly deep and tender mood reflecting the Passion. It recalls Mörike's *Karwoche* ("Holy Week") despite a difference in time of more than a century. Bach's style is first elevated to symbolical significance in the third stanza: the motive

not only paraphrases the c.f., but also makes the sign of the cross; the second motive

also derived from the c.f., depicts the bowed head of the Redeemer, his collapse on the cross.

The chromaticism of the following measures expresses "dejection" in a deeply moving manner, as the streams of lamenting voices pour down. And now the struggle is over; in the last line, "Grant us Thy peace today, O Jesu!"[360] angels carry the spirit to its heavenly peace. (Yet the performer must not interpret this ending as despair, but as triumph; cf. the end of "Valet will ich dir geben," VII, 50.)

Performance: The first stanza requires light foundation stops; in the second, the c.f. may be played on a separate manual or with 4' in the pedal—although Bach never placed ornamented parts in the pedal. The third stanza calls for *Organum Plenum,* and there is no need to reflect the changing emotional states in the registration. The tempo ought to be uniformly 𝅗𝅥 = 58. On p. 48, 2, 3, the tie in the pedal should be deleted.

7. *Nun danket alle Gott (VII, 43; BWV 657)* *Now thank we all our God*

a 2 Clav. e Pedale, Canto fermo in Soprano

360. *Tr.* Catherine Winkworth.

According to Spitta's pertinent characterization, this work "is strictly on Pachelbel's pattern, and without a flaw to mar it, to the very last note."[361] He then adds that "The jubilant shout that rises to the very clouds, and which Bach alone could raise, is here wanting." With this restriction the limitations of this composition are clear: it is worked out in mastery fashion, but still "worked out."

Here Bach's intellectuality has complicated Pachelbel's simple technique to such a degree that we might assume the chorale was first composed in Leipzig. The fact that no variant exists seems to support this opinion. Even more support is lent by the fact that the direct relationship with the instrument, which characterizes all the earlier works of Bach, is lacking in the compositions of the late master-period.

Performance: the c.f. with brilliant reed tone, the other parts with bright principals. ♩ = 84.

8. *Von Gott will ich nicht lassen (VII, 56; BWV 658)* *From God shall nought divide me*

(c.f. in the pedal)

The autograph assigns no pitch to the pedal. The BG restores "4'" after a copy by Oley—incorrectly, no doubt, since Bach's composition fills the alto area, but leaves the tenor area empty. Thus it seems more correct to restore "8'" (tenor).

The rapturous anticipatory imitation, with its "joy rhythm" ,[362] bends the descent of the melody back into a vigorous climb into the higher octave, and thus substitutes an ardent devotion for the serene faith the chorale expresses. At the end it is, as my old teacher Heinrich Lang once said to me, "as if a wanderer through the night were to see a consoling light flickering." A variant (VII, p. 102; BWV 658a) was improved merely in a few details, but always very characteristically (as in mm. 1, 4, 6, etc.). ♩ = 76.

9.—11. *Nun komm, der Heiden Heiland (VII, 45-47; BWV 659-661)* *Savior of the nations, come*

Internally the three arrangements belong together; each displays the chorale in a different light.

---

361. *Op. cit.*, I, 612.
362. Cf. the *Little Organ Book*, No. 18, p. 209.

The first setting (VII, 45; BWV 659), with embellished c.f.:

a 2 Clav. e Ped.

disguises the old Advent melody with scroll-work that reaches out far beyond the limits of the melody:

New imitations continually appear in the accompanying parts, and these involve the notes of the beginning of the c.f. in a mysterious way:

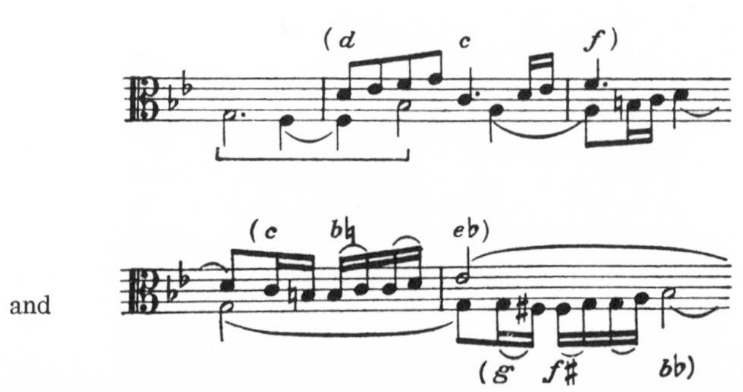

All in all, the work has a fantastic beauty that we never perceive fully. The solemn veiling of the melody is expressive of the impenetrable mystery of the Incarnation of God's Son.

A variant (VII, p. 92; BWV 659a) with the title *Fantasia* differs from the final version almost solely in the c.f. Bach made the coloration smoother in a number of places; for example:

Performance: C.f. with a light reed stop; l.h. light foundation stops, 8' and 4'; pedal uncoupled. ♩ = 42.

The second piece (VII, 46; BWV 660), a

Trio a due Bassi e Canto fermo

has puzzled all interpreters because of its curious style. What do the two basses signify, which climb tirelessly down into the depths? Was Bach perhaps thinking of Christ's descent into Hell?

Fuhr hinunter zu der Höll' Und wieder zu Gottes Stuhl?	The path to Hell at first He trod And then unto the throne of God.

Rust conjectured[363] that the composition resulted from the revision of a cantata-movement now lost. Two variants exist (VII, pp. 93 and 94; BWV 660a and 660b). In the second of these variants the c.f. occurs unembellished as melody in the pedal (with 4'—or, less probably, with 2'). Two chords in m. 15 and at the end are arpeggiated in the BG. Rust therefore suspected that this voice had been originally an obbligato 'cello part. Since the last note of the c.f. is sustained through the last measure in the variant (normally it would have ended five measures sooner) he assumed that this arrangement could not have been made by Bach. On the other hand, the second version (Variant 1), in which the c.f. is ornamented and transferred to the manual, Rust felt must have derived from Bach himself. In the final version it needed to be improved only in details.

Performance: This is a piece which is difficult to make sound well. In the first place, the two basses must be kept apart from each other. The first may be brightened up with 4', and a 16'-stop added to the second (in conformity with Variant 2, in which the two basses are shown an octave apart). ♩ = 56.

The third arrangement (VII, 47; BWV 661)

In Organo Pleno, Canto fermo in Pedale

sings the hymn of praise of redeemed humanity:

363. Preface to the BG, Vol. XXV. 2.

Lob sei Gott dem Vater g'tan,	Praise be God, the Father, done;
Lob sei Gott, seinem ein'gen Sohn,	Praise be God, His only Son;
Lob sei Gott, dem heil'gen Geist,	Praise be God, the Holy Ghost,
Immer und in Ewigkeit.	Always and for evermore.

Tr. H. H.

By "figuring" the first line of the chorale, Bach constructed an orchestral motive in which we imagine we hear violins being played with broad, vigorous strokes of the bow.[364] The chorale, grand and solemn, appears in the pedal.

All of Bach's organ chorales with the c.f. in the bass have the same fundamental idea: the chorale, as foundation, permeates and illuminates everything from the bass (cf. "Komm, heiliger Geist"; "Valet will ich dir geben," D major; "Fuga sopra il 'Magnificat' "; and "Kyrie, Gott, heiliger Geist"). Registration: see No. 1 (p. 247). 𝅗𝅥 = 69.

Again three arrangements of the same melody follow each other. Their inner relationship is less clear, however.

12.–14. *Allein Gott in der Hōh sei Ehr (VI, 9, 8, 7; BWV 662, 663, 664)*
All glory be to God on High

Here, also, an ornamented arrangement comes first (VI, 9; BWV 662):

one of the least familiar and least played, though possibly the most beautiful of all. We are reminded of A major as the Grail tonality by the other-worldly lustre that this piece radiates. The player who approaches it must do so in complete repose and in an attitude of prayer. Significantly, the advance imitation interrupts the rise of the melody with a descending seventh:

364. The similarity between the episodes of this work and the C Minor Fugue (III, 6; BWV 537) is striking.

—only four notes, but they bring heaven down to earth—and this motive is woven into the bass or one of the inner parts in every line of the chorale. In the deceptive cadence near the end the melody swings ecstatically upward with the freedom of a solo violin:

The *"accent,"* as a sentimental slurring of the melodic line, is less suited to the organ than to the clavichord, which has a tone that, though delicate, is capable of being modulated. Like the Lombardic rhythm (see p. 280), the ornament must be played in such a way that the first note seems accented while the second is very slightly detached, thus:

) = 60.

The second arrangement (VI, 8; BWV 663)

a 2 Clav. e Ped., Canto fermo in Tenore

is one of the most rarely played organ chorales of Bach. It is the only composition in which Bach places a florid c.f. in the tenor. In this apparently very early work, which is planned on the model of the North German chorale fantasies, the fantastic adornment of the c.f. has a downright smothering effect. Spitta speaks of "a tropical luxuriance of foliage with many-colored blossoms."[365] It is a jungle in which a listener can hardly find his way, despite the fact that the advance imitations, especially those in the pedal, are shaped quite clearly and simply. The variant (VI, p. 100; BWV 663a) shows only a few deviations, mainly in the c.f. 𝅗𝅥 = 66.

365. *Op. cit.*, I, pp. 615-616.

The third arrangement (VI, 7; BWV 664), a

Trio a 2 Clav. e Ped.

is a counterpart of No. 5, "Herr Jesu Christ, dich zu uns wend'." But it is even more loosely connected with the chorale than is No. 5, since only the first two lines of the c.f. appear at the end by way of supplementary confirmation. In brilliance and ease of writing it surpasses not only the trio just mentioned but also most of the sonata movements. It stands closest to the first movement of the G Major Sonata, particularly in its homophonic interludes; it is as though the heavenly hosts were soaring up and down. The more tranquil close may be interpreted as an illustration of the line: "Und als die Engel wieder von ihnen gen Himmel fuhren."

It is striking how the modulation scheme of the trio prefers the side of the subdominant (A—D—f♯—b—A). A variant (VI, p. 97; BWV 664a) exists here, also, an autograph which was refined and polished in its final revision only in details, to be sure, but in many characteristic features; for example, in the tied quarter notes, which throughout were given eighth-note anticipations:

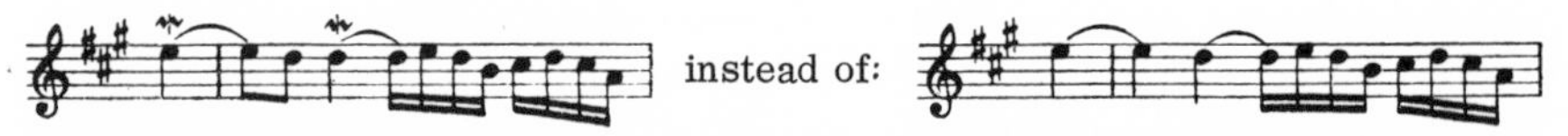

More extensive changes are found, from the entry of the c.f. especially. This work and No. 5 should be performed similarly. ♩ = 84.

Two arrangements of the old, austere Communion hymn by Luther follow:

15.—16. *Jesus Christus, unser Heiland (VI, 31 and 32; BWV 665 and 666)*
Jesus Christ, our Lord and Savior

(text, p. 284)

Even in Bach's time this hymn was on the verge of being supplanted by weaker Pietistic hymns.

All the scholars from Spitta through Schweitzer to Dietrich and Steglich have devoted special attention to the first setting:

Here, of course, Bach changes his style from line to line in such a striking way that it is only natural to look for a reason. The third line yields an explanation quite spontaneously: its refractory chromaticism expresses "the woe that Thee befell." In the fourth line, also, the mounting thirty-second notes may be interpreted as the deliverance "from the pains of hell."

Opinions as to the meaning of the first two lines differ widely. Schweitzer interprets the syncopations of the second line as "the strokes of God's wrath,"[366] while Steglich professes to see in them a "wresting," a "grasping struggle" for the love of God. On the other hand, Dietrich considers the large intervals a symbol of the "distance between God and man." Grace sees symbolized in the counterpoint to the first line the "carrying of the cross"; Steglich, "a yearning longing for and striving after" the Savior. As contradictory as these interpretations may be, they are nevertheless necessary attempts to understand Bach's conception. However, we should not overlook the structural uniformity of the work; in all four sections the succession of the entries of the c.f. is the same; namely, tenor, alto, bass, soprano. It is not the soprano that is felt to be leading, however, but the bass, so that the soprano comes in behind, as a kind of "after-imitation."

A variant (VI, p. 112; BWV 665a), which was revised only in quite unimportant details, shows by its marking *In Organo Pleno* that the pedal must be the bearer of the c.f., for Bach labeled only this type of chorale *Organo Pleno*. If he really intended this chorale for use during Communion, then on this point he is in strong opposition to our custom of permitting only subdued, often fulsome playing during that service. Here Bach has really transformed a magnificent text into not less magnificent musical speech. ♩ = 50.

The second setting (VI, 32; BWV 666)

is probably, like No. 2, a very early work, the only setting for manuals alone among the *Eighteen Chorales*. Only at the end, as in several youthful works of Bach, does the pedal enter with a supporting tone. This setting was doubtless the model for the larger one, as similarity in their formal structure shows; only its expression is more neutral, more vague. The relaxing sixteenths that enter with the third line lead to a youthfully exuberant ending. Steglich tried to establish a relationship between this chorale and the third stanza of the hymn, "Glaubst du das aus Herzensgrund." ♩. = 54.

366. *Op. cit.*, II, 73.

Curiously, the last two of the *Eighteen Chorales* have a connection with the *Little Organ Book*.

17. *Komm, Gott, Schöpfer, heiliger Geist (VII, 35; BWV 667)*
Come, Holy Ghost, Creator, come

In Organo Pleno, con Pedale obbligato

To the arrangement of this Pentecost chorale in the *Little Organ Book* (No. 33; see p. 218) Bach appended a second section with c.f. in the pedal and magnificent figuration occasionally reminding us of the C Major Prelude (II, 7; BWV 547).[367] As in all of Bach's treatments of a c.f. in the bass (cf. Nos. 11 and 16), here too, the meaning conveyed is that of all-penetrating power. The use of the minor subdominant at the end is to be interpreted, as in the G Major Fugue (II, 2; BWV 541), not as "intense sorrow," but as the ultimate heightening of joy and trust. ♩. = 50.

18. *Wenn wir in höchsten Nöten sein (VII, 58; BWV 668)*
When in the hour of utmost need
(Vor deinen Thron tret' ich hiermit)
(Before Thy throne, my God, I stand)

Vor deinen Thron tret' ich hiermit,	Before Thy throne, my God, I stand,
O Gott, und dich demütig bitt':	Myself, my all, are in Thy hand.
Wend dein genädig Angesicht	O show me Thine approving face,
Von mir betrübtem Sünder nicht.	Nor from Thy son withhold Thy grace.
(?) Bodo von Hodenberg, 1640.	*Tr.* Charles Sanford Terry.[368]

367. Spitta sees the procedure the other way around: the small chorale as having been splintered off the larger. *Op. cit.*, I, 611, and fn. 346.

368. *The Four-Part Chorals*, ed. Terry, No. 374.

The manuscript of this chorale is partly from Bach's own hand. Owing to serious trouble with his eyes, however, he dictated the greater part to his son-in-law Altnikol. The autograph portion breaks off in measure 26. The entire chorale is known to us from a manuscript owned by Philipp Emanuel and from which he added this chorale, as is well known, to the *Art of Fugue* (also left unfinished) as conclusion.

When Bach gave the chorale its second title,[369] he knew how soon he himself would be standing before God's throne. Now, ever since the *Art of Fugue* has once again been resounding in our concert halls, many thousands, deeply moved, have been united in prayer for the dead master, as if in a church service.

Consequently, it has acquired a symbolical meaning for us which far surpasses its true significance, much as the melody "O Haupt voll Blut und Wunden" has, for most educated persons, come to have a meaning associated with Good Friday. This, Bach's "swansong," however, was certainly not composed on his deathbed, but only dictated then. It probably originated in a much earlier period. If we look at it more calmly, we see an organ motet of the Pachelbel stamp, artistically worked out, rather than immediately felt. It is a counterpart of the small arrangement of "Aus tiefer Not schrei' ich zu dir" from the *Third Part of the Clavierübung*.

Particularly curious is Spitta's observation[370] that this arrangement may be considered as having been produced from the smaller one in the *Little Organ Book* (No. 42) by removing the coloration of the c.f. and adding advance imitations. As in "Alle Menschen müssen sterben," the peaceful calm of the melody is communicated to the whole composition. Only in the last measures do the shades of death seem to fall and transport us again in spirit to the deathbed of the master.

Its *rendition* should be tranquil and radiant, but not dragging. ♩ = 52. Of several small differences in the two readings, only the bass line in m. 10 is important; the reading in the Peters edition should be changed to  after the BG.

369. It is wanting in the Peters edition.
370. *Op. cit.*, III, 222.

CHAPTER 24

THE "SIX CHORALES"

Six Chorales
of Various Kinds
To be Performed
on an
Organ
With 2 Manuals and Pedal
Composed by
Johann Sebastian Bach
Royal Polish and Electoral Saxon Court Composer
Capellmeister and *Direct. Chor. Mus. Lips.*
Published by Joh. Georg Schübler in Zella at the Thuringian Forest
To be had of the Capellmeister Bach in Leipzig, of his
Sons in Berlin and Halle, and of the Publisher in Zella.[371]

So runs the title of this collection.[372] It could not have come out before 1746, for that was the year in which Friedemann first went to Halle. We can only speculate as to what may have led Bach to publish this volume, in which five out of the six chorales were not original works but transcriptions from cantatas. At that time arrangements of favorite pieces from operas and oratorios were, of course, no longer a curiosity (e.g., those of J. P. Krieger and Handel!). Transcriptions from church cantatas, however, were a novelty. Did Bach hope for a wider market for these melodious and easily understood chorales than that which the *Third Part of the Clavierübung* had had seven years before? His indications of pitch show that he was directing himself to a larger public. What competent organist would have needed to be told at the start that, in "Wachet auf, ruft uns die Stimme," the manual should be played with 8' and the pedal with 16'?

Bach selected from his Leipzig cantatas such pieces as could be played particularly well as trios on the organ. He succeeded in a measure, for no one who did not know it would ever notice that these chorales are "arrangements." In making these arrangements, Bach changed hardly a note; it is only the thorough-bass that is missing.

---

371. See *The Bach Reader*, p. 175.

372. We are discussing the *Six Chorales* before the *Third Part of the Clavierübung* because the cantatas from which Bach took the chorales were composed between 1728 and 1736.

If we compare the often copious figuring of the original with the writing for only two parts in the ritornellos of the organ trios, something essential does, in fact, seem to be lacking. Should the organist, then, try wherever possible to restore the figuring? I do not believe so, for the two-part beginnings of the six organ sonatas also permit no filling-in, while the corresponding beginnings of the violin sonatas are figured. Bach requires that the organist be capable of hearing mentally the tones represented by the figures.

Formally, the long periods of the ritornellos found in the *Six Chorales*—complete in themselves—represent for Bach the end of a long development. This began in his unoriginal counterpoints in the style of Scheidt and Pachelbel, and had as its constant goal an ever stronger individuality for the parts against the c.f. Important links in this development were the ritornellos of the first variations of the partitas and, in particular, the ritornellos of "An Wasserflüssen Babylon" (VI, 12a). Dietrich[373] is therefore correct in seeing in the Schübler chorales "the mighty keystone"[374] of Bach's production of organ chorales, "his legacy to the next two generations."[375] Dietrich also shows, in an organ chorale by Christian Gotthilf Tag, a pupil of Homilius, how this style was developed monodically.[376] Unfortunately it was a period of decline which took possession of this inheritance from Bach. But shouldn't we of today try to make a connection where the development was broken off?

1. *Wachet auf, ruft uns die Stimme (VII, 57; BWV 645)*
   Wake, awake, for night is flying

(c.f. in the tenor)

from Cantata 140 (with the same name), composed in 1731. The violins and violas play the figuration in unison; the tenors of the chorus sing:

"Zion hört die Wächter singen,	"Zion hears the watchmen singing,
Ihr Herz tut ihr vor Freude springen,	And all her heart with joy is springing,
Sie wachet und steht eilends auf," etc.	She wakes, she rises from her gloom," etc.
Philipp Nicolai, 1599.	*Tr.* Catherine Winkworth.

373. *Bach-Jahrbuch* for 1929.
374. *Ibid.*, p. 88.
375. *Ibid.*, p. 86.
376. *Ibid.*, pp. 86-88.

Underneath lies an elaborately figured bass.

In this celebrated piece Bach has written mystical wedding music of a truly bridal intimacy: "Zion," symbolized by the chorale, "hears the watchmen singing," whose love-melody sometimes sounds nearer, sometimes farther away, like an echo. Although one would suppose that what this music expresses surely could not be misunderstood, we frequently hear this wonderfully tender piece played too coarsely and clumsily by our organists. The player should restore the echo in mm. 3 and 4 after the original. Bach here added ornaments not found in the cantata; for the first and only time we encounter here the short grace-note. ♩ = 56.

2. *Wo soll ich fliehen hin (VII, 63; BWV 646)* or:
O whither shall I flee
Auf meinen lieben Gott
In God, my faithful God

(c.f. in the alto, with 4' in the pedal)

It has been customary to assume that the original of this trio was a movement of a cantata now lost. But if one compares its perfectly genuine organ style with the style of the rest of the chorales, the probability seems quite as great that it is an original composition or perhaps even a radical revision of an earlier, rather awkward trio in G minor[377] (see p. 243f.). The instruction "16'" for the left hand should be taken with a grain of salt; an 8'-stop will often sound better. Bach was composing the first text—the sixteenths seem to suggest "fleeing"; for if he had been thinking of the second (original) text, it would have been senseless to add the alternate heading. ♩ = 84.

Two four-part arrangements now follow. These have one feature in common: in the original, the relation between sung and played parts is the reverse of that in the other chorales. Here the counterpoints were sung and the c.f. sounded along with them like an instrumental quotation.

377. Curiously, Luedtke sees the procedure the other way around. *Bach-Jahrbuch* for 1918, p. 68.

3. *Wer nur den lieben Gott lässt walten (VII, 59; BWV 647)*
If thou but suffer God to guide thee

(c.f. in the tenor with 4' in the pedal)

This work is from Cantata 93 of the same name, composed in 1728. There it is a duet for soprano, alto, and b.c. on the fourth stanza of the hymn:

Er kennt die rechten Freuden-stunden,
Er weiss wohl, was uns nützlich sei,
Wenn er uns nur hat treu erfunden,
Und merket keine Heuchelei:

So kommt Gott, eh wirs uns versehen
Und lässet uns viel Guts geschehen.

Georg Neumark, 1659.

He knows the time for joy, and truly
Will send it when He sees it meet,
When He has tried and purged thee throughly
And finds thee free from all deceit,
He comes to thee all unaware

And makes thee own His loving care.

Tr. Catherine Winkworth.

Both the vocal parts paraphrase the c.f. expressively:

The expression of exuberance in the fifth line is especially beautiful:

In the cantata the c.f. is played by violins and violas in unison.

Here Bach does not specify the use of two manuals, possibly because of a few large reaches; nevertheless, the player should try to give the bass to a separate manual with 16'-tone. ♩ = 63.

4. *Meine Seele erhebt den Herren (VII, 42; BWV 648)*
My soul doth magnify the Lord

(c.f. in the soprano)

is from Cantata 10 of the same name, composed *ca.* 1735. There it is a duet for alto and tenor on the text "He hath holpen his servant Israel, in remembrance of his mercy."[378] Against the duet appears the Gregorian c.f. of the *Magnificat,* played by two oboes and a trumpet (see p. 196). The expressive principal motive symbolizes humbly bowing low and then becoming erect again. One should notice Bach's own articulation, intended to help in expressing this idea. The bass also fills the ritornello-like prelude and postlude with this motive. Twice—in mm. 13 and 24—too large an interval between the inner parts requires the assistance of the right hand, a situation which occurs very seldom in Bach's works written originally for the organ.[379] ♩. = 42.

5. *Ach bleib bei uns, Herr Jesu Christ (VI, 2; BWV 649)*
Lord Jesus Christ, with us abide

(c.f. in the soprano)

is from Cantata 6, "Bleibe bei uns, denn es will Abend werden" ("Bide with us, for now is night approaching"), probably composed in 1736. There it is an ornamented chorale on the first two stanzas of the hymn ("Lord Jesus Christ, with us abide" and "In these dark days that yet remain") for soprano, *violoncello piccolo* (in the alto clef) and b.c. The tempo is *allegro* and the eighth notes of the 'cello part are marked *staccato*. The figuration does not always sound well either on the 'cello or on the organ; what it is trying to express is not immediately clear. It begins with the c.f. almost in its purest form, but strays farther and farther from it, rambles up and down—a symbol of the evil unrest of this world—but then finally finds its way upward again into the comforting nearness of the chorale. ♩ = 92.

378. From the *Magnificat*, St. Luke 1:54.
379. For example, in "Herzlich tut mich verlangen," m. 12.

6. *Kommst du nun, Jesu, vom Himmel herunter?*
Art Thou, Lord Jesus, from heaven to earth now descending? (VII, 38; BWV 650)

(c.f. in the alto, with 4' in the pedal)

Kommst du nun, Jesu, vom Himmel herunter auf Erden?
Soll nun der Himmel und Erde vereiniget werden?
Ewiger Gott,
Kann dich mein Jammer und Not
Bringen zu Menschengebärden?

Art Thou, Lord Jesus, from heaven to earth now descending?
Shall now the earth with high heaven in union be blending?
Eternal God,
Can all my need and my woe
Bring Thee as man, Thy help lending?

Tr. H. H.

from Cantata 137, "Lobe den Herren, den mächtigen König der Ehren" ("Praise to the Lord! the Almighty, the King of Creation!"[380]), composed in 1732. There it is an alto aria with obbligato violin and b.c. on the second stanza of the hymn, "Lobe den Herren, der alles so herrlich regieret" ("Praise to the Lord! who o'er all things so wondrously reigneth"[381]). It is a mystery why Bach placed the words of an unfamiliar Advent hymn with the organ transcription, and it would certainly be better if we were to restore the original title and play the chorale as "Praise to the Lord, the Almighty, the King of creation."

The player might copy the elaborate articulation of the original in his volume of organ music:

380. *Tr.* Catherine Winkworth.
381. *Tr.* Catherine Winkworth.

This is the only time Bach made an alteration and improvement in the process of transcription: m. 2 is now rounder and smoother:

Although the c.f. is notated in 3/4 meter, the subdivisions of the beat are of course to be interpreted as triplets. ♩. = 54.

CHAPTER 25

THE "THIRD PART OF THE CLAVIERÜBUNG"

In 1731 Bach collected the six partitas for clavier under the title *Clavier Übung. . . .* Op. 1. Of these he had had one engraved on copper each year since 1726. In 1735 he followed this volume with a Second Part (Italian Concerto and French Overture in B Minor), and in 1739 with a Third Part entitled:

CLAVIERÜBUNG. THIRD PART.
Chorale Preludes and Duets

The subtitle read in detail: "Third Part of the Keyboard Practice, consisting of Various Preludes on the Catechism and Other Hymns for the Organ: For the Pleasure of Music Lovers and Especially of Connoisseurs of Work of This Kind Composed by Johann Sebastian Bach, Royal Polish and Electoral Saxon Court Composer, Capellmeister, and Director *Chori Musici* in Leipzig. Published by the Author."[382]

A nephew of Bach, Johann Elias Bach, in a letter to J. W. Koch, dated January 10, 1739, solicited a subscription at a reduced price: "My honored Cousin will bring out some clavier pieces which are mainly for organists and are exceptionally well composed. They fill eighty pages and should be ready for the Easter Fair."[383] After publication a copy cost three Reichsthaler.[384]

We do not know, of course, what could have led Bach to call a collection of compositions intended mainly for the organ "Keyboard

382. See *The Bach Reader*, p. 164.

383. Cf. Terry, *op. cit.*, p. 247.

384. The *Reichsthaler* was a coin, no longer made, worth approximately 3 German marks.

Practice" (*Clavierübung*).[385] But surely practical considerations were uppermost in his mind: he could count on selling more copies if outwardly he followed previous publications that had been well received by the public. Moreover, the new collection had a great deal to offer performers on the other keyboard instruments. The four Duets (large two-part inventions) had been included expressly for them. The main title mentions them explicitly, along with the chorale preludes, while the Prelude and Fugue in E♭ Major are not mentioned at all. The 11 small settings of the chorales were also available to performers on the other keyboard instruments, making 15 items out of a total of 27. The title selected, therefore, was not so misleading as it may seem at first glance.

A clear explanation of the dual purpose of this collection, intended for both organists and clavier players, has been necessary because of a recent attempt to characterize the *Third Part of the Clavierübung* as organ music exclusively and as a liturgical unit; namely, as "the German Ordinary of the Protestant Mass, usually sung every Sunday by the congregation."[386] The Duets are interpreted as organ music played during the Holy Communion. But, aside from the fact that their purely secular quality, better suited to the clavier, is decidedly opposed to their use in the Divine Service (including Holy Communion), there is no evidence whatsoever from Bach's period that organ music not based on a chorale was ever used during Holy Communion.[387]

Steglich[388] also tried to prove an inner connection between the Duets and the Chorale Preludes: "The relationship between the 'little world' (i.e., man) and God is the subject matter of the organ chorales. Can, then, the 'large world' (nature outside man as the creation of God) be the theme of the four Duets?" Steglich interprets them as sky, air, water, and earth. But isn't this explanation very artificial and far-fetched? Without knowing in advance, what player or listener could say which element the F Major Duet, for example, was intended to illustrate?

Thus, these attempts to combine the entire *Third Part of the Clavierübung* into one liturgical unit, although undertaken with great acumen, seem to me to proceed from false premises. The spiritual unity of the 21 chorale settings that constitute the chief part of the work, however, is clear. The heart of the collection consists of Luther's six chorales for the principal items of the Catechism: the

---

385. In Bach's day the word "clavier," while meaning "keyboard," was also used generically to mean the keyboard instruments other than the organ.

386. Wilhelm Ehmann in *Musik und Kirche*, 1933, *Heft* 2; following him, Frotscher and others.

387. The examples submitted by Ehmann (*op. cit.*, p. 83) do not admit of any such conclusions for Bach.

388. *Op. cit.*, p. 146.

Ten Commandments, the Creed, the Lord's Prayer, the Baptism, the Atonement, and the Holy Communion. Preceding these Bach placed the German hymns which, being translations of the Kyrie and Gloria, formed the first two main items of the Divine Service on Sundays.

Each chorale was given both a large and a small setting (corresponding to Luther's large and small Catechisms?). Only "Allein Gott in der Hōh sei Ehr" was arranged three times, each time in a different tonality. Was Bach intending here to give us a symbol of the Trinity, or was his reason merely that, because this chorale was used so frequently, an extra setting seemed desirable? Bach's settings of the other hymns (excepting "Dies sind die heil'gen zehn Gebot' ") are always in two different tonalities. Adlung gives us a contemporary opinion on this matter. In his *Musikalische Gelahrtheit*[389] he states that "When a few hymns, such as 'Allein Gott in der Hōh sei Ehr' or the large Creed, are sung every Sunday, the organist enjoys varying [the key from week to week]. Consequently, I play the former in E, F, F#, G#, A, and B♭; higher or lower [keys] I consider unsuitable."

It appears that Bach composed the greater number of the pieces intended for this collection especially for it, and included in it only a few earlier works. Hence, we have here the only chorale preludes that we may date with certainty in the period of Bach's greatest mastery. And a second point: in no other organ work are we so much impressed by Bach as a musical prophet and profound interpreter of the fundamental doctrines of Lutheranism as here. It is no accident that the chorales of the *Third Part of the Clavierübung* have remained misunderstood the longest, for here the purely musico-aesthetic standards are not applicable. In the late works of Bach another kind of beauty than that we look for in Classic or Romantic music has been revealed to our generation. On the other hand, it would be a mistake to expect to obtain the whole meaning from a purely "theological guide" through the range of ideas in these chorales: Bach was a musician, and he transformed every idea into music. It is wise, therefore, to interpret these organ chorales musically at first, before going into their symbolical meaning; but even then the correct interpretation is found only when the two coincide. The large settings seem monotonous and boring to one who does not live in their world; but the concept of length ceases to exist when one comprehends their *ordo*, their inner form and the laws they obey.

The following chorales seem to derive from the Weimar period: the first setting of "Allein Gott in der Hōh sei Ehr" (F major), similar in style to the Fantasy on "Christ lag in Todesbanden"

---

389. Erfurt, 1758. Facsimile edition (Kassel and Basel: Bärenreiter-Verlag, 1953), p. 676.

(VI, 16); the small setting of "Vater unser im Himmelreich," representing the type found in the *Little Organ Book;* the first version (variant) of the large arrangement of "Allein Gott in der Hōh sei Ehr" (G major, 6/8); and perhaps also the small arrangement of "Jesus Christus, unser Heiland," in style linked closely with the *Well-Tempered Clavier*. All the others, with great probability, were composed in Leipzig.

How is one to perform the *Third Part of the Clavierübung?* Surely not by playing it straight through from beginning to end, including the Duets; but by omitting the Duets and playing one each of the chorale-settings, which were conceived as alternatives. As a rule, the choice should fall on the large setting, since the fughettas do not present the complete c.f. One may, however, also use the small settings of "Aus tiefer Not" or "Vater unser im Himmelreich," since these, as organ chorales, bring the c.f. in its entirety. The sequence would then be:

Prelude in E♭ Major[390]
Kyrie—Christe—Kyrie (large)
Allein Gott in der Hōh sei Ehr (large)
Dies sind die heil'gen zehn Gebot (large)
Wir glauben all an einen Gott (large)
Vater unser im Himmelreich (large or small)
Christ unser Herr zum Jordan kam (large)
Aus tiefer Not schrei ich zu dir (large or small)
Jesus Christus, unser Heiland (large)
Fugue in E♭ Major.[390]

If each of these organ chorales is introduced by a choral setting of its melody, understanding will be greatly facilitated for most listeners. I performed the *Third Part of the Clavierübung* in this way for the first time in 1930 at the German Bach Festival in Kiel.

KYRIE

This *Kyrie summum* was intended for use at major feasts. It comprises three large arrangements. In the first of these Bach places the c.f. meaningfully in the highest voice; in the second section he conceals it in the tenor (Son of Man); and in the third section the c.f., from the bass, permeates all-powerfully the close texture of a five-part setting woven out of it. All three settings are "organ motets" of the most artistic kind, in which the c.f. appears in large, "supernatural" note values and is imitated in advance. Bach unifies this form by maintaining throughout the whole piece the advance

390. The Prelude and Fugue in E♭ Major are discussed on pp. 159ff.

imitation constructed at the beginning, and thus gives it a commanding thematic importance.

In the first section (VII, 39a; BWV 669)

Ky - ri - e, Gott Va - ter in E - wig-keit, groß ist dein Barm-her - zig - keit,
al - ler Ding ein Schöp-fer und Re - gie - rer, e - le - i - son!

Kyrie! God our Father evermore!
Mercy Thine in bounteous store,
Thou of all things Ruler and Creator!
Eleison!

Tr. Henry S. Drinker.

still suffused with the glamor of the E♭ Major Prelude, the advance imitation, consisting of a combination of the first two lines:

is treated in stretto from the very beginning, not only in direct motion, but also in contrary motion. The result is a composition so compact as to be understood by the player only if he singles out individual combinations of voices and tries to hear at first two, and then three voices together. Then, only, will he be able to play this piece as "vocally" in all the parts as is necessary. Both manuals and the pedal on a bright, but not too brilliant *Plenum.* 𝅗𝅥 = 60.

The second piece (VII, 39b; BWV 670)

Chri- ste, al - ler Welt Trost, uns Sün - der al - lein hast _ er - lost!
O__ Je - su __ Got - tes Sohn, un - ser Mitt - ler bist in dem höch-sten Thron,
zu dir schrei - en wir aus Her - zens Be - gier. E - - le - - i - son.

Christ our hope and comfort!
Thou who hast redeemed us
all from sin,
Jesus, Son of God, Mediator.

To Thee enthroned on high,
We Thy servants from our
hearts beseech Thee!
Eleison!

Tr. Henry S. Drinker.

is worked out in the same technique, though without inversion:

Bach splits the second and third lines of the c.f. each into two parts without discernible reason. In this section the tone quality should be more mellow than that used in the first section. 𝅗𝅥 = 66.

In the third section (VII, 39c; BWV 671):

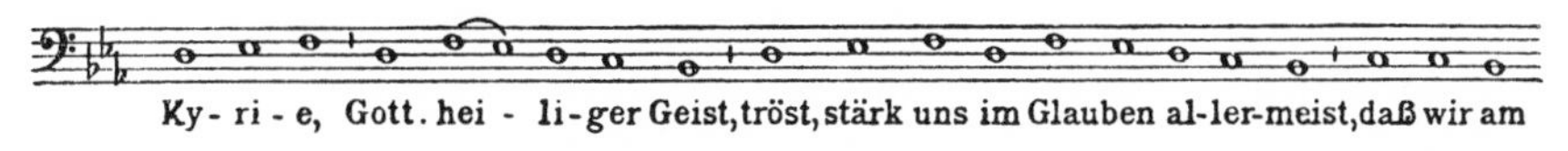
Ky- ri - e, Gott. hei - li-ger Geist,tröst,stärk uns im Glauben al-ler-meist,daß wir am

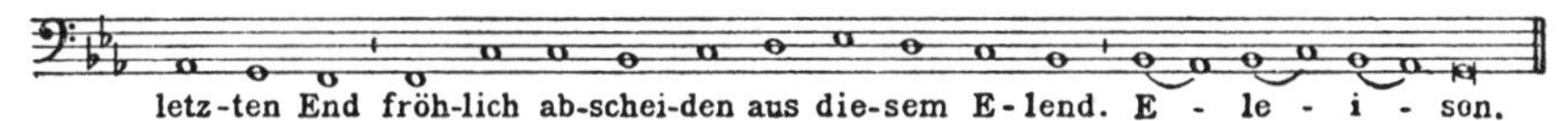
letz-ten End fröh-lich ab-schei-den aus die-sem E-lend. E - le - i - son.

Kyrie! O God, Holy Ghost!
Keep us firm of faith and true to Thee,
And when at last we die,
Joyful let us leave this Vale of Sorrows!
Eleison!

Tr. Henry S. Drinker.

the anticipatory imitation is treated from the very first in stretto of direct and contrary motion:

After the words "leave this Vale of Sorrows" the "Eleison" is expressed by a harmonic harshness that has a counterpart only in the "Crucifixus" of the *B-Minor Mass* and in the last counterpoint of the *Art of Fugue*. This, the most magnificent section of the triptych, requires a *Plenum*, with manuals coupled, and with strong reeds in the pedal. 𝅗𝅥 = 72.

The same, *alio modo* (small setting, VII, 40, a-c; BWV 672-674)

a)
(g
a
b)
b)
c)
(b
c
d)

It will always remain curious that in the *Third Part of the Clavierübung,* after such a long interval, Bach revived the unpretentious form of the prelude fughetta, which he had cultivated in a few youthful works. These fughettas, however, are by no means "of bewitching simplicity," as Schweitzer[391] thinks, but are representative of a style that is abstract and of the most exalted quality. Their form, too, is so polished that we discover their beauties only after long study. Only the second fughetta uses the whole first line of the c.f. as its subject. The other two limit their subjects to the first few notes, so that no one, without previous knowledge, would suspect they were chorale themes. As in the E♭ Major Fugue, the 9/8 meter of the third fughetta is to be interpreted here as a fusion of the 3/4 and 6/8 meters of the first two fughettas—as a symbol of the Holy Ghost,[392] "qui procedit e Patre filioque" ("Who proceedeth from the Father and the Son"). For the first fughetta, a mellow principal tone may be suggested; for the second, light foundation stops; and for the third, the *Plenum* of a subordinate manual. ♩ = 80; ♩. = 44; ♩. = 69.

GLORIA

Of the three settings of

Allein Gott in der Höh sei Ehr
All glory be to God on high

the large one is placed in the middle. The first, for three parts, *manualiter,* with the c.f. in the alto (VI, 5; BWV 675):

seems not quite worthy of the surroundings in which it appears. It may derive from Bach's first years in Weimar. The movement of the two parts that flutter about the c.f. symbolizes the beating of angels' wings. It is best to play the c.f. in the pedal with 4'; the piece also sounds well an octave higher (played with 4'; the c.f. 2'). ♩ = 80.

391. *Op. cit.,* I, 289.

392. Dietrich in the *Bach-Jahrbuch* for 1929, p. 20.

The second setting (VI, 6; BWV 676):

is a concerted trio in the style of the *Six Sonatas*, which combines in masterly fashion the construction and modulation scheme of a sonata movement with a presentation of a c.f. But in *cantabile* part-writing it surpasses even the sonatas. In the first (Weimar) version it was merely a three-part organ chorale with sextuplets in the middle voice (VI, Appendix, p. 96; BWV 676a). In revising it, however, Bach built a four-measure theme[393] from the sextuplet rhythm. This theme sparkles about the c.f. and provides the musical material that is shared by the two manual parts. Now and then a line of the c.f. slips unnoticeably into one or the other of these voices. On the repetition of the music containing the first two lines of the c.f. the two upper parts are exchanged. The next two lines are presented by manual and pedal in stretto, while the last line is repeated three times to produce a stronger conclusion. The first sketch was thus expanded to more than double its length. Bach achieved a significant effect by adding an ornament to the penultimate note of each line—as he did in the first two Kyrie chorales. In performing this piece it is advisable to bring the lines of the c.f. into prominence by the addition of a stop; otherwise the audience will notice them too late. ♩. = 56.

The third setting (VI, 10; BWV 677):

is a fughetta, which paraphrases the first line of the chorale in mm. 1-7, then paraphrases the second line, and in m. 17 brings the two in a spontaneous stretto. The work depicts a little angel concert in the most delicate colors. A rendition in accordance with this idea is indeed required by the original *staccato* marks. One should use soft but bright foundation stops, 8', 4', and 2'. ♩ = 84.

393. The progression up into the higher octave at the end has a counterpart in "Von Gott will ich nicht lassen" (p. 253.).

THE TEN COMMANDMENTS

The first, large, arrangement of

Dies sind die heilgen zehn Gebot (VI, 19; BWV 678)
These are the holy ten commands

(text, see p. 220)

has puzzled interpreters greatly. It is for five voices, *a 2 Clav. e Pedale;* the c.f. appears in canon between alto and tenor, and above these voices are two concerted soprano parts. Schweitzer interprets the parts that move about the c.f., that go their own way "without rhythm, without plan, without theme, and without regard for the others," as a symbol of moral confusion "as it reigned in the world before the Law," symbolized by the canon, "existed."[394] Quite understandably he finds that music cannot express satisfactorily this antithesis between order and disorder.

Dietrich[395] attributes to the opening passage (before the entrance of the c.f.) a whole chain of definite ideas: from the "sinless state of man in Paradise" to "Christ's work of redemption" in the chromatic "sighs of love," etc. Schering calls attention to the fact that, with the help of the canon, "the count of five chorale-lines is brought up to the sacred number ten."[396] Dietrich discovered that the entire construction of the piece comprised ten periods which, like Moses' Tablets of the Law, were divided into two halves of five each, etc.

Without doubt the writing of the c.f. in strict canon is supposed to signify the Laws of God laid inexorably before us. An understanding of the remaining parts is best arrived at, perhaps, through a comparison with the introductory chorus of Cantata 77. Here the melody of "Dies sind die heilgen zehn Gebot" is also heard in canon between trumpet and fundamental bass in augmentation. Meanwhile the choir is singing: "Thou shalt love the Lord thy God with all thy heart, and with all thy soul, and with all thy strength, and with all thy mind, and thy neighbor as thyself." This movement interprets the Bible with impressive grandeur. Bach seems to have had thoughts of this kind in the organ chorale, as well. The contrapuntal parts mean neither "moral disorder" nor the "Pauline doctrine of justification." On the

394. *Op. cit.*, II, 59.
395. *Bach-Jahrbuch* for 1929, p. 80.
396. *Bach-Jahrbuch* for 1925, p. 48.

contrary, they bring warmth to the inflexible, inexorable c.f. in the Christian thought, "God is love." Serene faith and imploring sighs are the two poles of this feeling, as Bach expresses it here. With the chromatic progression in the last line, "Kyrie eleis'," sorrowful feelings predominate, corresponding, perhaps, to the close of the whole hymn, "Es ist mit unserm Tun verlorn, verdienen doch eitel Zorn" ("Our own work is a hopeless thing, Judgment alone it can bring."[397]).

Performance of this work must seek to unite austerity and deep emotion. The c.f. is displayed best on two manuals, the tenor leading on the lower, the alto somewhat less strong on the upper. ♩ = 92.

The second, small, setting (VI, 20; BWV 679)

seems even more difficult to interpret satisfactorily. It is a fughetta on a paraphrase of the first line of the chorale, in the rhythm of a *gigue*, and with bouncing leaps and an almost playful mood of high spirits! The subject appears exactly ten times, in fact, if one counts three incomplete entries. That it occurred to Bach that its compass (g—f) comprised ten half-steps[398] seems to me most unlikely. We should be equally justified in remarking that it is ten quarters long. But all this does not yet establish any inner connection with the chorale. Wilhelm Weismann seems to me to come much closer to the truth when he sees in the piece a kind of "New Testament antithesis, a symbol of man born again through Christ, a *vita nuova*. . . no longer through the Law, but through the power of rebirth in God"—actually, therefore, something akin to "the joyous dance of the new man." In its style it is more than just another piece in the *Third Part of the Clavierübung;* it is a brilliant clavier piece, and a satisfying performance on the organ is achieved only with difficulty. ♩. = 76.

397. *Tr*. George MacDonald.
398. Dietrich in the *Bach-Jahrbuch* for 1929, p. 20.

THE CREED

The large setting of

Wir glauben all an einen Gott (VII, 60; BWV 680)
We all believe in One true God

(in Organo pleno)

does not present the complete chorale melody, and is the only one of the large settings that does not. Possibly the reason is, as with the organ chorale (IX, 24; see p. 231), that the c.f. is too long. Instead, Bach substitutes a fugue on the first line. To the vigorous subject[399] is added a *basso ostinato*—probably a unique instance in a fugue—whose firm tread signifies reliance on faith. At the end, surprisingly, the last line enters, unembellished, in the tenor: "Es steht alles in seiner Macht" ("By whose mighty power alone All is made, and wrought, and done."[400]). Bach thus sums up the entire hymn in its first and last lines. As in the Great G Minor Fugue, here also the episodes are brought back literally in a different key in the manner of a concerto movement; compare mm. 27-40 and mm. 60-72.

In *performance* one should make no change of manual, however much the two episodes may seem to invite it. On the other hand, one should take care to separate the manual and pedal clearly by their tone quality. The tempo is often taken too fast; however, the beat note is not the quarter, but the eighth; therefore, about ♪ = 138.

The small setting (VII, 61; BWV 681),

a fughetta in the rhythm and style of a French overture, elevates the symbol of princely dominion to that of Godly Omnipotence. Like the preceding fughetta, it also shows throughout the style of a work for the clavier, especially in the expressive declamation of the last five

399. Schweitzer calls it "tender and musing" (?). *Op. cit.*, II, 60: "It consists of a gentle, almost dreamlike fantasia upon the motive of the first line of the chorale text."

400. *Tr.* Catherine Winkworth.

measures. The mature Bach replaced the notation , which was earlier the usual one, by the accurate . Tempo, ♪ = 104.

THE LORD'S PRAYER

Luther's hymn,

Vater unser im Himmelreich (VII, 52; BWV 682)
Our Father, Thou in heav'n above

Ulrich Steigleder called "the song of all songs, the prayer of all prayers." The large five-part arrangement of this chorale (*a 2 Clav. e Pedale, Canto fermo in Canone*) is the most complicated and most difficult to understand of all Bach's chorale settings. Contemporaries probably had pieces of this kind in mind when they expressed the opinion that "by their bombastic and intricate character they obscured their beauty with all too great art."[401] The apparent confusion, however, turns into a deeply thought-out scheme, when we grasp what Bach wanted to express. In the following paragraph I reproduce an interpretation by Wilhelm Weismann which, I must confess, gave me an understanding of this piece for the first time:

"The prayer for deliverance from all evil runs through almost all nine stanzas of the chorale like a c.f.: deliverance from false doctrine (2), the wrath of Satan (3), flesh and blood against God's will (4), discord, strife, etc. (5), guilt (6), the evil one (7), and hard times (8). The monstrous piece with its various rhythms is, then, nothing short of a symbol of the 'hard, cruel world,' through which the Christian must pass, with this world all around him, but with the Lord's Prayer in his heart (the Divine Law in him = canon)."

"The symbol of this world, however, is the individual, as Bach depicts him in the almost distorted chorale melody of the first three measures: unredeemed and full of distressing anxiety. From him, in the next measures, the view broadens out onto world affairs, and the tragedy of adverse circumstances, of sorrow, and of pain. For the chains of sighs, intensified by the Lombardic appoggiaturas, and interspersed again and again with chromatic passages, tell us very clearly that in this sinful world there is suffering, painful suffering.

---

401. Cf. a quotation from J. A. Scheibe in *The Bach Reader*, p. 238.

Thus the monumental panorama is unrolled before the listener: a world situation in which all those forces prevail which are dealt with in the individual stanzas of the chorale. Particularly remarkable is the bass, the foundation of this world. In sinister monotony it strides along, stopping again and again, and yet eternally invariable. Even the tempo, therefore, is to be determined by it (slow eighth). . . ."

But there are almost insurmountable obstacles to be overcome if this work is to sound well. As in the five-part "Christe, du Lamm Gottes" of the *Little Organ Book,* Bach links together one c.f.-part and one florid part; in conformity with their style and what they express they should contrast with each other as clearly as possible. According to Bach's instructions, however, this is quite impossible. I have never yet heard the piece performed by *one* player in an even halfway satisfactory manner. The only alternative seems to me to be to play only the two florid parts oneself on two manuals and have another organist play the two canonic parts on a separate manual or, on a 4-manual organ, on two manuals! Then, only, can one distinguish both the c.f. and the two florid parts clearly from each other,—and then the prerequisites—in sound, at least—for understanding have been provided.

The so-called "Lombardic rhythm" ( ) constitutes the second difficulty; i.e., the slurring of a short accented note and a longer unaccented one. We encounter it in Frescobaldi (the *Toccata per l'Elevazione*) and in Handel (the *concerti grossi*), but very seldom in Bach. (Notice, however, an example in the eleventh measure of the preceding Fughetta.) Only the stringed instruments, obviously, can execute this "limping" rhythm, since only they can accent the first note and play the second more softly. The keyboard instruments, particularly the organ, can achieve the impression of an accent only by releasing the second, unaccented, note. Moreover, the usual notation did not mean—even for the strings—a literally exact execution, but allowed complete freedom between and . All that mattered was its expressiveness. Any organist who takes pains to execute the rhythm in "Vater unser im Himmelreich" as accurately as possible will only torture himself and his audience and, moreover, will violate the meaning of the music. Since the prevailing rhythm is that of triplets, the execution will be approximately like this (mm. 14-15):

In measures in which no triplets occur, as in m. 4, the execution may be brought still closer to ♬.[402] ♩ = 48; the mode is transposed Dorian.

The small arrangement (V, 47; BWV 683),

a smooth organ chorale in the style of the pieces in the *Little Organ Book*, is, in its simplicity, in the greatest conceivable contrast to the preceding arrangement. Originally the lines were separated by interludes, and ritornellos appeared at the beginning and at the end. In this form the chorale occurs in Vol. V, p. 109 (BWV 683a), as a counterpart to the variant of "Wer nur den lieben Gott lässt walten" (V, p. 111). Bach struck out these sections and hardly needed to change a note of the chorale setting. Mild foundation stops. ♩. = 48.

OF THE BAPTISM

Christ, unser Herr, zum Jordan kam	To Jordan's stream came Christ our Lord,
Nach seines Vaters Willen,	Saint John beside Him standing,
Von Sankt Johann die Taufe nahm,	Baptized Him there in Jordan's ford
Sein Werk und Amt zu erfüllen;	At Mighty God's commanding;
Da wollt er stiften uns ein Bad,	He thus prepared for us a bath
Zu waschen uns von Sünden,	In which to drown death's terror,
Ersäufen auch den bittern Tod	To wash away all sin and wrath,
Durch sein selbs Blut und Wunden,	Efface for each his error,
Es galt ein neues Leben.	And fire anew our courage.
Martin Luther, 1541.	*Tr.* Henry S. Drinker.

402. Spitta had reminded us of these matters (*op. cit.*, III, 47, fn.) but without attracting much attention.

The large arrangement (VI, 17; BWV 684)

is in C Dorian, since the c.f. on 8' in the pedal would otherwise have ranged too high; below, in the bass there is an incessant flow of sixteenth notes as an image of the waters of the Jordan, which are interpreted in the last stanza of the hymn as a symbol of the blood of Christ, which washes away all sins, both inherited and personal.[403] But what is the meaning of the upper parts, which rise and fall and become entwined with each other? Could Bach, in these, have been depicting Christ and John the Baptist: John the Baptist's rising, their stepping down, the clasping of hands, and the immersion? If so, the picture for which the chorale supplied the subject is complete.

Performance: r.h. with foundation stops (mellow principals) 8' and 4'; l.h. with 8' and 16'; the c.f. with an 8'-reed. ♩ = 76.

The small setting (VI, 18; BWV 685):

is even more difficult to interpret than the large one in its extremely concentrated counterpoint. To the subject of the fughetta is added as countersubject a "diminution" constructed from the subject. Both these voices are answered in contrary motion. And this occurs three times! Does this treatment, then, signify immersion (inversion) three times during the baptism? Looked at in this way, the piece is not "an amazing antique,"[404] but an impressive work having the power to evoke imagery, such as was possible only to Bach.

Performance: Principals. ♩= 80.

---

403. Cf. Spitta, *op. cit.*, III, 216, "as a symbol of the atoning Blood of Christ."
404. Dietrich in the *Bach-Jahrbuch* for 1929, p. 24.

OF THE ATONEMENT

The large setting (VI, 13; BWV 686) of

Aus tiefer Not schrei' ich zu dir
Out of the depths I cry to Thee

Pro Organo Pleno, Manuale e Pedale doppio, a 6 voci

the only organ composition by Bach for six real parts, is an example of the organ motet in its most monumental, quite unsurpassable form. From the squared stones of the Phrygian chorale Bach erects a structure of unheard-of grandeur and austerity of architecture. At the very first appearance of the c.f. in double pedal, two manual parts move in stretto with it. Every line is introduced and given a contrapuntal treatment in the same manner. In the last line the "rhythm of constancy" ♩ ♫ ♩ gains more and more headway. But it does not imply a sudden change of mood to a triumphal ending (as Schweitzer[405] and Heuss claim): the ending in major was self-evident, and the homogeneity of the piece would be invalidated by an interpretation of that kind. And yet there is some truth in what they say: in its elemental force the work has something magnificent, something uplifting about it, so that both performer and audience go forth, not crushed by it, but strengthened.

Scheidt wrote two six-part compositions with double pedal for the *Tabulatura Nova,* and we find a c.f. in double pedal in Tunder's "Jesus Christus, unser Heiland."[406] A performance that will sound satisfactory can be imagined only on an organ with two pedal keyboards.[407] Under normal circumstances, with a pedal *Plenum* based on 8', the c.f. will not be heard to any degree except by a careful articulation of the lower pedal part. Under other circumstances one may have the c.f. played by trombones along with the five-part setting for the organ, or performed by another player on a separate manual.

Performance: a full *Plenum* (without brilliant mixtures) on the *Hauptwerk;* a *Plenum* with penetrating 8' reed tone in the Pedal. 𝅗𝅥 = 69.

---

405. *Op. cit.,* II, 70.
406. See Karl Straube, ed., *Choralvorspiele alter Meister* (Peters 9124),

407. In the collegiate church in Stuttgart, for example.

The second setting (VI, 14; BWV 687)

is in F♯ Phrygian and is written for four parts with the c.f. in the soprano. This work could be considered a "large" arrangement, if the tremendous six-part arrangement did not precede it. Like the latter it is an organ motet with anticipatory imitation of each line. In its use of the notes of the c.f. at a quarter of their value for this imitation, it resembles the organ chorale "Vor deinen Thron tret' ich hiermit," but in its continual use of strettos of both direct and contrary motion it is much more strict. As the massive structure of the large setting to some degree nullified the deeply sorrowful mood of the hymn, Bach's technical mastery here is so transcendent that a similar effect is the result.

Performance: the piece will sound best with the c.f. on a 4'-stop in the pedal; not too "small" in sound, and with a feeling of urgency in the tempo. ♩ = 46.

OF THE HOLY COMMUNION

Jesus Christus, unser Heiland,
Der von uns den Gottes Zorn wandt,
Durch das bittre Leiden sein
Half er uns aus der Höllen Pein.

Tr. Martin Luther, 1524, of John Huss's "Jesus Christus nostra salus."

Jesus Christ, our Lord and Savior,
Turn, we pray, God's anger from us;
Through the woe that Thee befell,
Protect us from the pains of Hell.

Tr. Henry S. Drinker.

Je-sus Chri - stus, un-ser Hei - land, der von uns den Got-tes Zorn wandt,
durch das bit-tre Lei - den sein half er uns aus der Sün - den Pein.
(d
a
g
a)

The large arrangement (VI, 30; BWV 688)

is for three voices, *a 2 Clav. e Pedale*, and has the c.f. (as a tenor) in the pedal, where it stands like a "*rocher de bronze*" in the midst of a powerfully surging and heaving movement. The work is so extraordinary in its idiom that a number of commentators have experimented with it, though none with convincing results. Spitta, with fine sensitivity, contemplates the fifth stanza of the hymn, "Du sollst glauben und nicht wanken" ("Thou shalt have faith and not waver"), and finds expressed in it "Faith, lively and immovable, together with the solemnity of a consciousness of sin. . . ."[408] Schweitzer[409] claims to see in it the difference between Luther's and Zwingli's dogmas concerning the Holy Communion. Dietrich[410] sees in the decreasing size of the intervals in the first four measures "the lessening of the distance between God and man; i.e., the passing of God's wrath through the death of Christ." Steglich[411] sees in the "reaching out of the theme beyond the interval of the octave, for Bach the reaching out toward the Almighty, and, in the gradual drawing-in, the shrinking of the superhuman to the human measurement of the sixth. . . lively endeavor, fervent longing, and personal striving toward the goal, the duality which is realized in the Holy Communion. . . . 'Solch gross Gnad und Barmherzigkeit sucht ein Herz in grosser Arbeit' ('Though great our sins and sore our woes His grace much more aboundeth')."[412] (6th stanza of the hymn.)

What is meant by the really extraordinary progression of the manual parts? First, the chorale is contained in them in various ways: in whole notes (see the musical example) and in the motive f e d, which is derived from the end of the first line. Like embittered fighters, the two manual parts charge at each other with mighty lunges. The chorale strides through, between these hostile powers, like Dürer's knight between death and the devil—powers which symbolize the wrath of the God of the Old Testament and his "strife" with man, from which Jesus Christ redeemed us through his bitter Passion.

Only rarely will a player succeed in achieving a satisfying performance of this colossal work, even though he may be considered a master of his profession. He might select for comparison the first movement of the D Minor Concerto for clavier which Bach transcribed for organ and placed at the beginning of his cantata "Wir müssen durch viel Trübsal."[413] Too fast a tempo obliterates the turbulence in the manual, which must also be intense and big in tone, but which must be victoriously outshone by the c.f. ♩ = 104.

---

408. *Op. cit.*, III, 215.
409. *Op. cit.*, II, 61.
410. *Bach-Jahrbuch* for 1929, p. 64. fn.
411. *J. S. Bach*, p. 123.
412. *Tr.* Catherine Winkworth.
413. Cantata 146 (see p. 165).

The small setting (VI, 33; BWV 689):

is in F Dorian, and is the only small setting to differ in pitch from the corresponding large one by the interval of a third. It is not a fughetta, but a fugue with the dimensions of the fugues in the *Well-Tempered Clavier*. It acquires its distinctive characteristics from the raised fourth-step in the subject and from the displacement of the measure which occurs when the subject appears in the middle of the fugue:

but particularly from the strettos, of which no less than five different ones occur: in mm. 10, 16, 23/24, 37/38, and (in augmentation) m. 57. From this point on, the augmenting part retains the subject to the end, possibly as a symbol of the *unio mystica* of man and God in the Holy Communion.

In order to make the progression of the parts come out clearly everywhere—in particular, to make the strettos audible—one may distribute the four voices of the fugue on two manuals and pedal. The tone should be a full principal tone; the tempo, ♩ = 76.

The Fugue in E♭ Major, which forms the conclusion of the *Third Part of the Clavierübung*, was discussed on p. 161f.

CHAPTER 26

THE CANONIC VARIATIONS

"A Few Canonic Variations on the Christmas Hymn 'Vom Himmel hoch, da komm ich her'" (V, p. 92; BWV 769)

"for an organ with 2 manuals and pedal"

"He joined the Society for Musical Sciences in the year 1747. . . . Our lately-departed Bach did not, it is true, engage in deep theoretical speculations on music, but was all the stronger in the practice. To the Society he handed over the chorale 'Vom Himmel hoch, da komm ich her,' completely worked out; this was afterwards engraved on copper." So reads the report in the obituary—with a light touch of sarcasm directed at theorists.

The meaning of the last sentence is somewhat obscure. Spitta interprets it as follows: "Bach worked out a composition based on the chorale 'Vom Himmel hoch,' had it engraved on copper, and then laid the finished work before the Society."[414] It was brought out by Balthasar Schmidt in Nuremberg, and according to the publisher's number it would already have appeared in 1746.

The Society was established in 1738 by the Swabian Lorenz Mizler, and it had the aim of improving and raising the level of music through research into its rational foundations. For this reason it did not accept any who were merely instrumentalists or singers, but only composers and scholars. When Bach was persuaded to join, after having held aloof for some time, he submitted to the membership on admission two works which combined erudition and art: a six-part triple canon and the variations for organ. A contemporary remarked, "I cannot persuade myself that the most difficult demonstration in geometry would have required reflection any more profound or more extensive."[415]

The *Canonic Variations* are, in fact, entirely worthy of being placed beside two other works of Bach's old age: the *Musical Offering* (1747) and the *Art of Fugue* (1749-1750). Common to all three works is the almost abstract quality of their style: all thought of a specific instrument recedes—hence the many different attempts to conceive the *Art of Fugue* in terms of sound. Only for reasons of an association of ideas almost obvious did Bach assign these chorale variations to the organ.

The abstract-philosophical nature of the work was prominent more especially in the publication engraved for the Society. There the first three canons were not written out in full; only the first notes of the imitating voice were given. Hence it was impossible to play from this version! The work, therefore, has characteristics quite different from those of a partita, and it is surely not right to say that Bach here reverted to the forms of his first youthful works; a comparison with Scheidt's chorale cycles is more justified.

Yet even this resemblance is only external. In expression the variations are at the opposite pole from the objective idiom of Scheidt; they bring the highest exaltation to an expressive, subjective

414. *Op. cit.*, III, 295.
415. See Jacob Adlung, *Anleitung zu der musikalischen Gelahrtheit*, p. 692.

style. Spitta expressed this idea with warmth when he said that the very complicated forms, to which, by preference, Bach devoted himself in the last years of his life, did not fascinate him because of their difficulties alone; his musical perception had grown more and more profound, and it drew him to these forms. "These partitas are full of a passionate vitality and poetical feeling. The heavenly hosts soar up and down, their lovely song sounding out over the cradle of the Infant Christ, while the multitude of the redeemed 'join the sweet song with joyful hearts.' "[416]

Bach made a copy of the work for himself during the last years of his life, wrote out the first three canons in full, improved the work in a number of details, and so rearranged the order of the variations that the last variation now came in the middle; i.e., 1, 2, 5, 3, 4. Credit is due Friedrich Smend for having clarified this whole matter in a valuable critical-aesthetic study in the *Bach-Jahrbuch* for 1933. Recently he published the variations[417] in the order of the last autograph, and rejected the engraved edition as a "grave misrepresentation" in which Bach's participation "must be considered out of the question."

As grateful as we must be to Smend for passing on the corrected readings to us, and for his many shrewd observations concerning the work, most musicians will not be able to reconcile themselves to the rearrangement, inasmuch as the plan of the engraved edition—which, after all, probably represents Bach's original conception—is more convincing than the later one, the result of Bach's own changes.

In the first order of arrangement the last variation is plainly contrasted with the first four. In the first four variations the counterpoints are treated canonically, at first in a simple way, and then more and more artificially, against the unornamented c.f. appearing in large note values. In the last variation the c.f. itself becomes a canon—in fact, four times in all—corresponding to its appearance four times in the first four variations. But if any doubt should still remain as to the *finale*-quality of this variation, in spite of these arguments, this doubt should be removed when we consider the celebrated, unique stretto, in which all four lines of the chorale are presented simultaneously in a six-part passage:[418]

416. Spitta, *op. cit.*, III, 221.
417. Publications of the *Neue Bach-Gesellschaft*, XXXIV, 2.
418. Cf. Keussler in the *Bach-Jahrbuch* for 1927, pp. 106ff.

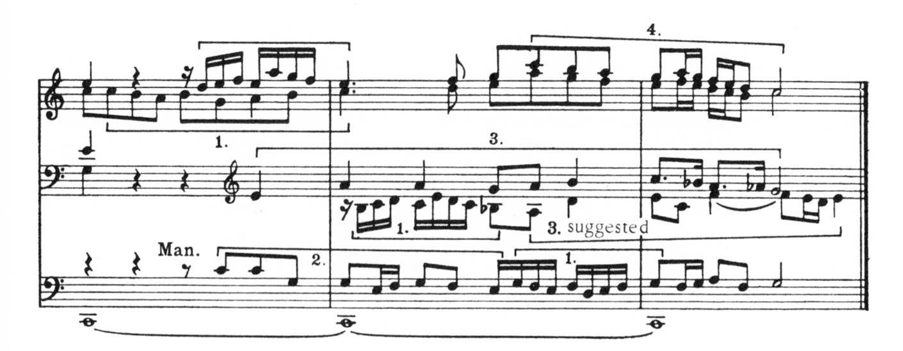

Nevertheless, the fact remains that Bach subsequently revoked this order, so that the climax now came in the middle: "The path leads to an ever larger and more considerable clearing." Smend thus characterizes the relaxation that occurs after this climax.

I should like to regard it as probable, or at least possible, that Bach continued to work at this piece mentally: he rejected the first new order, set up another, and would have changed even this, perhaps, had he got around to it, since—in spite of Smend's clever arguments—it is less convincing than the first. The plan of the work according to the engraved edition is as follows:

A. Canons in which the c.f. is accompanied by two parts that are treated in canon.
   a) Two three-part canons:
      No. 1: at the octave between soprano and bass; the c.f. lies in between as tenor;
      No. 2: at the fifth below between soprano and alto; the c.f. lies below as tenor or bass.
   b) Two four-part canons, in which a fourth, free part is added to the c.f. and the two canonic parts:
      No. 3: in canon at the seventh between bass and tenor; the c.f. lies in the soprano, the free part (marked *cantabile*) in the alto;
      No. 4: in canon at the octave between soprano and bass, the latter being in augmentation; the c.f. lies in the pedal as tenor, the free part in the alto.

B. The c.f. itself is treated canonically:
   Var. 5: which contains four canons in itself: the first two in three parts, like Variations 1 and 2; the next two in four parts, with a free part added, like Variations 3 and 4. All four canons answer the c.f. in contrary motion: the first at the sixth; the second (with roles exchanged) at the third; the third at the second (in

which a vigorous florid part in sixteenth notes is introduced in the soprano, *forte*, as fourth part); the fourth at the ninth[419] (the sixteenths go over into the tenor); in the fifth measure from the end the word *diminuzione* hints that the sixteenths

present the first line in diminution. Thus the last variation balances the first four canons in every respect.

From the first canon to the third the thematic relationship between the canonic parts and the c.f. becomes more and more close: In the very first variation, the descending scale in sextuplets makes reference to the last line of the c.f. (This dependence escaped Smend.) In the second, the canonic parts bring an anticipatory imitation of the first line (even the second is cited). And in the third, the eighth notes treated canonically are woven tightly from the c.f.; the motive of the continuation:

could be a reminiscence of the early organ chorale (VII, 55), where the third line is imitated in advance like this:

Only the canon by augmentation is entirely free of thematic reminiscences; it numbers 42 measures; the part of the soprano imitated by the bass ends exactly in the middle, on the third quarter of measure 21. From there on, the soprano continues freely (Bach also writes more freely from here on than in the first half); several quotations of the chorale also appear here, and are woven in unnoticeably. The close of this variation is truly magnificent music, while the fifth variation, especially its first half, is rather dry. Did this fact perhaps lead Bach to re-arrange the movements?

The cardinal question, then, more important than all theoretical analysis, is: did Bach succeed in converting all this stupendous erudition and artificiality into music? And a second question: how

419. So that now all the intervals from the second to the ninth have been represented once, if we include the fifth below in the reckoning as a fourth.

shall the player set about making it "sound"? That these variations are more than merely abstract counterpoint, only the person who makes an exhaustive study of them will learn. They will hardly reveal themselves to the unprepared listener.[420] And for the player, the idea expressed by Griepenkerl in the Preface to Vol. V is particularly valuable here: "It is not desirable for anyone to form an opinion of the effect of all these arrangements of chorales until he has discovered the right stops with which to play them."

First of all, attention should be directed to the distinctness of the individual voices and their separation by tone quality. The third variation actually needs to be played on three manuals—another player for the c.f.—in order to sound well. Foundation stops must predominate in the registration; a *Plenum* is required only for the last variation. The following tempi may be suggested, those assigned by Schwebsch being given in parentheses: Var. I, 𝅗𝅥. = 56 (52–54); Var. 2, ♩ = 69 (56); Var. 3, ♪ = 104 (80-84); Var. 4, ♪ = 88 (80); Var. 5, ♩ = 88 (92).

CONCLUSION

In the works of his last years Bach ascends into the realm of philosophical music, which can no longer be explained by the traditional concepts of style. One of the greatest changes in recent music history was taking place around him: the change in style from the Late Baroque to Sentimentalism and through the period of Storm and Stress to a new Classicism.

Philipp Emanuel's "Prussian Sonatas" appeared in the same year (1742) as did his father's *Fourth Part of the Clavierübung*, and in the same decade Stamitz wrote his revolutionary orchestral trios, *Opus 1*. Almost automatically all of the older music, especially church and organ music, was put out of circulation by this revolution.

This sudden sharp decline would not have been possible, however, had everything still been in order in the church behind the baroque façade of splendor. In reality the church was greatly weakened, even though it preserved a semblance of the old well-being in its orders of service. The brightly gleaming fire of the Reformation period had already become dim during the period of Humanism and the Counter Reformation. In the chaos of the Thirty Years' War it was trans-

420. We should like to recommend as good preparation and as valuable music for use in the home the transcription of the variations by Erich Schwebsch (Kallmeyer); the poetic interpretation of the work in the Preface also gives evidence of subtle, sympathetic understanding.

formed into a smouldering haze, and burned lower and more quietly during the half century after the great war. In the unfruitful defensive struggles against the Reformed Church and against Pietism, and later against the general assault of the Enlightenment, the Lutheran Church had to exhaust its best powers. At about the time of Bach's death its ability to construct forms seems to have been worn out.

In music the leadership passed over from the Protestant North to the Catholic South; it was no accident that almost all of the great composers of the next period were Catholic: the Mannheimers, Gluck, Haydn, Mozart, Beethoven, and Schubert. Only with Schumann and Wagner, and, a generation later, with Brahms, did the Protestant North Germany again step into the arena, even though in the works of these masters, especially the two first-mentioned, only weak traces of the old Lutheranism may be detected.

The pupils of Bach were thus faced with the decision whether to change over to the new style and, in so doing, give up the heritage of their teacher, or to adhere to the old style against an overwhelming counter-current.

With the decline of the old orders of service and of "regulated church music,"[421] the standing of church musicians had also declined. Therefore only a small band of pupils and "grand-pupils" preserved the old traditions and held them over into the new period. The organ sonatas of Philipp Emanuel Bach demonstrate in an almost unnerving way the relation of the new style to the organ; in these sonatas almost no traces of a true organ style remain.

The organ works of Justin Heinrich Knecht, who "played the clavier" on the organ in Mozartian turns, stood even lower, of course; as did also the program symphonies of the most successful organ virtuoso of all time, Abt Vogler. From the death of Bach, therefore, to the re-awakening in the nineteenth century, the result was a kind of vacuum.

Even though the organ works had a relatively early part in the re-awakening, particularly through the service rendered by Griepenkerl's edition, important prerequisites were still lacking. In the church service, which had become sterile in the nineteenth century, there was no longer any place for this art, and doubtless there would have been no one who wanted to listen to it. But the instruments, especially, were quite inappropriate, as may be imagined. To cite one example: Homeyer, in his selection of organ works by Bach (creditable for its period) meant by *mf* all the 8' flue stops with Bourdon 16'.

---

421. See Bach's letter to the parishioners of the Church of St. Blasius in Mühlhausen requesting dismissal, *The Bach Reader*, p. 60.

Thus the attempts at revival of Bach's organ music in the nineteenth century did not stand under a favorable omen. To be sure, a number of men interested themselves in its behalf: primarily, the indefatigable Christian Rinck, who is today underestimated; among composers there were M. G. Fischer, Hesse, Merkel, and others, including the highly gifted Louis Thiele. Above all, though, we must mention the name of Julius Reubke, who died in his youth, yet whose only surviving organ work, the Sonata in C Minor, "The 94th Psalm," surpasses anything written for the organ in the nineteenth century, César Franck's works not excepted.

In the second half of the nineteenth century, primarily the reputation of Rheinberger gradually earned higher respect for the organ, but by most musicians and laymen as well it was considered a soulless instrument which permitted no comparison with the expressive capabilities of the grand piano or even the orchestra. Only the simultaneous appearance of Max Reger as composer and Carl Straube as his interpreter marked a turning point. While around 1900 Straube interpreted the organ works of Bach in an ingenious, subjective way hitherto unheard of, and in particular placed the transitional dynamics of the "modern" organ fully at the service of expression, nevertheless he gained ground for the organ which had been lost for a century. It was a Bach seen through the temperament of a modern man who had grown up with Beethoven and Wagner,—but otherwise the generation around 1900 could not have understood him.

After this mission was fulfilled, the renunciation of this style and the return to the true historical Bach was effected with compelling results. What Schweitzer had begun around 1906, the German Organ Movement completed around 1925. Only now can we set about really taking possession of the heritage that we have had handed down to us in Bach's organ works. Art works, however, are not inanimate objects that one can possess and preserve, but are living entities and as such are subject to the laws of life—they have their day.

By far the greater part of all music has only a very limited life; of most music one can say with Hanslick, "It was once beautiful." Even the large constellations of art are not constantly in the heavens, but rise, stand at the zenith, and slowly set again. Probably several works of Beethoven, earlier highly celebrated—for example, the *Sonate Pathētique*—have passed beyond the zenith that they had reached in the second half of the nineteenth century; others—perhaps Op. 106—were only rising at that time. Bach's art also began to shine only in the nineteenth century. Not all of his works at the same time: only in recent decades have the late works risen for us, while some of the large organ works of long-established fame—like the D Minor Toccata, the G Minor Fantasy, and the Passacaglia, among others—already stand almost at the zenith.

All great art has its own laws and is based on them; even Bach we can understand ultimately not from his period, nor from his humanity, nor even from his conception of man's ultimate destiny—so far as we know anything about his views—but solely from his music. As important as may be the relation of the texts to the chorale preludes, we still cannot understand these works from the texts alone. Bach transforms these ideas and images into music; that is to say, he converts them into works of art which live by their own laws.

We can hope to meet the master, not by lingering in the outer courts, but by trying to find the entrance to the interior of the temple. Only the artist is received there; but scholarship can help him to find the entrance and prevent him from going astray. For the person who is occupied with Bach's art, therefore, the sobriety and objectivity of the scholar are quite as necessary as are the inspiration and sympathetic understanding of the artist.

May some measure of this dual spirit be felt in this book and be communicated to the reader!

APPENDIX

THE ORGAN WORKS OF BACH

Following the title, in the absence of other indications, are given first the volume and number of the Peters edition; following these, the *Jahrgang* and page of the edition of the *Bach Gesellschaft.*

*By J. G. Walther. See p. 175.
**By François Couperin. See p. 141.

*Not by Bach, but by J. G. Walther. See p. 175.

*By G. P. Telemann. See p. 141.

THE ORGAN WORKS OF BACH LISTED IN THE ORDER OF THEIR DIFFICULTY

Comment: This classification may prove useful to organists, and more particularly to teachers of organ. It offers, of course, only general suggestions, since many points of difficulty are naturally influenced by personal conceptions, noticeably in the selection of the tempi in which the various works are to be played.

A. FREE ORGAN WORKS

Easy to Medium Difficult

Pastorale in F Major, 1st movement (I, 8); Prelude in C Major (VIII, 7); *Larghetto* from the Concerto in D Minor (separate publication); Fantasy in C Major (VIII, 9); *Fantasia con imitazione* in B Minor (IX, 1); Eight Little Preludes and Fugues (VIII, 5); Fugue in C Major (VIII, 10); Prelude in C Major (VIII, 8); Fugue in G Major (IX, 7); Preludes and Fugues in C Minor (IV, 5), E Minor (III, 10), and A Minor (III, 9); Canzona in D Minor (IV, 10); Little Harmonic Labyrinth (IX, 9); *Pedalexercitium* in G Minor (IX, 11); Prelude in G Major (VIII, 11); Fugues in B Minor (IV, 8), G Minor (VIII, 12), and C Minor (IV, 6); *Allabreve* in D Major (VIII, 6); Prelude in A Minor (IV, 13).

Medium Difficult to Difficult

Fantasies in C Minor (IV, 12) and G Major (IX, 4); Trios in D Minor (IV, 14), C Minor (IX, 10), F Major [Aria] (IX, 5), and G Major (IX, 8); Fugue in G Minor (IV, 7); Fantasies and Fugues in C Minor (III, 6) and A Minor (IX, 6); Preludes and Fugues in F Minor (II, 5), C Major (II, 1), and G Minor (III, 5); Concertos in G Major (VIII, 1), C Major (VIII, 3), and C Major (VIII, 4); Sonata in D Minor (I, 3); Fugue in C Minor (IV, 9); Fantasy in G Major (IV, 11); Toccata in E Major (III, App. and 7); Sonata in E Minor (I, 4); Trio in G Major (IX, 3); Toccata in D Minor (IV, 4); Preludes and Fugues in A Major (II, 3), B Minor (II, 10), C Minor (II, 6), D Minor (III, 4), and G Major (IV, 2); Dorian Toccata and Fugue (III, 3); Concertos in D Minor (separate publication) and A Minor (VIII, 2); Sonata in E♭ Major (I, 1); Fugue in G Major (IX, 2).

Difficult to Very Difficult

Preludes and Fugues in C Major (II, 7), A Minor (II, 8), and G Major (II, 2); the Passacaglia in C Minor (I, 7); Fantasy and Fugue in G Minor (II, 4); Prelude and Fugue in E♭ Major (III, 1); Toccata and Fugue in F Major (III, 2); Toccata in C Major (III, 8); Preludes and Fugues in D Major (IV, 3) and E Minor (II, 9); Sonatas in C Minor, C Major, and G Major (I, 2, 5, and 6).

B. ORGAN WORKS BASED UPON CHORALES

Easy

V: 2, 5, 9, 10, 20, 23, 27, 30-32, 36, 39, 43, 48, 52, 53, Partitas 1 and 2; VI: 1, 11, 15, 16, 21, 25; VII: 53, 55; IX: 12, 15, 19, 20.

Medium Difficult

V: 1, 3, 6-8, 11-19, 21, 22, 25, 26, 29, 33, 37, 38, 40-42, 44-47, 49, 51, 54, 55, 56, Partita 3; Appendix: 1, 2, 4-7; VI: 2, 4, 5, 8-10, 12b, 14, 17, 18, 23, 24, 26, 28, 29, 31-34; VII: 35, 37-40, 42, 45-50, 56-61, 63; IX: 13, 14, 16-18, 21-26.

Difficult

V: 4, 24, 28, 34, 35, 50, Canonic Variations; Appendix: 3; VI: 3, 6, 7, 12a, 13, 19, 20, 22, 27, 30; VII: 36, 41, 43, 44, 51, 52, 54, 62.

LIST OF THE COLLECTED ORGAN WORKS OF J. S. BACH IN THE ORDER OF THE PETERS EDITION

Vols. I-VIII, edited by Griepenkerl and Roitzsch
Vol. IX, edited by Hermann Keller

Vol. I (Peters No. 240)

1. Six Sonatas for 2 manuals and pedal: E♭ Major, C Minor, D Minor, E Minor, C Major, and G Major
2. Passacaglia in C Minor
3. Pastorale in F Major

Vol. II (Peters No. 241)

1. Prelude and Fugue in C Major
2. Prelude and Fugue in G Major
3. Prelude and Fugue in A Major
4. Fantasy and Fugue in G Minor
5. Prelude and Fugue in F Minor
6. Prelude and Fugue in C Minor
7. Prelude and Fugue in C Major
8. Prelude and Fugue in A Minor
9. Prelude and Fugue in E Minor
10. Prelude and Fugue in B Minor

Vol. III (Peters No. 242)

1. Prelude and Fugue in E♭ Major
2. Toccata and Fugue in F Major
3. Toccata and Fugue in D Minor
4. Prelude and Fugue in D Minor
5. Prelude and Fugue in G Minor
6. Fantasy and Fugue in C Minor
7. Prelude and Fugue in C Major
8. Toccata and Fugue in C Major
9. Prelude and Fugue in A Minor
10. Prelude and Fugue in E Minor

Vol. IV (Peters No. 243)

1. Prelude and Fugue in C Major
2. Prelude and Fugue in G Major
3. Prelude and Fugue in D Major
4. Toccata and Fugue in D Minor
5. Prelude and Fugue in C Minor
6. Fugue in C Minor
7. Fugue in G Minor
8. Fugue in B Minor
9. Fugue in C Minor
10. Canzona in D Minor
11. Fantasy in G Major
12. Fantasy in C Minor
13. Prelude in A Minor
14. Trio in D Minor

Vol. V (Peters No. 244)

Part I: 56 kürzere Choralvorspiele

1. Ach wie nichtig, ach wie flüchtig
2. Alle Menschen müssen sterben
3. Christe, du Lamm Gottes
4. Christ ist erstanden
5. Christ lag in Todesbanden
6. Christum wir sollen loben schon
7. Christum wir sollen loben schon (Fughetta)
8. Christus, der uns selig macht (with Variant)
9. Da Jesus an dem Kreuze stund
10. Das alte Jahr vergangen ist
11. Der Tag, der ist so freudenreich
12. Dies sind die heil'gen zehn Gebot
13. Durch Adams Fall ist ganz verderbt
14. Erstanden ist der heil'ge Christ
15. Erschienen ist der herrliche Tag
16. Es ist das Heil uns kommen her
17. Gelobet seist du, Jesu Christ
18. Gelobet seist du, Jesu Christ (Fughetta)
19. Gott, durch deine Güte
20. Gottes Sohn ist kommen (Fughetta)
21. Helft mir Gott's Güte preisen
22. Herr Christ, der einig Gottes Sohn
23. Herr Christ, der einig Gottes Sohn (Fughetta)
24. Herr Gott, nun schleuss den Himmel auf
25. Herr Jesu Christ, dich zu uns wend
26. Herr Jesu Christ, dich zu uns wend
27. Herzlich tut mich verlangen
28. Heut triumphieret Gottes Sohn
29. Hilf Gott, dass mir's gelinge
30. Ich ruf zu dir, Herr Jesu Christ
31. Jesu meine Freude
32. Jesus Christus, unser Heiland
33. In dich hab ich gehoffet, Herr
34. In dir ist Freude
35. In dulci jubilo
36. Liebster Jesu, wir sind hier
37. Liebster Jesu, wir sind hier (with Variant)
38. Lob sei dem allmächtigen Gott
39. Lob sei dem allmächtigen Gott (Fughetta)
40. Lobt Gott, ihr Christen, allzugleich
41. Mit Fried und Freud ich fahr dahin
42. Nun komm, der Heiden Heiland
43. Nun komm, der Heiden Heiland (Fughetta)
44. O Lamm Gottes, unschuldig
45. O Mensch, bewein dein' Sünde gross
46. Puer natus in Bethlehem
47. Vater unser im Himmelreich (with Variant)
48. Vater unser im Himmelreich
49. Vom Himmel hoch, da komm ich her
50. Vom Himmel kam der Engel Schar
51. Wenn wir in höchsten Nöten sein
52. Wer nur den lieben Gott lässt walten (with Variant)
53. Wer nur den lieben Gott lässt walten
54. Wer nur den lieben Gott lässt walten
55. Wir Christenleut
56. Wir danken dir, Herr Jesu Christ

Part II

1. *Partite diverse sopra:* Christ, der du bist der helle Tag *(manualiter)*
2. *Partite diverse sopra:* O Gott, du frommer Gott
3. Variationen über: Sei gegrüsset, Jesu gütig
4. Einige kanonische Veränderungen über das Weihnachtslied: Vom Himmel hoch

5. Appendix: Seven hitherto unpublished chorale-preludes on: 1. Gelobet seist du, Jesu Christ. 2. Jesus, meine Zuversicht. 3. In dulci jubilo. 4-5. Liebster Jesu, wir sind hier. 6. Lobt Gott, ihr Christen allzugleich. 7. Vom Himmel hoch, da komm ich her.

Vol. VI (Peters No. 245)

34 grössere und kunstreichere Choralvorspiele

1. Ach Gott und Herr*
2. Ach bleib bei uns, Herr Jesu Christ
3.—5. Allein Gott in der Höh sei Ehr
6.—8. Allein Gott in der Höh sei Ehr (Variant)
9. Allein Gott in der Höh sei Ehr
10. Allein Gott in der Höh sei Ehr (Fughetta)
11. Allein Gott in der Höh sei Ehr (Fugue)
12a. An Wasserflüssen Babylon
12b. An Wasserflüssen Babylon (Variant)
13.—14. Aus tiefer Not
15. Christ lag in Todesbanden
16. Christ lag in Todesbanden (Variant)
17.—18. Christ, unser Herr, zum Jordan kam
19.—20. Dies sind die heil'gen zehn Gebot
21. Durch Adams Fall ist ganz verderbt (Fugue)
22. Ein feste Burg ist unser Gott
23. Gelobet seist du, Jesu Christ
24. Gott der Vater, wohn uns bei (Variant)*
25. Gottes Sohn ist kommen
26. Herr Gott, dich loben wir
27. Herr Jesu Christ, dich zu uns wend (Variant)
28. Ich hab mein Sach Gott heimgestellt
29. Jesu, meine Freude (Variant)
30. Jesus Christus, unser Heiland
31. Jesus Christus, unser Heiland (Variant)
32. Jesus Christus, unser Heiland
33. Jesus Christus, unser Heiland (Fugue)
34. In dich hab ich gehoffet, Herr (Fughetta)

Vol. VII (Peters No. 246)

29 grössere und kunstreichere Choralvorspiele

35. Komm, Gott, Schöpfer (Variant)
36. Komm, heiliger Geist, Herre Gott (Variant)
37. Komm, heiliger Geist, Herre Gott (Variant)
38. Kommst du nun, Jesu
39a. Kyrie, Gott Vater in Ewigkeit
39b. Christe, aller Welt Trost
39c. Kyrie, Gott heiliger Geist
40a. Kyrie, Gott Vater in Ewigkeit
40b. Christe, aller Welt Trost
40c. Kyrie, Gott heiliger Geist
41. Magnificat (Fugue)
42. Meine Seele erhebt den Herren
43. Nun danket alle Gott
44. Nun freut euch, liebe Christen g'mein *or* Es ist gewisslich (Variant)
45. Nun komm, der Heiden Heiland (Variant)
46.—47. Nun komm, der Heiden Heiland (Variant)
48. O Lamm Gottes, unschuldig (Variant)
49. Schmücke dich, o liebe Seele
50. Valet will ich dir geben (Variant)

*By J. G. Walther. See p. 175.

51. Valet will ich dir geben
52.–53. Vater unser im Himmelreich
54. Vom Himmel hoch (Fughetta)
55. Vom Himmel hoch (Fugue)
56. Von Gott will ich nicht lassen (Variant)
57. Wachet auf, ruft uns die Stimme
58. Wenn wir in höchsten Nöten sein
59. Wer nur den lieben Gott lässt walten
60. Wir glauben all an einen Gott
61. Wir glauben all an einen Gott (Fughetta)
62. Wir glauben all an einen Gott
63. Wo soll ich fliehen hin

Vol. VIII (Peters No. 247)*

1. Concerto in G Major
2. Concerto in A Minor
3. Concerto in C Major
4. Concerto in C Major
5. Eight Little Preludes and Fugues: C Major, D Minor, E Minor, F Major, G Major, G Minor, A Minor, and B♭ Major
6. *Allabreve* in D Major
7. Prelude in C Major
8. Prelude in C Major
9. Fantasy in C Major
10. Fugue in C Major
11. Prelude in G Major
12. Fugue in G Minor

Vol. IX (Peters No. 2067)

I. Fantasies, Fugues, etc.

1. *Fantasia con imitazione* in B Minor
2. Fugue in G Major
3. Trio in G Major
4. Fantasy (Concerto) in G Major
5. Aria in F Major**
6. Fantasy and Fugue in A Minor
7. Fugue in G Major
8. Trio in G Major***
9. Little Harmonic Labyrinth in C Major
10. Trio in C Minor
11. *Pedalexercitium*

II. Chorale Preludes

12. Ach Gott und Herr *(per canonem)*
13. Ach Gott, vom Himmel sieh darein
14. Allein Gott in der Höh sei Ehr
15. Auf meinen lieben Gott *(per canonem)*
16. Aus der Tiefe rufe ich
17. Das Jesulein soll doch mein Trost (Fughetta)
18. Herr Jesu Christ, dich zu uns wend
19. In dulci jubilo (Trio)
20. Nun freut euch, liebe Christen g'mein (Trio)
21. Vater unser im Himmelreich
22. Wie schön leuchtet der Morgenstern (Fantasy)
23. Wir Christenleut
24. Wir glauben all an einen Gott
25. Wo soll ich fliehen hin

*The Concerto in D Minor (not in Vol. VIII) is published separately as Peters No. 3002.
**By François Couperin. See p. 141.
***By G. P. Telemann. See p. 141.

III. Chorale Variations

26. *Partite diverse* on: "Ach, was soll ich Sünder machen"

The collections of Chorale Preludes in the order of the autograph appeared also as a special edition in three volumes:

Vol. I. *Little Organ Book* (Peters No. 3946)
Vol. II. *Six Chorales* and *Eighteen Chorales* (Peters No. 3947)
Vol. III. *Third Part of the Clavierübung: Chorale Preludes and Duets* (Peters No. 3948)

INDEX OF PERSONS

LIST OF ABBREVIATIONS

II, 3	= Bach, *Organ Works*, Peters Edition, Vol. II, No. 3.
p. 22, 3, 4	= page 22, brace 3, measure 4 of the volume of organ works in question. By this method of citation the reader will be spared the time consuming task of counting measures.
BG	= Bach's works in the edition of the Bach Gesellschaft
BWV	= *Bach Werke Verzeichnis*, ed. Wolfgang Schmieder (1950)
HW, BW, OW, RP . .	= *Hauptwerk, Brustwerk, Oberwerk, Rückpositiv*
OB	= *Orgelbüchlein* (Little Organ Book)
b.c.	= *basso continuo*
c.f.	= *cantus firmus*
c.p.	= counterpoint
m. (mm.)	= measure (measures)
man., ped.	= manual, pedal
r.h., l.h.	= right hand, left hand
Tr.	= translated by